SALTWATER SOCIALITY

SALTWATER SOCIALITY

A Melanesian Island Ethnography

Katharina Schneider

Berghahn Books

New York • Oxford

Published in 2012 by
Berghahn Books
www.berghahnbooks.com

Library of Congress Cataloging-in-Publication Data

Schneider, Katharina.
   Saltwater sociality : a Melanesian island ethnography / Katharina Schneider. —
1st ed.
      p. cm.   Includes bibliographical references and index.
   ISBN 978-0-85745-301-3 (hardcover : alk. paper) — ISBN 978-0-85745-302-0
(ebook : alk. paper)
   1. Ethnology—Papua New Guinea—Bougainville Island Region.   2. Matrilineal
kinship—Papua New Guinea—Bougainville Island Region.   3. Bougainville
Island Region (Papua New Guinea)—Social life and customs.   4. Bougainville
Island Region (Papua New Guinea)—History—Autonomy and independence
movements.   I. Title.
   GN671.N5S33 2012
   306.099592—dc23   2011037824

British Library Cataloguing in Publication Data
A catalogue record for this book is available from the British Library.

Printed in the United States on acid-free paper

ISBN: 978-0-85745-301-3 (hardback)
ISBN: 978-0-85745-302-0 (e-book)

CONTENTS
. . . .

List of Tables   ix

A Note on Languages   xi

Preface   xiii

Acknowledgements   xxiii

Maps   xxv

INTRODUCTION • Pororan and Buka, 2004   1
Buka History: An Overview   2
Pororan, 2004   8
The Buka Mainland, 2004   12
Movements: An Ethnographic Focus   15
Studying Movements: Some Methods   17
Movements as Objectification   20

CHAPTER 1 • Fishing People   25
Anywhere, Any Time, Anybody   26
Gardening and Fishing   30
Fishing Methods   33
Going Around at Sea   38
Return from the Sea   42
Sia and Hulu   46

CHAPTER 2 • Kin on the Move   51
Watching, Discussing and Eliciting Movements   52
Mothers and Children   57

Pinaposa Gatherings   63

Fathers, or 'Making Grow'   66

The Ninja   71

Fishermen and Gardeners   74

Matrilineal Kinship: A View from Pororan   75

CHAPTER 3 • Mobile Places   80

Ancestral Settlement   82

Colonial Gathering   86

Present-Day Pulling   89

Leitana and the Little Thing   93

Stones   95

Image section   101

CHAPTER 4 • Pinaposa   107

Matrilineages 'by the Hair'   107

Pinaposa Relations across Buka   112

The Pororans on Ancestral Roads   114

Reconnecting with Mainland Relatives   118

Migration Stories   121

Hatsunon   126

Conclusion   131

CHAPTER 5 • Marriage and Mortuary Rites   136

Sinahan   137

Tightening a Relation   142

Mortuary Rites   145

Persons at Death   146

Objects of Forgetting   150

Bung Malot: The End of Mourning   153

Hahur: 'A Mark of Being Human'   157

Finishing Mourning on the Mainland   161

CHAPTER 6 • Movements and Kastom   164

'Writing Down the Clans'   169

Straightening Traditional Leadership   172

Straightening the Ground   177

A Pororan Kastom Event   182

CONCLUSION   186

The Argument   186

Pororan, Melanesia   192

Pororan, at Sea   195

Glossary. Hapororan and Tok Pisin Terms   199

Appendix A. Pororan Travel Routes, 2004–05   203

Appendix B. Some Fishing Terms   207

Appendix C. Tok Pisin and Hapororan Kin Terms   209

Appendix D. Stories and Solomon   211

Bibliography   215

Index   227

TABLES

· · · · · · ·

Chapter 1

Table 1.   Weekly Schedule, Pororan Village   28

Chapter 4

Table 2.   Plisoh *Pinaposa* Relations   115

Chapter 5

Table 3.   Schedule of Pororan Mortuary Rites   146

Appendices

Table B.1   Fishing Methods and Species Caught   207

Table C.1   Tok Pisin and Hapororan Kin Terms   209

A NOTE ON LANGUAGES

· ·

The fieldwork on which this book is based was conducted in two languages, which are commonly mixed on Pororan. One of these languages is Papua New Guinea Pidgin, or Tok Pisin. The other language is Hapororan, the local language spoken on Pororan and Hitou Islands. Hapororan words and phrases are *italicized*, and Tok Pisin words and phrases are underlined in the text.

Key ethnographic terms are rendered in the original language in the text, following the example of several earlier ethnographers working in the area. The translations that are sometimes used locally for conversations with foreigners are over-used and carry unwanted connotations in anthropology, and I have thus avoided them. Furthermore, keeping the original terms will make the text more useful for people with ethnographic or other interests in the Buka area. All these terms are explained in the text. For consistency, Hapororan terms are used even where reference is made to my own or other ethnographers' research in other Buka language areas. Where the Halia and Haku terms differ from Hapororan ones—as they usually do only very slightly—they are noted in the glossary.

Furthermore, there are some words and phrases that Pororan Islanders used either very frequently or emphatically, the exegesis of which has contributed to the development of my argument. I often, though not always, render these terms in the original, both in order to highlight their importance to the ethnography and to establish connections across the text. A translation is given in brackets when a word is first used. All words are also listed, and are either translated or briefly explained in the glossary.

My Tok Pisin spelling is based on local usage, as learned from notice boards in Buka Town and from hymn lyrics handed out during mass on Pororan. My spelling of Hapororan is based on teaching material used at the Pororan elementary school. It diverges in two points from the spelling used in Beatrice Blackwood's (n.d.) Petats vocabulary list and two gospel translations, one by the London British and Foreign Bible Society (1934) and one by the Summer Institute of Linguistics (1976). A vowel pronounced as a closed English 'o' or 'ou' is written '*o*.' A diphthong between the English 'ch' and 'ts' is written '*ts*.' There are no plural markers in Hapororan, and none have been added here.

PREFACE
· · · · · · · ·

In July 2004, I went on a first visit to Pororan Island, a small island on the fringe reef of Buka Island in Bougainville, a region in the far east of Papua New Guinea (PNG). Colin Filer and Mike Bourke at Australian National University had suggested Pororan as a field site for doing research on saltwater-bush relations in Melanesia, as I had told them I wanted to do. Colin had put me in touch with one of his former students, Roselyn Kenneth, from the Haku language area in northern Buka. Roselyn was working at the United Nations Development Project office in Buka Town in 2004. She picked me up from the Buka airport and put me up in the spare bed in her room in Town. A few days later, as part of a broader round of introductions among her colleagues, relatives and friends, Roselyn introduced me to her 'uncle' Lawrence—neither of them was clear about how exactly they were related—from Pororan, who was running a hotel and restaurant in Buka Town and whose house on the island stood empty. Lawrence seemed to like the idea of me staying there. He said he would be glad if I could keep an eye on his mother there, who tended to over-work herself in an attempt to defy aging. About a week later, Lawrence asked his brother Albert to take Roselyn and me along when he left for Pororan on his fibreglass boat, powered by a 60-horsepower outboard motor. Albert agreed, and Roselyn and I packed a few things and enjoyed a pleasant two-hour journey across the lagoon.

We approached Pororan just as dark was falling. Roselyn deeply inhaled the smell of grilled fish that hung over the island, spoke about her memories of Pororan and imagined what it would be like for me to live there: 'Ah! Pororan is a fishing place. We used to come here as children, I remember, for eating fish. We stayed with our relatives and ate and ate and ate. You can never get this much fish on the mainland. Smell it!' she said to me. 'You will grow fat on Pororan fish if you stay here, lucky you! Just be sure to go and see my mother at the market at Kessa [at the northwestern tip of Buka Island, where Pororan and Hitou Islanders exchanged fish for sweet potatoes and other garden produce every Saturday in 2004]. You can bring her some fish, and she will give you sweet potatoes. Otherwise you will not have any sweet potatoes to eat. The Pororans don't have enough sweet potatoes. Their gardens are too small. This island is tiny, you know. So make sure you don't miss the market.' My first thought was that I hadn't even got a fishing line yet. Roselyn seemed to have read my thoughts as she said: 'Of course, <u>mama</u> will be happy, too, if you give her money instead of fish. Certainly until you have settled in on the island and learned how to catch fish over here.'

A few boys who had come to greet the boat led Roselyn and me to the hamlet of Kobkobul, where we met Lawrence's mother, Roselyn's <u>bubu</u> [grandmother], the old lady Kil. Kil was in a rage. 'Where are my forks?' she shouted in Tok Pisin, whizzing through the hamlet from one kitchen table to another outside different houses. She cleared a fishing basket off a bench to look underneath, cursed her daughter Denise who was away at this crucial moment when she needed to find forks for her visitors, and hit at her giggling grandchildren who were getting in her way. 'Oh, I have visitors, and the forks are not there', she lamented. 'This woman from Haku, I have not seen her for—how many years? I thought she had forgotten all about her old grandmother on Pororan! I did not even know if she was still alive! You, how are you?' she asked Roselyn almost accusingly and wiped tears off the corner of one eye. 'You and your sisters, and your old mother, that woman Ngasi? I never see her, she never comes round to visit, did they mess her up over there?' It was only much later that I learned to understand this as a reference to sorcery. Roselyn was listening patiently for a while, but then her eyes started dancing nervously. Finally, she managed to interrupt Kil's lamentation: '<u>Mama</u> is fine, <u>bubu</u>. We are all fine. Here, I have brought you some sweet potatoes', she said and pointed to a basket that we had bought in Buka Town in the morning. Kil threw a glance at the basket and was off onto another topic, sitting down now but not losing momentum in her speech. 'This is not very much. You know, we have been hungry on the island. For four months, we have been hungry now. Your people in Haku, they have been greedy with their sweet potatoes. The markets have been very bad. Too few sweet potatoes. Our fish, we had to take it back with us. It rotted on the way back in the sun. Not enough sweet potatoes. You tell your mothers and sisters to bring some sweet potatoes to the market, for their relatives on Pororan. You know, I am glad I have two good sons working in Town. They are good boys, Albert and Lawrence, they help me, they send rice.' Indeed, Albert had dropped a big bag of rice off along with Roselyn and me. 'Without the rice, I don't know what we would do', Kil added. Roselyn quickly told me that the past four months had been extremely hard for everyone in Buka, as bad weather had spoiled the sweet potatoes in the ground. Her relatives had had trouble keeping themselves fed, and there were no leftovers to take to the market and exchange for fish.

In the meantime, a woman who was introduced to me as Marta and who I later learned was the daughter of Kil's late husband's sister, had put some plates in front of us with enormous heaps of rice on them, topped by pieces of fish boiled in coconut milk. She had not been able to find the forks and apologized that we would have to eat with spoons. Roselyn and I started eating, but Kil did not. She was worried about something else now: we had to stay somewhere. What had Lawrence been thinking when sending us over without letting her know beforehand, she wondered. Where was she to put us? In her kitchen house, perhaps? Of course, Lawrence's house was empty, but it had not been cleaned recently, and now it was dark. Should she clean it in the dark? Roselyn, thankfully, had made her own preparations for the night. As soon as we got off the boat, she had asked one of the boys on the beach to fetch Ardie, an in-law of hers from Haku, and one of her students when she had worked as a teacher at Buka High School several years back. Just as Kil was starting to get really agitated over the issue of our lodging, Ardie arrived at Kobkobul and invited Roselyn and me to stay with her in her big house at the Pororan Primary School compound, where she lived as a teacher. Her husband, a nephew of Roselyn's, was away working in Buka Town. After finishing our meal and chatting with Kil and Marta for a while, we followed Ardie across the village to her house at the school.

After breakfast the next morning, Ardie took Roselyn and me along to a neighbouring hamlet, where she said she used to spend a lot of her time. The hamlet was called Lulutsi. 'They are nice people', she told me. 'They saw I was here on my own, and they just called me over and took me in. The young women there are my sisters now. Their baby, Tarasih, is my child, too.' A woman called Jennifer welcomed us as we approached the hamlet, and her one-year old, Tarasih, stretched her arms out for Ardie to carry her. We sat down under the big house in the centre of the hamlet. I asked who lived there. 'That's my parents' house', Jennifer told me in very fluent English. '<u>Papa</u> is a carpenter. Have you seen him in town? He works there for Chris [another son of Kil's]. He used to work for the provincial government in Arawa [the former capital of Bougainville Province]. He retired in 1987, and we all came back. <u>Mama</u> and <u>papa</u> and my sister Sagi and her husband and I and my husband, we all live in this house with our children. My brother Tsunon lives in the small house in the back.' She called over to a woman sweeping the stairs of that house: 'Tambu [in-law], we have visitors! Come and sit down with us.' Jocelyn came, bringing along her youngest son Goman, and I spent some time chatting with her and Jennifer. Jennifer, it turned out, had attended high school in Arawa. Thence her good English. Jocelyn, too, spoke English fluently. She came from Hahalis Village on the Buka east coast, and she, too, had attended high school. While we chatted, Ardie played with Tarasih. Roselyn wandered off to the beach for a swim.

When Roselyn came back, she asked about a heap of *mamop* [clam-shells] that she had seen just off the hamlet in the shallow water. *Mamop* are a delicacy in Buka, and Roselyn had speculated on the boat to Poro-ran if we would be able to get any to take to her mother in Haku. 'We put all the *mamop* there that we find when we go out gathering shells that are too small to be eaten yet. When we want *mamop*, we just go and get them from this "garden"', Jennifer explained. Then she invited Roselyn and me to come and gather some *mamop* that Roselyn could take to her relatives on the Buka mainland. Roselyn was delighted, and we spent the next half hour or so on the shallow reef, opening clamshells and cutting the flesh out. When we had a small basket full, we took it back to the hamlet for cooking.

Just as we walked up from the beach, a wiry little lady, a bit younger than Kil, with hair pointing off her head in all directions came into the hamlet from a path that wound south between mangroves and coconuts. She carried a bush knife in one hand and an apparently heavy basket on her back, which was kept in place there by a rope running over her shoulders. The woman called Jennifer over to help her take the basket off her back. We handed our shells to Jocelyn, who put them on the fire for us and followed Jennifer to meet this lady, who had to be her mother. While straightening her back, she enquired with Jennifer about us. Jennifer explained who we were, and why we were there. Then she turned to me. 'This is my mother. Don't mind her hair. She is mourning a relative. She has not cut or washed it for almost a year now. On the anniversary of the death, she will cut it and look smart again.' I did not mind Salu's hair at all but thought she looked very friendly. She had lively eyes.

In the late morning, there was a village meeting. Kil's brother Tsireh, the *tsunon* [chief, traditional leader] of her *pinaposa* [matrilineal group], took me there so that I could introduce myself to the villagers and for-mally ask the *tsunon* of all *pinaposa* on the island for permission to stay and conduct research on Pororan. We arrived early at the soccer field in the centre of the village, and Tsireh left us there on our own for a while. Roselyn pointed out a small hut with open walls and slit-gongs in three different sizes inside that stood on the long side of the field.

I was excited. The slit-gongs had to be the *tui*, which were used for accompanying dances on ritual occasions and, in the past, for sending messages across the area. Gordon Thomas, a planter on the Buka west coast who had undergone male initiation on Pororan before World War II, had mentioned them in an article that I had read (Thomas 1931). Roselyn confirmed that they were *tui*, and said: 'And if you have read the Rimoldis' book (Rimoldi and Rimoldi 1992), then you will also know that this house is a *tsuhan*, the men's house where the *tsunon* hold their meetings, and where the young boys used to sleep in the past and be taught by the *tsunon* of their *pinaposa*, their matrilineal group.' I nodded. Just as Roselyn explained to me that women had to walk around the *tsuhan* at a distance, and that only men were usually allowed inside, Tsireh came over and led me straight into the *tsuhan* for shaking hands with the old and very old men who were sitting on the benches forming the walls. Each of them told me their name, and some mentioned their *pinaposa*. Then Tsireh took me outside again and told me to introduce myself in a loud voice to the villagers, some of whom were following the proceedings at the *tsuhan* from their own houses—what a convenient way, I thought, of attending a meeting. I asked if I could do so in English, with Roselyn translating, as I was concerned that my two-week-old Tok Pisin might cause misunderstandings. This was granted. I told the villagers that I was an ethnographer and would like to stay on the island for a year or so and find out how they lived, and the *tsunon* murmured approvingly. Then, Tsireh and some other *tsunon* made a few announcements about communal work and other village affairs, and the meeting was over.

Later that day, a boat going to Buka Town dropped Roselyn, me and Ardie, who had decided to pay a quick visit to her mother, off on the reef off Kessa, the market place on the northwestern tip of Buka. Although Roselyn had sent word from Buka Town for a car belonging to her sister's company to pick us up there, none was around. So we walked to Tegese, the hamlet of Roselyn's people at Lontis Village. There, I met Roselyn's mother Ngasi, the highest-ranking *hahini* [woman of rank] of Roselyn's matrilineal group, and her father, Maru, a prominent *tsunon* in Haku. I also met Roselyn's children, who were staying with their grandmother. Maru, who had read *Both Sides of Buka Passage* by the anthropologist Beatrice Blackwood (1935), told me that Ngasi was the daughter of Balai of Lumankoa Village, Blackwood's main informant in the Haku language area.

After a chat with Tom and Ngasi, Roselyn took me over to a house across the street. 'This is the house of my auntie Elmah', she said. 'Elmah is <u>mama</u>'s younger sister. <u>Mama</u> is the *hahini*. She knows a lot about our *pinaposa*, who is related to whom, where we came from originally, and so on. But because she has a position [of rank], she will not speak about it. But Elmah, she will talk. She talks on behalf of <u>mama</u>. She knows everything that <u>mama</u> knows. So, if you want to know something, you ask her. Don't ask <u>mama</u>. And here is another good person to ask', she added as we reached the house and a man sitting underneath got up to greet us. 'This is Pascal, Elmah's husband. He used to be the research assistant of Bill Sagir, whose PhD thesis you might have read (Sagir 2003). It's about chieftaincy in Haku. Bill worked closely with Pascal. Pascal knows a lot.' 'Sure', Pascal said lightly. 'Anything you want to know. I have helped my <u>tambu</u> Bill Sagir. I will help you, too.'

We had dinner with Elmah, who came downstairs with two of her children in tow, and with Pascal. We spoke about Buka ethnography, and I was thrilled to find out that these people were obviously capable of putting the texts that I knew critically alongside their own knowledge of life in Buka. Elmah and Pascal impressed on me that earlier ethnographers had been right to point out that <u>bihainim mama</u>, or matrilineal kinship, was the most important thing in Buka. I should never forget that. They made sure that I knew that there are two main matrilineal groups in Buka, the two birds. They are *manu* [the eagle], the big bird or bird above, and *kekeleou* [the bush fowl], the small bird or bird below. Each bird is divided into several *pinaposa*, or matrilineal groups. These, in turn, are divided into *ngorer*, which Elmah and Pascal told me referred to an umbilical cord. Within the *ngorer*, each person can trace kin relations to a single ancestress, which is why people within a *ngorer* consider themselves siblings, or people 'of one mother'. 'Within one village, each *pinaposa* has its own hamlet', said Pascal. 'Tomorrow when it is light, you will see. Tegese here belongs to Elmah's people, Ngasi's people. I come from Gogonuna. Maru, too, comes from there. He is the *tsunon* of Gogonuna. Each hamlet has its own *tsuhan*, belonging to the *pinaposa* that lives there. You will see tomorrow.'

Elmah took over. 'But even within the hamlets, you can see who is who, exactly. Each *ngorer* lives in its own part of the hamlet. They all live around the house of their *tsunon* and *hahini*. You know about *tsunon* and *hahini*? They are the firstborn son and daughter of the firstborn woman in each generation. For example, our *hahini* now is Ngasi. Roselyn will follow her when Ngasi dies. After that, it will be Ayesha [Roselyn's daughter]. We have already started to acknowledge her status. She already has a position. The other children cannot mess about with her, and she herself must behave properly. Lloyd, her brother, will be Ayesha's *tsunon*. Their position is really very high. Because our *ngorer* is the highest-ranking *ngorer* in our *pinaposa*. And our *pinaposa* is very important among the Nakarip here in Haku.' Pascal added: 'Of course, here you will find disagreements. Bill Sagir has written about this. Not everybody agrees on who came first, and who therefore ranks highest. Don't be stupid. Don't let yourself be taken in by anybody's particular opinion on this.'

It was great to have a conversation with people who spoke with such clarity and confidence about ethnographic issues that it had taken me a long time to understand when I was reading about them. I was interested, though, in hearing if all that—matrilineal kinship, the *tsunon*—would be the same on Pororan as on the mainland. In principle, said Elmah, it should be the same. 'Our <u>kastom</u> [culture] is the same all over Buka. You see, we are all relatives. Both *pinaposa* and *ngorer* are scattered across Buka, that is, people have *pinaposa* and *ngorer* relatives all over the area. On Pororan, too.' On Roselyn's question, Elmah told her that Kil was a *ngorer* relative of Ngasi's father Balai. That was why Roselyn had to address Kil as her <u>bubu</u> and Lawrence as her uncle.

Pascal, however, warned her against over-emphasizing that the Pororans were relatives. 'True, they are relatives. But you see, Pororan is a little strange. They are another kind of people [<u>arakain man</u>], those islanders. They are our relatives, but we don't really know about them. They do things differently sometimes. I am not sure how much they know about their own culture. They seem a little confused sometimes.' Roselyn told him that she had been able to identify only a single *tsuhan* on Pororan, the one where the village meeting had been held. She had not seen any others. Pascal nodded. 'You see, this is not proper. Every *pinaposa* should have its *tsuhan*. Perhaps they are just lazy. Or they have no money. Building a *tsuhan* is expensive. You need to kill pigs at several points in the process. Or perhaps the Pororans have forgotten how to build a *tsuhan*. What to do first and second, and when to kill pigs, and how many. Perhaps it is that. And now they are afraid to build one, because if they try and cannot finish it, or if they mess up the procedures, the ancestors will be angry. The spirits might kill someone. They might kill the *tsunon* or *hahini* of that *pinaposa*, because they are above all the others.' I thought the Pororans were clever people for avoiding all this trouble, but Roselyn looked somewhat concerned. 'How is she going to learn about <u>kastom</u> from those people', she asked Pascal, nodding in my direction. 'It will be difficult for her. It's not like here.' Pascal shrugged. 'If it is too difficult, she can always do her research here with us. We have a lot of experience working with anthropologists.' Turning to me, he added: 'Meanwhile, if you have any questions, just come and ask. We will help you.'

At that point, when we had almost finished our dinner, Ardie appeared at the edge of the house and asked if Roselyn and I would come over and have a cup of tea with her mother and stepfather. We said goodbye to Elmah and Pascal and slowly made our way down the main road towards the Lontis village school, where Ardie's mother lived as a teacher. As I sat down on a bench outside the house next to Ardie, someone suddenly emptied a cup of cold water over my legs. I was perplexed. Roselyn smiled. 'You don't know about <u>wasim leg</u>? You should. This is an old custom. When the *tsunon* and *hahini* come to a new place, the people there pour water over their legs, to wash the salt off after the journey and to show them that they recognized their status. When the *tsunon* and *hahini* go back to their own place, their own people pour water over their legs again, to wash the salt off after the journey and show their recognition of their status. Ardie's father just poured water over your legs to show his recognition of you as an important visitor. Welcome!'

On the truck that took Roselyn and me back to Buka Town the next morning, I thought how lucky I was. I had wanted to come to an area where I could study the relations between 'bush people', gardeners on larger islands, and 'saltwater people', fishing people with access to only very little land. Within a week of having landed in Buka, I was already in the middle of those relations. I had been taken to a saltwater location by a woman from the Buka mainland—the term 'bush people' has connotations of backwardness to some Buka people, and I will therefore avoid it when referring to them—had seen her difficulties of making sense of what she saw, and had heard her relatives' comments on the saltwater people, who were at the same time relatives and 'strange people' who 'do not know about our culture'. This apparent paradox became central to my research on Pororan.

Several moments recounted above gained significance for me later, when I began to understand the differences between Pororan and mainland modes of engaging in social relations. Then, I realized that Kil's fuss over forks and lodging, and her claims that she was unprepared for our coming while Lawrence had, in fact, warned her several days ahead, were not at all accidental. They were a great demonstration of the Pororans' particular way of dealing with new people [*u ka a binits*]. By fussing over little things, she showed her surprise at new people turning up at her hamlet, and she showed her excitement over the novel, unexpected and so far undetermined relations that our coming held out. The Pororans find new relations extremely exciting for the so-far unlimited potential that they are seen to hold—both positive and negative. Because of that unlimited potential, one cannot know how to handle these relations at first. Things are perceived to get out of hand, as Kil impressed on us through her exaggerated search for the missing forks.

People feel out of control and get nervous, angry, or otherwise emotional as a result. Kil's reproachful comments that Lawrence had not warned her sufficiently, her tears over seeing a woman whom she had not seen for so long [and no longer knew how to deal with], her anger over the absence of her forks, and her refusal to eat out of worry over where we would sleep were thus all appropriate to the occasion. They drew attention to novel relations emerging, whose value lay precisely in their indeterminacy, as of the moment. Had the table been set, forks been around, the house clean and ready for me to use, this value would not have been properly acknowledged.

On the mainland, I was received in a strikingly different way. By pouring water over my legs and in explicit statements to this effect, the people at Lontis emphasized that they treated me and would treat me in future according to already established precedents [as an important visitor, as an anthropologist]. I learned to appreciate this, later on, as being consistent with the value that mainlanders place on setting up relationships according to already established patterns that make them [relatively] predictable. They call it *kura maror*, following the road. Mishaps such as the absence of forks when visitors arrive are not at all staged and appreciated as an indication of the emergence of novel and open-ended relationships. Instead, they are perceived to demonstrate a lack of knowledge of appropriate procedures, 'roads', or a lack of skill in following them. That one should know what is appropriate when a new person arrives is assumed on the mainland. The Pororans, who apparently don't know this—who, in fact, make a show of not knowing it, for if they pretended they knew, they would risk putting a limit on a relation that they would rather leave wide open—appear ignorant or strange in the mainlanders' eyes. The evening we had with Kil was certainly not easy for Roselyn.

As Roselyn noticed during our brief visit, only one *tsuhan* existed as a physical structure in 2004, and people did not live in different hamlets according to their *pinaposa* membership. Nevertheless, *pinaposa* and their locations of power are important, on the island just as on the mainland. I learned during fieldwork that Pororan Islanders recognize and acknowledge people's *pinaposa* membership and the power of the *tsunon* and locations of power belonging to different *pinaposa* in ways that differ from those on the mainland. I also learned to appreciate that their particular way of life and mode of engaging in social relations did not sit easily with Buka mainlanders' understandings of what Buka kastom—*pinaposa, tsunon* and *tsuhan* in particular—was all about. As the islanders themselves state the matter, their particular mode of engaging in social relations is intimately connected to their preoccupation with fishing and their marine environment. Thus, I call the Pororans' sociality a 'saltwater sociality'. Describing it is the aim of this book.

In the course of my first brief visit to Pororan, I also met the people who remained the most important ones for me and my research on Pororan. These were Kil, her children and her relatives of the *pinaposa* called Plisoh at the hamlets of Kobkobul, Hapagas, Hutjen and Hinoping; and Salu, her children and her relatives of the *pinaposa* called Takap at Lulutsi. In the course of my fieldwork, I stayed with each of them for some time. My affiliation with two 'mothers', Kil and Salu, and two *pinaposa*—relations between which, moreover, were not particularly good at that time—caused some confusion on the island. However, I could not have done without the insights, contacts provided and general support from the two sides.

Kil's brother Tsireh and the highest ranking *tsunon* of the Plisoh, Francis, became my key sources of information for the more formal aspects of island life, including what is locally called <u>kastom</u>, or culture. Because other people referred me to Tsireh for authoritative statements about island life, he will be cited frequently in the following pages. Through Tsireh, who made sure that others understood the purpose of my stay on the island, I met many other *tsunon*, who all contributed to my understanding of island affairs. Ardie became a friend, and through her, I made contacts among the schoolteachers that were extremely useful for my research.

When visiting Town, I stayed with Roselyn or one of her sisters, and I spent much of my time at the restaurant run by Lawrence and the workshop run by his brother Chris. There were many Pororan men working there during the week, and in the weekend, these places were popular with islanders who rested here during trips to Town for shopping and other purposes. Lawrence's comments on island life have been crucial to the development of my own understanding of it. Furthermore, he made sure that nobody in Town, which people from all over the Bougainville region visited, could get the idea that I was 'just a floating piece of driftwood'. I belonged to the Pororans and enjoyed their support and protection.

On extended visits to the Buka mainland, I enjoyed the hospitality and the insightful comments of Roselyn's relatives at Tegese, and of the late Hilary Masiria, his wife Loretta and her relatives at Gagan Village in the Solos language area. Here, I gained insights into life on the mainland.

This study is my account of my time with the Pororans and my hosts on the mainland, what I observed during this time, and what they taught me.

ACKNOWLEDGEMENTS

* * * * * * * * * * * * * * * * * * * *

At Cambridge, my greatest debt is to Professor James Leach. I am grateful for his support during my PhD and afterwards. Marilyn Strathern and Michael Scott have encouraged me to publish what used to be a thesis, and I have tried my best to implement their suggestions. Marilyn Strathern's suggestions and her expression of support at various points were crucial to the direction that the research for this book has taken. Two anonymous reviewers have provided very helpful suggestions.

An Internal Graduate Studentship from Trinity College has provided funding for my doctoral research, and Dr David McKitterick and Mrs Rosemary Jolley have offered advice and support both in obtaining it and later on. Financial support for fieldwork in Papua New Guinea was provided by the Smuts Memorial Fund, the Richards Fund, Anthony Wilkins Fund, and the Bartle Frere Memorial Fund at Cambridge.

I-Chun Lin, Tomek Religa, Kerim Suruliz, Kamil Szczegot and Gabor Szekelyhidi have helped me with fieldwork preparations. For support and stimulation during writing-up, I thank the writing-up group at Social Anthropology, and especially Poline Bala, Ludek Broz, Liana Chua, James Doubleday, Rebecca Empson, David Leitner, Andrew Moutu and Lee Wilson. The staff at the Pitt Rivers Museum, Oxford, has kindly permitted me to view the Beatrice Blackwood Collection. Tim Bayliss-Smith at Cambridge has made many suggestions, and he and Lissant Bolton at the British Museum have patiently discussed my research with me.

In Port Moresby, I thank James Robins at the National Research Institute and the NRI library staff for their hospitality during library research in 2006.

In Buka Town, I am indebted to Roselyn Kenneth, who hosted me, facilitated crucial contacts and discussed various aspects of my research. I thankfully acknowledge the practical support and advice of the staff of the United Nations Observer Mission in Bougainville and UNDP and thank Melanie Baines and Steve Nairn for their hospitality.

On Pororan, the *tsunon* of the village kindly agreed to host me and help me with my research. Among them, Francis and Tsireh of Plisoh and their *hahini* Anna and Kil have been excellent teachers. For making knowledge of the past available to me, I thank Rokayo and Hulagum of Keketin; Laguin and Siatun of Naboen I; Tonio Silak and Ninio of Naboen II; Kitou and Hulagam of Natasi; Peter Hapot, Tsik, Kihi, Lucy and Tsimat of Mulul; Salu and Tom of Takap; Gisa of Holu II; and Philip of Put.

As requested, I have used people's names in the text so as to make each person's particular contribution to my research visible. Beyond that, I especially thank my two island mothers, Kil of Plisoh and Salu of Takap, as well as Salu's daughter Jennifer and Kil's son Lawrence for their generous hospitality and support. Without their help, I might not have learned to see on the island. The generous hospitality, friendly curiosity and patience of all Pororan Islanders I have had the privilege to meet have impressed me deeply. For the many betel nuts, cups of tea, fish, bananas, galip and other signs of kind attention I received, *e nigan-toano, elomi hobot areban ipinapu. Mei lul.*

At Tegese hamlet, at Lontis Village, I thank Ngasi and Maru, their daughters, and Elmah and Pascal for stimulating discussions. At Gagan, I thank the family of the late Hillary Masiria for inviting me into their home and teaching me Solos culture. Helen Hakena discussed my research with me, and Moses Havini kindly commented on an early draft of my thesis.

In Hong Kong, I thank Fiona Chung, her parents and her husband Eric, Linda Olson and Levi Gao, Natasha and An Xiang for their great hospitality after fieldwork and during the preparation of the manuscript. Levi Gao found me a job that kept me happy and left me time for writing. Bill Fore has sent innumerable inspiring emails. Most importantly, I thank my parents.

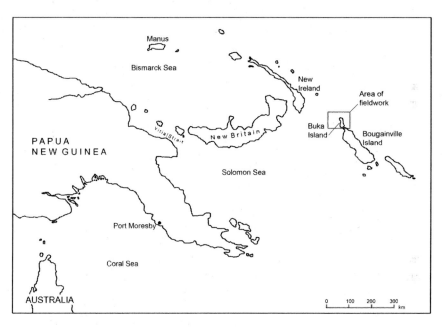

Map 1 • Papua New Guinea

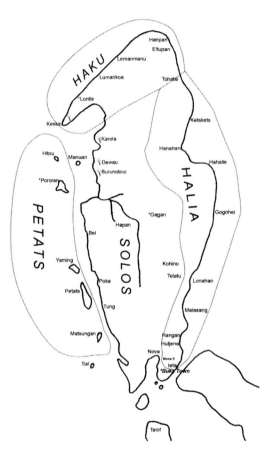

Map 2 • Buka

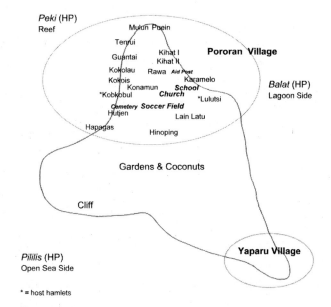

Peki (HP)
Reef

Mulun Puein

Tenrui

Guantai

Kihat I
Kihat II

Pororan Village

Kokolau

Kokois
Konamun

Rawa *Aid Post*

Karamelo

School

Balat (HP)
Lagoon Side

*Kobkobul

Church

*Lulutsi

Cemetery Soccer Field

Hutjen

Lain Latu

Hapagas

Hinoping

Gardens & Coconuts

Cliff

Pililis (HP)
Open Sea Side

Yaparu Village

* = host hamlets

Map 3 • Pororan Island

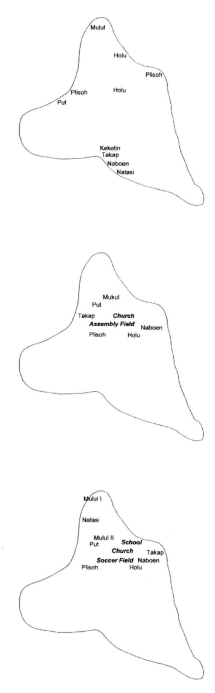

Map 4 • Pororan Places—
In pre-colonial times, in colonial
times, and in 2004.

Pororan and Buka, 2004

After my first visit to Pororan, I returned to Buka Town, packed my belongings and moved to the island, taken in already by the prospect of working with people who 'don't know much about our culture', as Pascal had said. However, things weren't that simple. A long and hard 'hungry season' was just coming to a close in Buka at the beginning of my fieldwork. Food was extremely scarce on Pororan. So I took the advice of my hosts on Pororan and spent two months moving back and forth between the island, Buka Town and Lontis and Gagan Villages, trying to gain a sense of what life was like in the different locations in the area, and working out how I might begin investigating the contrast between saltwater people and mainlanders.

The contrast is familiar from the ethnographic literature from various locations in the Solomon Islands, Papua New Guinea, Vanuatu and the Torres Strait, and from pre-colonial as well as colonial and post-colonial times.[1] Saltwater people are fishing people who live on small islands, often with little land of their own. They exchange fish and other marine resources for starch food and other garden produce with their mainland, 'mountain' or 'bush' neighbours. Mainlanders live as gardeners in the interior of larger islands, with no or limited access to the sea or no interest in fishing but access to abundant garden land. Often, there is an intermediate coastal category with access to both sets of resources. In many areas, the distinction has been either eradicated (e.g. Küchler 1993) or altered significantly due to colonial resettlement projects (Hviding 1996). Nevertheless, in many locations, it has persisted and remains a powerful aspect of people's identity (Pomponio 1990, 1992). Ethnographers have investigated the distinction from various theoretical angles, for instance as an outcome of particular roles that each side plays in exchange, both subsistence and long-distance (Harding 1967); as a result of their access to different factors of production (Carrier and Carrier 1985); as emergent from contrasts in subsistence activities (Astuti 1995); and through attention to history and human-environment interactions (Hviding 1996). In the following sections, I will introduce the approach that I have found most productive for making sense of my ethnographic observations in Buka. First, however, a brief introduction of Buka history, according to the written sources available, and of the political conditions under which I conducted my first two months of fieldwork may help orient readers.

Buka History: An Overview

Relatively little is known about life in Buka in pre-colonial times. Archaeological research has shown that Buka was populated in two major waves of immigration before the arrival of Europeans (Spriggs 1997, 2005). The first wave arrived more than 28,000 years ago (Wickler and Spriggs 1988). The second wave, arriving from about 2,700 years ago, were Austronesian-speakers known as the Lapita Culture for their distinctive pottery style. They originated probably in Taiwan or South China and brought a fully agricultural lifestyle and domesticated animals with them when they settled Southeast Asia and the Pacific (Spriggs 1997). The current distribution of languages on Buka and Bougainville—nine Austronesian and seventeen non-Austronesian—suggests that, here as elsewhere, they displaced the earlier inhabitants towards the interior of a larger island (Tryon 2005).

In 1767, the British explorer Carteret sighted Buka (Oliver 1973). Buka's name derives from the inhabitants' reported shouts of 'boucabouca' (used in 2004–05 to express surprise or direct attention somewhere) upon the sight of a sailing ship. In 1768, the French explorer Bougainville named the larger island to the south. From the 1820s onwards, French, British and American whaling ships cruised the wider region, and the crew of at least one ship traded with Buka people (Oliver 1973). In the 1870s, Buka and Bougainvillean men first signed on with 'blackbirders' (labour recruiters) for work on plantations in Fiji, Samoa and Queensland (see, e.g. Friederici 1910; Oliver 1973; Parkinson 1907; Sack 2005).

From 1886 to 1914, Buka was part of German New Guinea, ruled under Imperial Charter. In 1914, the Germans quietly left the area. In 1921, Australia took over the rule of former German New Guinea under a League of Nations C-Mandate. Three German colonial policies had a lasting influence on the region: pacification, probably achieved by 1903 (Hahl 1904), the resettlement of people from many small hamlets into a large village, and the introduction of a system of indirect rule through luluai [village chiefs] and tultul [their assistants] probably after 1905 (Sagir 2005). Beyond that, Buka was not a focus of colonial administrative activity, either in German or in Australian times. It was judged to be too far away from the administrative centres, too densely populated and its population too war-like for opening the area either for large-scale plantations or for European settlement (see Sack 1973, 2005). However, Buka men gained a reputation as reliable labourers, members of the colonial police force, and personal bodyguards (see, e.g. Melk-Koch 2000; Rimoldi 1971; Seidel 1911).

Marist missionaries were the second group of foreigners with an influence in the Buka area. They arrived on Pororan in 1901 (Laracy 1976). In 1910, two Marist Fathers and one Brother set up a mission station at Burunotoui, opposite Pororan on Buka, where they trained local men as catechists. By 1936, Buka was predominantly Catholic.[2] At the time of my fieldwork, Pororan Islanders displayed pride in having been the first whom the missionaries had visited in the area. They told me of the 'strong belief and good Christian lifestyle' of their ancestors, who were among the first catechists at Burunotoui.

Political experiments since the early twentieth century have given the Buka area a reputation in mission records and in the anthropological literature for 'cargo cults' (see Laracy 1976; Rimoldi and Rimoldi 1992; Worsley 1968). In 1914, Molein (or Muling) from northern Buka was imprisoned for accusing the missionaries of withholding goods sent to Buka people by the ancestors. In 1932, Pako at Malasang Village claimed that ships would come and deliver goods to Buka soon. He gained a large following, but was imprisoned and died. In 1934, Sanop at Gogohei revived the movement. Into the atmosphere of recurrent 'cargo' activity and mistrust of the Whites fell the Japanese occupation of Bougainville in World War II (see esp. Nelson 2005; Oliver 1973). Buka people's relations with the Japanese were generally friendly at first, as many of them welcomed the departure of the Australians. However, Buka-Japanese relations deteriorated from late 1943, when the Allies began bombing Bougainville and when the Japanese, under pressure, began raiding native food gardens. Historians have estimated that 25 per cent of Bougainvilleans might have lost their lives during the war (Nelson 2005). In August 1945, the Japanese forces surrendered to the Australians, and in March 1946, Australian civilian administration was re-established. By then, villages were destroyed and no or only few new gardens had been made (Archer 1945–46).[3] Taro, the staple crop before the war, had been decimated by Japanese consumption of both roots and leaves, and had suffered from disease and possibly from Allied spraying of gardens with napalm (see also Nelson 2005). Sweet potatoes and cassava became the new staple.

After World War II began the time that the Pororans call <u>nau</u>, the present. The economic and political development of the territories of Papua and New Guinea became a matter of increasing interest to the Australian administration. In Bougainville, Agricultural Officers helped establish cooperative societies (Rimoldi and Rimoldi 1992).[4] For the purpose of educating the population to the Australian-introduced political system, to administrative work and to a sense of nationhood, Local Government Councils (LGCs) were introduced. The Buka council was set up in 1961. However, its function was hardly understood in Buka, even by those who participated (Griffin 1977; Kavop 1977; Regan 2000; and see Ogan 1970, 1971 for accounts from Kieta, Bougainville).

In this period, social movements emerged in many parts of PNG that Ron May has analyzed in terms of 'micronationalism' (May 1982). Followers of these movements tended to withdraw from the administration's projects and aimed to achieve development on their own instead. One example from Buka was the Hahalis Welfare Society.[5] It was founded on the Buka east coast in 1960, in explicit opposition to the administration's suggestion of a Buka LGC, and by 1966 claimed the support of almost half of Buka's population (see Hagai 1966). The Welfare remained politically isolated until 1972, and divisions between Welfare supporters and supporters of the LGC remained salient in Buka in 2004–05. My Pororan hosts were non-Welfare people.

Two processes began in Bougainville in the 1960s that affected the region as a whole: firstly, the construction and operation of a giant copper mine at Panguna in central Bougainville, and secondly, the increasing integration of Bougainvillean LGCs and oppositional political movements in discussions over Bougainville's political future after PNG's independence. The construction and maintenance of the Panguna copper mine, which began operating in 1972, and the rapid economic development and social differentiation it caused has changed many Bougainvilleans' lives dramatically.[6] The mine had a number of multiplier effects and stimulated rapid economic growth in the area around it. Many Buka people who had worked for the mining company, Bougainville Copper Limited, told me with awe of the giant mine. Their particular notion of economic development, as expressed in 2004–05, was clearly derived from first-hand experiences of living and working at Arawa, the mining town and then provincial capital.

Unlike the Buka, who mainly benefited from the mine, the Nasioi who lived in the mining area had to abandon their land, the basis of their social, political and economic life (Dove et al. 1974).[7] Moreover, they perceived in-migration of mainland Papua New Guineans (sometimes derogatively called 'redskins' by ['black'] Bougainvilleans) and the presence of unemployed squatters (including Bougainvilleans) as a threat to social order (Mamak and Bedford 1974). Thirdly, the rapid influx and uneven distribution of large amounts of money in mining royalties made social relations in the Nasioi area increasingly volatile (Filer 1990, 1992). Many Bougainvilleans accused the colonial administration of sacrificing their welfare to the economic feasibility of Papua New Guinean independence, to which revenues derived from the Panguna mine contributed significantly.

This final point leads to the second important process that began in Bougainville in the 1960s, 'Bougainvillean nationalism' or 'separatism'.[8] After a complex process of public consultations, negotiations among different political bodies and organizations in Bougainville and at the national level, Bougainvillean leaders unilaterally declared the independence of the Republic of the North Solomons on 1 September 1975, two weeks ahead of PNG's independence. But because the North Solomons remained internationally unrecognized, they accepted re-accommodation into PNG in early 1976, and became PNG's North Solomons Province in August 1976. Between 1982 and 1989, three successive North Solomons Provincial Governments asked for a review of the mining agreement, unsuccessfully (Sohia 2002). Eventually, increasing social differentiation and demands for secession entangled and grew into the bitter and long-term conflict commonly referred to as the 'Bougainville Crisis'.

The Bougainville Crisis, its causes and developments were a sensitive topic of conversation in Buka in 2004–05, and I can merely sketch out the outlines of the conflict here. The Crisis began in November 1988, when militant landowners from the mining area committed acts of sabotage that forced the mine to shut temporarily. In March 1989, the PNG government sent riot squads and Papua New Guinea Defence Force (PNGDF) soldiers to Bougainville. They burnt the houses of so-far uninvolved villagers, and as a result, the militant landowners gained more widespread support. Francis Ona founded the Bougainville Revolutionary Army (BRA), and in May 1989, the mine was closed permanently. Unable to defeat the BRA, the PNGDF withdrew. On 17 May 1990, the newly formed Bougainville Interim Government (BIG) unilaterally declared independence. The PNG national government then declared a complete economic and communications blockade over Bougainville. It lasted until August 1990, when the PNGDF was re-deployed. Up to 3,000 Bougainvilleans are estimated to have died of malnutrition and preventable diseases between early 1990 and the beginning of 1991 (Amnesty International 1993). Buka people remember the early 1990s as a time of suffering and fear of BRA assaults.

In September 1990, a group of traditional leaders in the Haku language area therefore invited the PNG military back to Buka.[9] They established the BLF (Buka Liberation Front), which was supplied with weapons by the PNGDF. From then onwards, so-called Resistance Forces were founded in many parts of Bougainville to combat the BRA. Factional fighting caused civilian deaths and internally displaced persons. Human rights abuses were reportedly committed by members of the PNGDF, especially in the care centres that were set up in order to protect civilians, as well as by the BRA (Amnesty International 1993).

In 1991, the national government changed its strategy from negotiating with the BIG/BRA, whose representatives' agreements were not necessarily accepted as binding by the fighters, to negotiating with regional and 'traditional' leaders. In Buka, those were the *tsunon*. Community schools and some health facilities, as well as a limited form of local government were re-established. In response, the BRA intensified its lobbying efforts abroad (Miriori 2002). However, an informal, highly tentative peace process gained increasing numbers of supporters, not the least among women. In 1994, an 'all-Bougainvillean' peace conference was held in Arawa in 1994. In April 1995, provincial government could be re-established, in the form of the Bougainville Transitional Government (BTG). However, when a BIG/BRA delegation was ambushed by PNGDF troops after returning from talks in Australia soon afterwards, the peace process collapsed, at least publicly. In early 1997, PNG Prime Minister Chan, among others, was forced to resign after the revelation of the 'Sandline Affair', an attempt to solve the Bougainville Crisis through the deployment of foreign mercenaries (see Dorney 1998).

A breakthrough was eventually made when New Zealand hosted two rounds of talks in Burnham, and a truce was signed in October 1997. Violence between the main protagonists ceased, freedom of movement was gradually established and the care centres dissolved (Regan 2002). An unarmed regional Truce Monitoring Group, later renamed Peace Monitoring Group, helped to give Bougainvilleans a sense of security (see Wehner and Denoon 2001). In April 1998, a ceasefire was signed. From late 1998 until 2005, the United Nations Observer Mission to Bougainville observed the peace process. In June 1999 the Bougainville People's Congress, a representative body without legal basis, put forward a Bougainvillean negotiating position for a final peace agreement. It demanded a guarantee of a referendum for Bougainville on its independence, and the highest possible level of autonomy until the referendum was to be held (Regan 2002). All groups in Bougainville except for Ona's supporters who had set up a 'No Go Zone' around

Panguna agreed to this position, and the Bougainville Peace Agreement was finally signed in August 2001.

With the Peace Agreement began a period that Buka people called 'post-Crisis'. My fieldwork in 2004–05 included the transition from 'post-Crisis' to 'autonomy', which began in May 2005, when the first Autonomous Bougainville Government was elected. Partial regional autonomy within PNG is planned to last from 10 to 15 years, when a referendum over independence will be held. In 2004–05, Buka people were busy with what they called kirapim bek ples [getting the place up and going again]. This included rebuilding burnt-down houses and clearing new gardens; holding reconciliation ceremonies between ex-combatants and their families; micro-finance projects, agricultural projects, road building and maintenance; and drafting the constitution of the Autonomous Region of Bougainville, with financial and other support through observers and advisors from the United Nations and bilateral donors, especially the Australian AusAid. Towards the end of my fieldwork, when preparations directly related to the elections of the first Autonomous Bougainville Government began to dominate these efforts, kirapim bek ples came to be called wok blong otonomi [work of autonomy]. When people formally or informally discussed these activities and their progress, they were said to toktok long otonomi [talk of autonomy]. Information on matters pertaining to autonomy was shared by people across Buka to a considerable degree, mostly by daily radio broadcasts and by word of mouth.[10]

A concern that underpinned most of the activities and discussions about autonomy in Buka and that people across the area made explicit was how politics and economic activities in the Autonomous Region could be conducted 'in a Bougainvillean way'.[11] Buka people explained to me that they became aware of the strength of local, past or ancestral ways of doing things [kain pasin blong mipela yet long hia, kain pasin blong bipo, pasin blong tumbuna] during the difficult times of the Crisis. At that time, government services were disrupted, supplies from beyond Bougainville were temporarily cut off completely, and people stayed mostly within their own villages for fear of attack by armed forces. Here, they came to appreciate the resilience of matrilineal kin relations and the protection offered by the tsunon. Many of those politically active in 2004–05 argued that it was necessary to actively revive knowledge and sentiments of matrilineal kinship, traditional leadership and other aspects kastom, or culture, in the villages. When I arrived, many of the people I met were hoping that I, as an anthropologist, would share their interest in kastom and might be able to help them revive it. Most were surprised that I spent most of my time with the Pororans—who had a reputation for not knowing, and perhaps not even wanting to know about <u>kastom</u>.

Pororan, 2004

Pororan is a tiny place 'packed with people—it might sink soon', as the islanders themselves say, half laughing and half concerned. It is located at approximately 5°07' degrees southern latitude and 154°31' degrees eastern longitude, is about two square kilometres in size and had a population of 1,225 in 2000, the year of the most recent census at the time of my fieldwork. Most of them lived at the northern village of Pororan, with Yaparu Village, on the southern tip, being much smaller. The figures are estimates at best, however, because Pororan Islanders are highly mobile. They leave the island for high school or training, for employment in Buka Town or in other urban centres of Papua New Guinea, or for making gardens of sweet potatoes on the Buka mainland, as the island's own landed resources are insufficient for keeping its population fed. People staying or working elsewhere return on the weekends, once their mainland gardens are harvested, or at least once a year, usually for Christmas or Easter. Besides these more long-term absences, children and adults alike may choose to visit relatives for as little as a day or as long as a month or two, 'just for fun' or in order to request 'help', usually starch food. Furthermore, close links exist between the people of Pororan and neighbouring Hitou, a much smaller island with a population of about 80. Hitou children attend school on Pororan, and some of them live with relatives on Pororan during school terms. Many adults visit relatives on Pororan frequently and are closely involved with affairs of their *pinaposa* and thus of the community at large on Pororan. Pororan Islanders, conversely, may go and live with relatives on Hitou for some time, for making use of the fishing grounds there or in order to be away from Pororan after an argument with relatives, for instance. Thus, there is a constant coming and going on Pororan. People move by canoe or by dinghy. Five dinghies owned by different people on the island were active at Pororan Village and another three were active at Yaparu at the time of my fieldwork.

In their frequent 'going around', as they call it—leaving the island for 'finding food', for work or 'just for fun', and returning, in unpredictable patterns—the Pororans are continuing the habits of the ancestors, they say. Their ancestors were members of different matrilineal groups who set up fishing camps on the island when it first fell dry. Temporary at first, the settlements grew permanent over time. However, the members of the different matrilineal groups on Pororan maintained close connections to their relatives on the mainland. Although small gardens were made on Pororan, they continued to depend on mainland relatives for most of their starch food. Already in pre-colonial times, markets [*toan*] were arranged on the Buka west coast. Tense affairs prone to headhunters' attacks, they turned into regular gatherings once or twice a week after pacification, in the beginning of the twentieth century. In 2004–05, the Pororans obtained most of their starch food at those markets, either in exchange for fish or for money that mainlanders gave them for their fish and shellfish. Additional sources of starch food were gardens that individual family members from Pororan made on land belonging to mainland relatives, and whose harvest they brought with them upon their return to Pororan.[12] Finally, some cassava, sweet potatoes and bananas were grown in two garden areas in the interior of the island. Gardens were tiny compared to those on the mainland, however, fallow periods were short, sweet potatoes didn't grow very well, and few islanders claimed to be enthusiastic gardeners. They preferred 'going around at sea' [*roror itasi*, fishing], and 'going around over there in the bush' [*roror ilatu*], that is, visiting mainland relatives and exchanging fish for starch food.

This preference made the islanders highly vulnerable to shortages of sweet potatoes on the mainland. Tsireh told me that this was why most households aimed to have at least one member in paid employment in Buka Town, who would bring money, rice, tinned meat and fish and instant noodles from the trade stores in Buka Town on weekends, along with salt, washing powder, matches, cooking pots, towels and some other items of everyday use, and clothing. Some households fared better with this strategy than others, as alcohol consumption made 'money go missing' on a regular basis in some cases. A further problem was wind, which in mid-2004 often left employees stranded in Town on Fridays or stranded on Pororan on Mondays. Some quit their jobs, as they lost too much money staying in Town over weekends, and others were sent away by their employers when they turned up for starting the week on Wednesdays. This was not a problem in mid 2004, since the season for sea cucumber harvesting was on and the Pororans knew that they could make much more money gathering sea cucumbers and selling them to Chinese traders than they could working in Town. However, sea cucumber harvesting is restricted in Buka to about four months every four years, so as to not over-exploit this highly valuable marine resource. It was not yet clear what the laid-off men harvesting sea cucumbers would do three weeks later. (They all found employment again, though not all of them in Buka.) This, however, was 'island life', according to the Pororans: not knowing when one would be where, if one would 'find money' or not, if one would be able to obtain sweet potatoes for one's fish at the market, or when someone supposed to bring supplies to the island would arrive.

Boat owners whom I asked on Tuesday and Friday nights whether or not they would go to the market the next morning, and if I could come along usually responded with 'what if I lie to you' [nogut mi gia-manim yu]. The reason that they feared ending up lying to me, as Tsireh explained patiently when I asked him, was that human beings change their mind about where they want to go and what they want to do all the time. How could they tell in advance? Moreover, they might run into another person on their way to the boat that morning that might convince them to go somewhere other than the market. Who could know that, Tsireh asked. 'You go back in the morning, you check if they are getting ready to go, and then you get on the boat.'

I began to understand how boat journeys and other things worked on Pororan when I watched Kil arrange a boat trip for herself one day. She had been sitting and 'relaxing' in front of her kitchen house with her daughter Denise and a couple of other female relatives. They had been commenting endlessly—it seemed to me—on the movements of people unfolding around them: who had gone to Buka Town on whose boat in the morning, for doing what; who could be seen walking along the beach towards the coconut plantations; who had arrived at the neigh-bouring hamlet with a large basket of sweet potatoes for their relatives there; the young boys of what *pinaposa* had carried a radio around the village again instead of contributing to community work; who had been among the women who took an old boat whose engine was broken and had paddled it across the lagoon to Buka Island for making firewood there early in the morning; and who of Kil's younger relatives was now loading copra onto Kil's son Chris's boat, which he would bring to Town. They were busy drawing tentative conclusions about the current state of social relations from their pooled observations, interrupted by silences as they chewed betel nuts and spat out the juice. Suddenly, Kil got up, took her bilum [woollen bag] off its hook on the outside of her kitchen house and said: 'I think I might go to Town with Chris.' Denise, her daughter, said what one says on Pororan when somebody leaves: 'You go. We stay.' 'When will she come back?' I asked. 'Who knows about her', said Denise.

When I asked Tsireh if he did not mind people—Kil—coming and going in manners that must make it very difficult to plan any coopera-tive undertaking, he said: 'That's how it is over here, at sea'. He pointed to a piece of driftwood. 'You see', he said, 'this one, too, comes and goes. Who knows where it came from? It got stuck here three days ago, that's when I first saw it. Now it is stuck here. But who knows what will happen next? Maybe tomorrow, the tide will carry it away again. Maybe it will drift all the way to Rabaul [the capital of East New Britain Province], or to Samarai [Milne Bay Province], or maybe it will end up in the Philippines, who knows?' He paused. His eyes lit up, and he called out to the piece of driftwood: 'Hey, you! If you end up in the Philippines, I want you to come back here to Pororan and tell me what it is like over there!' He laughed and turned to me: 'Imagine, if it went to the Philippines, what stories it could tell afterwards! It's the same with me. It's the same with my children. It's the same with my sweet potatoes. I don't worry about them going missing here and there. Who knows, maybe they will come back some time, and what will they bring?'

Tsireh's was only the first in a series of comments on driftwood that I recorded in those early weeks. Kil made another one a week later, on a fishing trip that we took in her canoe. Suddenly, she pointed her paddle towards a piece of driftwood on the reef: 'You see?' she said. 'This one got stuck there. It has been there for a while. Birds are gathering on it now. They will bring seeds from the mainland. This is how Pororan began. Perhaps this one will grow into an island, too.' Upon my inquiries, she and Tsireh told me that Pororan is a place of very recent origin. When the Pororans' ancestors first reached the Buka west coast on their migration from their origin place on the mountain of Punein on Buka Island, at an unspecified point in the not-so-distant past, Pororan was still submerged in water. Only gradually, as domestic rubbish and bits of flora travelled from the mouth of the Gagan River and 'heaped up' around elevated reef parts, did dry spots suitable for habitation emerge. 'You see this white sand beach over there', Tsireh asked, pointing towards the northeastern tip of the island. I nodded. 'This has grown very recently. When I was young, this was all sea. And Puein [the hamlet just inland] was a swamp. Nobody lived there. It fell dry over time. They drained it. You ask Tsik [the *hahini* of the people living there]; she will tell you how she helped her parents drain the spot when she was small. So, on this side, the island is growing, but at other spots, the sea is coming inside.' Kil's son Lawrence, who was visiting, fell in: 'Our house did not stand where we are now when I was small. It was way out there, on the reef. The spot at which I grew up is sea now. The ground of the island is changing all the time. The currents deposit sand here, and they wash the cliff away over there.' 'Our little island', said Kil, shaking her head with a mix of concern and amusement. 'Who knows what will happen? Who knows where it is going?'

The Buka Mainland, 2004

Roselyn, when I shared those accounts of boat owners, driftwood and shifting ground with her, shuddered: 'That's those saltwater people, *tsomi* [sorry].[13] Who would want to live like that? If it gets too rough for you, you come and stay with us, at Tegese. You will always have enough to eat there. Have you been to the gardens yet? No? You will see, they are big, and they are well kept and there is always food there, plenty of food of various kinds: sweet potatoes, cassava, even taro.[14] And if you want to come to Town, you just get on one of our trucks. Huki's [her sister's] company trucks go every morning. You just let her know that you want to get on, no problem. It's not like on Pororan, when there are regular boats only once a week, and even then, you never know if they will actually go. My people are different. Our place is different.'

The Buka mainland had a different feel to it, indeed. Its pre-colonial name, Leitana, means 'high ground' or 'high land'. With a land area of 611 square kilometres inhabited by 33,800 people in 2000 (Bourke and Betitis 2003), it is far more substantial than Pororan, the 'small thing'. My experiences on the mainland come from two different locations, Lontis Village in the Haku language area on the Buka north coast, and Gagan Village in Solos, in the interior.[15] In some respects, they could not be more different. Lontis is the northernmost of a series of villages whose hamlets are strung up next to each other on both sides of the Buka main road, the road that leads from Buka Town along the east and north coast all the way to Kessa, the northwestern tip of the island. Population density is high along the coast, and often, the boundaries of villages and of hamlets within them consist of no more than a thick shrub separating houses on either side. Garden areas are located inland from the hamlets. Gagan, by contrast, has a church and a few houses located on a feeder road, but most people here live in scattered hamlets hidden amidst gardens and coconut plantations in the scarcely populated interior. While Lontis women do their laundry at the opening of an underground freshwater source on the beach, Gagan women do theirs in small streams flowing down from the mountains. (They avoided the Gagan River itself, where it passed near the village. It was brackish, and people were nervous about sea crocodiles.)

Despite the contrasts in scenery and certain differences in everyday life and subsistence activities that came with it, people's accounts of their place were much the same in the two locations. People drew my attention, first of all, to the soft, thick ground of the footpaths that they said must be a pleasure for me to walk on, after Pororan's coral rubble. They also pointed out the thick green of the gardens and the height of the mountains in the interior visible from a distance; the moist, soft and heavy soil inside gardens, and the size of the root crops that grew in it; the size and heaviness of banana trees, that are said to carry more and larger bananas than anywhere else, and finally, the persistence of the cloud formations over the mountains in the interior that never seem to move, compared to those over the small fringe islands, which come and go, and nobody ever knows when or why. 'Life on the mainland is very good', they said to me. 'You see, our gardens are full of food. Our land is strong and soft.'

Their land, as people at both Gagan and Lontis told me repeatedly and without my asking about it, afforded them privacy and a sense of strength resulting from the fact that they were 'staying on the land of the ancestors.' They continued: 'It is our land, and nobody can boss us around here. And whatever else happens, we always have our land and can live here.' They took care to show me the boundary of their land, both their hamlets and their garden areas, indicating, too, where those boundaries were disputed. They warned me against strolling over onto other people's land, or engaging with those others on my own. 'We don't go around here like that. We stay in our own place. If you want to go and talk to those people over there, for your research, let us know and we will accompany you. Don't go on your own. Don't eat with them. They are other people, and you belong to us.'

People gave me two different explanations, separately and jointly, when I asked why this was so important, and when I told them that on Pororan, I was used to wandering around freely and being invited for tea by anybody whose house I happened to pass by. One explanation was simply 'those are our ways here on the mainland'. The other was the Bougainville Crisis. Loretta, my host in Gagan, was primarily worried about my safety when she told me not to stray too far from the hamlet on my own. Her place, she said, was secure. Her husband was the police minister, and as a former leader of one of the Crisis factions in Solos, he was feared in the area.[16] Nevertheless, the tension that held his relatives in its grip was obvious. Younger male relatives of Loretta's, not visibly armed but obviously watchful, were guarding the hamlet at night. Loretta's daughters, 18 to three in age, moved around the hamlet and the garden areas freely, but never left 'our land' without the company of some of the 'boys'. Her husband had not reconciled yet, Loretta explained, with some of her relatives, who had fought 'on the other side'. She herself had begun 'straightening relations', but painful memories that she did not specify further made this a slow and difficult process. Under those conditions, people were careful to move in ways that did not offend or frighten anybody. They carefully avoided trespassing onto the land of other people, took care not to startle others by approaching their houses or hamlets from the back, and avoided 'going around randomly' in places where they had no business. Loretta said it was important that I, too, did not 'roam around'.

Concerns for my safety, which predominated in Gagan but were made less explicit among my hosts at Lontis were complemented by considerations of propriety. No young woman should be seen 'wandering around randomly' among 'other people' [*mis a katun*], as Roselyn's mother Ngasi told me one day while we were making buns that she would sell at her daughter's trade store later on. I asked how I could go about my research then, which would have to include people outside my host hamlet. Ngasi told me to 'follow the road' [*kura maror*], just as everybody else did, and I would be all right. She took another load of buns out of the iron drum she had turned into an oven, and I had no occasion to ask her what 'following the road' involved. I learned that a couple of days later from her sister Elmah. I was making a map of Tegese and was just crossing an empty space between two houses, no more than five meters wide, when Elmah called out to me: 'What are you doing over there! Don't mess up the road!' Elmah explained that the houses belonged to members of different *ngorer* within the *pina-posa*, and that I had just crossed a boundary between different parts of the hamlet that one should not cross. She took me by the shoulders and walked me all the way to the main road on 'our' footpath, along the main road and then into 'their' footpath that branched off the main road parallel to ours. Only then did she let go of me. 'This is how you do it. And next time you want to go around to other people's places, let me know. I will go with you. You are messing up the road with your ways of going around randomly.'

Another instance of 'messing up the road' occurred during my second visit to Gagan, and it made me aware how important 'following roads' was to people concerned with peace and with the ways of the ancestors on Buka. A man was found dead on the feeder road linking Gagan to the Buka main road one morning. He had a knife in his back. My hosts were deeply disturbed. That someone had 'messed him up, that poor guy' [bagarapim em, *tsomi*] was not particularly surprising to them. They did not know the man, but assumed that his death was Crisis-related. What troubled them more was that the killer had apparently killed and had then left his victim on the road. He had 'messed up the road', besides messing up a particular person. 'This is our road. It was paved again after the Crisis finished. We are only just beginning to use it again. We are only just beginning to travel again to meet matrilineal relatives elsewhere, to reconcile with those who fought on the other side, and to catch up with people whom we could not meet during the Crisis, because travel was dangerous. The small roads in the bush, they are still not safe, so this one is very important. Now this man was killed on it, people will be afraid again', Loretta explained, sad and furious. She then wondered who this killer was. 'Whoever it was, he has no respect for the peace process', she said. 'He has no respect, either, for the ways of our ancestors, whose footsteps we are tracing in keeping in touch with matrilineal relatives in other locations. What are we to do if not even this road is safe?'

Movements: An Ethnographic Focus

In my initial inquiries into everyday life and people's understandings of themselves and their place, I was not pursuing a particular track yet. I was merely trying to settle in and ease my way into research when I inquired into the numbers of people of Pororan and tried to find out how they kept themselves fed, when I went fishing, talked to Tsireh, negotiated with boat owners, baked buns with Ngasi and made a map of Tegese, and learned about the Bougainville Crisis from Loretta in Solos. Across this range of undirected inquiries and activities, however, something appeared again and again and began to preoccupy me. This was the enormous interest that people, both on Pororan and on the mainland, took in observing and manipulating the physical movements of persons, and to a lesser degree, of food, money and driftwood.

On the mainland, the importance that people attached to 'following roads' struck me. In the first two months of my fieldwork in Buka, I acquired no more than a rough idea of what 'following roads' meant in practical terms. Moreover, I knew close to nothing at that time about the history and the capacity for manipulation of those roads, and thus could not see the value that Elmah, for instance, saw in following them [and in making me follow them]. Nevertheless, it was clear already then that if I wanted to live on the mainland, and if I wanted to learn anything about mainland sociality at all, I would have to investigate those roads and people's ways of 'following them'.

On Pororan, I marvelled at the opposite to the mainlanders' interest in 'following roads'. This was the islanders' insistence on the inherent indeterminacy of movements, human and non-human alike, 'at sea'. I was interested in their ways of drawing tentative conclusions about social relations from watching these movements unfold. Their abstention from predicting the future of those movements or claiming knowledge of their past beyond that part that they had been able to observe themselves fascinated me. I knew nothing then about the linguistic finesse of the Pororans' discussions of movements, or about their skills at manipulating movements in everyday life and on ceremonial occasions. Nevertheless, the close attention that the Pororans paid to movements unfolding around them was sufficient indication that on Pororan, I would have to study not roads but people's everyday movements.

I will mostly be concerned in this study with the highly indeterminate movements from which people drew tentative conclusions about social relations on Pororan. Mainlanders' interests in 'following roads' will only concern me here insofar as it was significant to island-mainland interactions. My reasons for choosing a saltwater focus, about two months into what was originally intended to be comparative research, were threefold. First of all, I realized that an in-depth investigation of both roads and indeterminate movements would exceed the scope of a doctoral project. Secondly, a fair amount of ethnographic research, including recent research, is available on the Buka mainland (see esp. Kenneth 2005; Rimoldi 1971; Rimoldi and Rimoldi 1992; Sagir 2003, 2005; Sarei 1974). From the Western Islands, by contrast, no book-length study is available to date.[17] Finally, hearing Tsireh link the unpredictable movements of Kil, and hearing Kil link the unpredictable growth and diminishment of the island she lived on to the movements of driftwood and other things floating by at sea struck an anthropological cord, with resonances deep into several sets of anthropological writings.

The first and smallest set of literature consists in ethnographies of fishing people in Melanesia, especially those that have already drawn attention to movements, including highly indeterminate ones (Munn 1986); to the dialectical processes of closing and opening relations, with a focus on the latter (Battaglia 1993, 1999; Küchler 1987, 1988, 2002); to surprise (Rutherford 2003) and to the contingency of human action, in contrast to ancestral perfection (Battaglia 1990). Beyond those specifically saltwater-oriented writings lie theoretically highly sophisticated analyses of innovation and convention (Wagner 1981), and of the uncertainty of outcomes and gradual processes of revelation in Melanesia (M. Strathern 1988). These have been very influential in Melanesian anthropology and have drawn upon and contributed to research into a broad range of theoretical issues beyond Melanesia, including gender, kinship, exchange and property.[18] I shall explicitly link the Pororans' interests in highly indeterminate movements to these broader anthropological concerns, and shall utilize them for comparative purposes beyond the saltwater literature, by employing some of the theoretical tools that this literature provides throughout my analysis.

In addition, Pororan comments on driftwood resonate with writings on space, place and the environment, from Melanesia and beyond.[19] I am specifically interested in approaching from a saltwater perspective the question formulated most succinctly by Corsín Jiménez (2003: 137): 'What happens when people's identity is not land-related?' The highly particular connections that Kil and Tsireh drew for me between 'our ways here at sea', human movements, the movements of driftwood, and the processes of island growth and diminishment offer a promising starting point for pursuing this question further. Moreover, overlapping with research on space and place but with interests of its own, there is a literature on land and marine tenure in Melanesia that this study builds upon and aims to speak to. As anthropologists have long pointed out, land plays a crucial role in relations of kinship (see, e.g. Langness 1964; Leach 2000, 2003a; A. Strathern 1973), citizenship (e.g. Bolton 2003; Filer and Sekhran 1998) and cosmology (e.g. Rumsey and Weiner 2001, 2004). It is thus crucial to the constitution of Melanesian sociality, but in ethnographically specific ways. Anthropologists have provided insightful commentaries on the need of taking this specificity into account in the context of development.[20] Compared to the large body of research on land and land ownership, notions of the sea and practices of marine tenure have received relatively little ethnographic attention (Hviding 1996: 20).[21] Specifically, Hviding argues that a new kind of 'processual analysis' (21) is needed that describes how marine tenure works, not as a set of rules pertaining to resources but as a system of relationships between persons, and between persons and their environment. Such analyses appear increasingly urgent in the face of intrusions of foreign commercial fishing vessels into Melanesian waters. Pororan interests in movements, in contrast to Buka mainlanders' interests in roads, offer a unique occasion for investigating marine tenure in relation to land tenure in the same area. In the following chapters, I shall investigate the Pororans' interests in movements through the analytic tools and guiding questions provided by these diverse anthropological sources.

Studying Movements: Some Methods

First, however, having decided to take the Pororans' interests in movements as an ethnographic focus, I needed a methodology for studying them systematically. Haphazardly at first and in a more conscious and organized manner later, I utilized four methods, each drawing on familiar ethnographic methodology but adjusted to the purpose of learning about movements. One involved employing my eyes and ears for detecting people's everyday movements in the same way as Pororan Islanders did. I observed and followed the example of Kil's female relatives who occasionally came by her house for a chat and stayed on for hours, doing nothing but watching and commenting on the movements of people visible or audible from this spot. From them, I learned not only to watch but also to 'listen to' the shifting locations of people in space as Pororan Islanders do, most importantly by tracing the long drawn out '*oo*' that people call out when greeting someone passing by. Through those '*oo*', a person's changing positions in space could be detected beyond one's field of vision. I also learned to distinguish the sounds of the engines of the different Pororan boats, and to pay attention to the direction in which they were going.

However, watching and listening to people shift positions in space alone would not have been sufficient. As Merleau-Ponty (1966: 311–13) has pointed out, our understanding of movements is always disproportional to our understanding of a sequence of positions of a mobile item in space. The more we focus on positions, the less we can grasp the movement as a whole. My method for grasping the 'whole' of the movements that were relevant to Pororan Islanders was to pay careful attention to verbs of movement (especially going, coming, causing to go/come, throwing away, pulling, putting, leaving, arriving, returning) that the Pororans used when discussing everyday affairs, when telling stories of the past, or when commenting on the current state of social relations on the island. Gradually, I learned the significance of these linguistic forms that people employed in a highly sophisticated manner in their accounts of movements. Then, I began to recognize movements matching specific linguistic terms, as Pororan Islanders did, in people's everyday comings and goings. Being able to participate intelligibly in Pororan discussions about movements they observed was a big step towards looking like a person to the islanders.

Words alone, however, were not enough, for especially in highly significant moments, Pororan Islanders tended to fall silent. I learned, however, that particular verbs of movement were often accompanied by distinctive movements of the speaker's hand and arm or eyes and head. Having identified those, I could detect relational meaning that people attributed to others' movements even in the absence of any verbal commentary, just by looking at the movements of their hands, arms or heads. As I myself learned to employ these linguistic and gestural forms (more or less) correctly, the Pororans began to draw me into more sophisticated, and sometimes more esoteric discussions of movements past and present, which often continued deep into the night.

Thirdly, I moved with the Pororans, in everyday life and on ritual occasions. Much of the ethnographic material on which this study is based was collected on boats and trucks, and while walking along the reef gathering shellfish or along the footpaths to the garden areas in the interior. I gained significant insights into Pororan-mainland relations when I accompanied Kil on a visit to matrilineal kin there whom she had not seen for many years. My understanding of island history made rapid progress when Salu, towards the end of my stay, arranged for me to visit the pre-colonial village site of Keketin, together with Rokayo, who held the position of paramount *tsunon* on the island in 2004–05. Finally, my analysis of marriage and mortuary rites is based on observations that I made while attending such events with Kil or Salu, or while moving back and forth between the two of them. In doing so, I noticed the difference that movements made to perception.

The final important method for learning about Pororan movements and through them about island relations was to strategically deploy my own movements and record people's reactions. At first accidentally and later on deliberately, I occasionally failed to conform to Pororan habits of moving, and in doing so, I learned what understandings underpinned those habits. My occasional trips to the mainland became a part of this strategy. I used them to elicit verbal commentaries on their own relatives and experiences there, which the islanders were otherwise not very forthcoming with. If I asked those questions in the abstract—'do you have any relatives on the mainland? Where do they live? When did you last see them?'—I usually got to hear a vague 'who knows about them? I haven't seen them for a long time. How would I know now if I have relatives in the bush?' By contrast, telling the islanders where I had been on the mainland, whom I had met there or who had mentioned to me that they had relatives on Pororan usually led into lively story-telling about trips to the mainland, adventures there or ancestral migration routes that linked the Pororans to people 'in the bush'.

It took me some time to develop these methods into a consistent research strategy that convinced the Pororans as well as myself. At first, the islanders were puzzled as they watched me spend my time walking around the island, going fishing and watching other people's movements with them. What I was doing was not what they knew anthropology to be about. Anthropology, as they were fully aware, was about kastom, or culture, as they reminded me in English. However, since I knew already before my arrival that the Pororans thought of themselves as being ignorant about kastom, I downplayed this aspect of anthropological interests and highlighted my wish to find out how they lived and what was important to them. The Pororans remained sceptical, nevertheless. For months, people asked me every now and then if I didn't have any questions I needed them to answer about kastom, about the clans, for instance, or about traditional leadership [and see Chapter 6 for the outcomes of the discussions that we did have about <u>kastom</u>]. Over time, however, the Pororans and I myself became confident that I was learning something from them that important, although they did not call it <u>kastom</u>. I shall investigate this 'something' in the following chapters as the Pororans' mode of 'objectifying' relations in movements (M. Strathern 1988).[22]

Movements as Objectification

Movements, on Pororan, are the most immediate 'manner in which persons and things are construed as having value, that is, are objects of other people's subjective regard or of their creation' (M. Strathern 1988: 176). This definition of the term 'objectification' has a particular history in Strathern's Hagen ethnography, and the term does specific theoretical work in her writings. Both have been made explicit (see esp. M. Strathern 1999, chapter 1). I argue that Pororan movements are both sufficiently similar to the ethnographic moments that Strathern describes for being usefully investigated through this term, and are different from these moments in theoretically interesting ways.

Neither the Euro-American/Melanesian contrast nor the argument about gender in which Strathern employs the term is explicitly taken on here (see M. Strathern 1984, 1988). My interest is, instead, in the origin of the term, and its re-capture for theoretical purposes of particular Hagen revelatory strategies. One such moment especially has influenced Strathern's anthropology in significant ways (M. Strathern 1999: 10–11). This is a moment at which shell wealth is transferred between men in exchange, or their display when the shells are just about to be given away. This moment of objectification is an assemblage of valuable objects, here things, that makes relations between persons visible in a particular form. The assemblage draws together and draws attention to the value and power of particular relations. At the same time, spectators are also invited to consider other relations, which the display conceals within itself.

Pororan movements are comparable to these moments. Like Hagen wealth displays, they make the capacities of persons and their relational constitution apparent in particular forms. They reveal persons and relations as entities with particular qualities and value attached to them, in ways that are constrained by particular conventions of form. As among Hageners, these conventional forms are gendered. In addition, Pororan movements, like Hagen wealth displays, hold in tension revelation and concealment. As Hageners do with wealth displays, Pororan Islanders 'decompose' (see also Mosko 1985; M. Strathern 1992c) a movement into the intentions and capacities of persons who are observed to perform and who are stipulated to have caused it. The relational composition of persons is apprehended in their 'coming from', 'going to' or 'returning to' particular others (the distinction is significant on Pororan). These similarities make it plausible to extend the term objectification from Hagen wealth displays to Pororan movements. Pororan movements are 'objects', both of Pororan Islanders' scrutiny and regard, and of my argument here.

At the same time, it is worth asking what difference it makes that these objects are movements, and not material objects, as displays of wealth are. My analysis builds upon one observation in particular. This is that definite form of a movement only becomes apparent as a movement is halted (and thus ceases to be a movement, until it starts and changes form again). Movements thus highlight the contingency of outcomes, and pose questions about the relation between single forms and the sequences of forms through which they appear, and that they might hold as a potential. I do not wish to suggest an absolute contrast to Hagen wealth displays here. Strathern's analytic unfolding of these displays proceeds by gradual revelation, just as Pororan Islanders commentaries do when they watch one another's movements unfold. Strathern has also made it clear that the power of Hagen wealth displays as moments of objectification has become fully apparent only retrospectively (M. Strathern 1992c: 12–13). The moments of objectification of Strathern's interest thus do not 'have less' temporal depth than Pororan objectifications of relations in movements. However, movements, whose gradual unfolding Pororan Islanders enjoy watching, make an object of the temporality of revelation, and of the relation between single and multiple forms, in a way that neither Hagen wealth displays nor roads on the Buka mainland do. Thus, using Strathern's notion of objectification for investigating Pororan movements seems an appropriate strategy of drawing my ethnography towards the first, Melanesian set of anthropological writings mentioned above. It helps me set up comparisons between movements on Pororan and roads on the mainland, comparisons of the Pororans' saltwater sociality to saltwater ethnographies elsewhere in Melanesia, and beyond that, theoretical comparisons of the Pororans' interests in the indeterminacy of human movements and relations with similar interests elsewhere, in saltwater or in landed settings.

I begin my analysis with a chapter on fishing. In their fishing activities, the islanders' characteristic interests in highly indeterminate movements and in keeping relational possibilities open become most strongly apparent. By starting here, I intend to set the tone of open-ended inquiries with surprising outcomes for everything that follows. In order to retain this sense of open-endedness throughout an account that nevertheless, by academic conventions, must achieve some degree of closure, I shall do as the Pororans told me and use the real names of the people I lived with and who contributed to my research. Where people are not referred to by name, it is either because they asked me not to mention their name in a particular context, or, more frequently, because I stand to them in a relation of <u>tambu</u>, in-law, that would have made it inappropriate to use their name. In being specific about what particular people did or said in certain moments, and about how this has informed what I have come to think and write about Pororan, I hope to retain the sense that things could as well have turned out differently, which is so strong in all Pororan undertakings.

NOTES

1. See esp. Hocart 1922: [76–77]; Hviding 1996; Ivens 1930 (for the Solomon Islands); Carrier and Carrier 1985, 1989; Harding 1967; Parkinson 1907: 201–202; Pomponio 1990, 1992 (for Papua New Guinea); Bonnemaison 1984: 94; Rodman 1987: 17 (for Vanuatu); and Sharp 2002 (for the Torres Strait). This list is limited to texts that discuss the distinction, as opposed to many more that mention it in passing.
2. Buka had 6,144 baptized Catholics in 1936, out of an estimated population of 6,810 (Laracy 1976).
3. Fred Archer was the manager of a plantation on Yaming, the island between Pororan and Petats. He had also worked as a coast watcher in the early phase of the Japanese occupation.
4. See also Connell's (1978) work on cooperatives in Siwai, and Ogan's (1972) on Kieta.
5. The ethnographers Max and Eleanor Rimoldi (1992) have provided a detailed account of the history and political philosophy of the Welfare.
6. See, e.g. Connell 1997; Davies 2005; Dove et al. 1974; Filer 1990, 1992; Mamak and Bedford 1974; Momis 1974; Momis and Ogan 1973; Ogan 1972, 1996, 1999; Oliver 1973; and Regan 2005.
7. Perhaps most widely known is the case of Rorovana, a coastal village whose site was selected for the mining port. Here, police eventually removed women who tried to block the bulldozers' way (Oliver 1973: 165).
8. E.g. Crocombe 1968; Ghai and Regan 2002; Griffin 1973, 1977; Hannett 1969a, 1969b; Luana 1969; Mamak and Bedford 1974; Premdas 1977; Tsibim 1967.
9. Maru, pers. comm. One might sense doubts about this 'invitation' in a central Bougainvillean leader's wording: 'It was said that the military had been invited back by the chiefs in Buka' (Miriori 2002). Alternatively, one might understand this phrasing as a discouragement to investigate further into an issue that remained contentious in 2004–05. Presented here is the opinion prevalent among my Buka hosts.
10. In contrast to some areas on Bougainville, which remain inaccessible by trucks, cars or boats.

11. In extension of Bernard Narokobi's (1983) 'Melanesian Way'.

12. Some islanders used to cultivate a larger block of land belonging to people at Karoola, just opposite Pororan, to which one of their *tsunon* had negotiated access for them. However, disputes over the ownership of this land among the mainlanders led to food being 'stolen' from the Pororans' gardens, and by 2004, the Pororans had given up on working there. The Catholic church, too, had given the islanders permission to garden on some of its land on the Buka west coast, but the continuation of this arrangement was uncertain in 2004–05 as the church wanted to use the land for other purposes.

13. *Tsomi* is translated as 'sorry', but only higher-ranking persons use it towards lower-ranking ones, or adults towards children. It is a statement of power as much as of empathy.

14. Taro used to be the staple food on Buka until World War II, but was then replaced by sweet potatoes. The reasons include taro blight in the 1930s, the consumption of roots and leaves by the Japanese forces that occupied Bougainville and suffered hunger there in World War II, and possibly also Allied spraying of gardens with napalm (see Nelson 2005). Some taro grew in 2004–05 in the gardens in the interior, and was considered superior to sweet potatoes.

15. All Buka languages belong to the Meso-Melanesian sub-group of the Oceanic sub-group of the Austronesian language group, and are largely mutually intelligible. Linguists have distinguished three of them: Halia spoken on the east and north coast, Solos spoken in the interior, and Petats spoken on the Western Islands (Tryon 2005). Buka people, however, consider the Haku dialect of Halia that is spoken on the north coast to be a separate language. Similarly, the Pororans claim that they and their neighbours on Hitou speak Hapororan, which derived from Petats but contains elements of Haku, Solos and Tok Pisin, as well. This is said to be due to their close interactions with mainlanders, mostly from Haku at present.

16. Hilary Masiria died in an accident in 2007.

17. Beatrice Blackwood lived on Petats in 1929, but shifted her field site to northern Bougainville because she felt the islanders had been too thoroughly exposed to the influence of the Methodist Mission just across the island on Buka (Blackwood 1935). I thank the staff at the Pitt Rivers Museum in Oxford for granting me access to her unpublished field notes (Blackwood n.d.). In addition, an article by a Buka plantation owner who lived on the west coast for a long time and underwent male initiation on Pororan gives some details about island life in the 1920s (Thomas 1931).

18. For research on gender, see esp. Gillison 1993; M. Strathern 1980, 1984, 1988. On kinship, see esp. Bamford and Leach 2009; Konrad 2005; Leach 2003a; M. Strathern 1992a, 1992b, 2005; Wagner 1967, 1974, 1977a. On exchange, see esp. Crook 2007; Foster 1995; Lederman 1986; McKinnon 1991; Piot 1999; M. Strathern 1988, 1992d; Wagner 1986b. On property, see esp. Hirsch and Strathern 2004; Kalinoe and Leach 2001; Leach 2003b; 2004; Riles 2004; M. Strathern 1998, 1999, 2001. On meaning, symbols and their transformation, see Wagner 1972, 1977b, 1986a, 1987, 2001; Weiner 1988. On partial connections and chaos, see Mosko and Damon 2005, M. Strathern 1991, Wagner 2001. On networks and institutions, see Riles 2001; M. Strathern 1996, 2000.

19. See esp. Basso 1996; Bender 1993; Feld and Basso, 1996; Hirsch and O'Hanlon 1995; Ingold 2000; Leach 2003a; Rodman 1985, 1992; Weiner 1991.
20. E.g. Bell 1953; Connell 1978; Crocombe 1971; Epstein 1969; Filer 1990, 1992, 1997a, 1997b; Filer and Sekhran 1998; Hogbin and Lawrence 1967; Hviding 1996; Hviding and Bayliss-Smith 2000; Larmour 1991; Leach 2000, 2003a; Mitchell 1982; Ogan 1971, 1972, 1996; Otto 1998; Rumsey and Weiner 2004; Weiner 1998, 2001b.
21. This does not mean no studies existed, and more have since appeared. See, e.g. Akimichi 1995; Aswani 1999; Carrier 1981; Carrier and Carrier 1983; Foale 2005; Hayes 1993; Hyndman 1993.
22. Various other notions of objectification in anthropology (see, e.g. Handler 1984; Keane 1997; Miller 1987) and in the feminist literature (Nussbaum 1995) are not immediately relevant to my argument.

CHAPTER 1

Fishing People

Pororan is a fishing place, as Roselyn told me on my first visit. At Pororan Village, the proximity of the sea and the importance of fishing to the inhabitants were apparent everywhere in 2004–05. Spear guns and paddles leaned against house walls, and fishing baskets usually had to be cleared off benches and tables before meals. Large, store-bought fishing nets were hanging between trees in some hamlets. The beach and the canoes[1] on it provided the visual background to most Pororan domestic scenes, and the smell of smoked fish hung over the village in most evenings. Men and women, from early childhood to very old age, were involved in fishing and movements at sea more generally on a daily basis. Every morning and every night, all islanders except for the very smallest used to go and wash in the sea. A significant portion of children's time was spent on the reef around the island. At high tide, they paddled around the island in groups in their small canoes, collected seaweed, or caught small fish that they then roasted on the beach. At low tide, they caught mud-crabs in the mangroves or gathered shellfish on the reef. Older children went out more purposefully for gathering shellfish, spearing small reef fish, and diving for fish in the smaller passages. Young people went diving with goggles and fins in the deeper passages. Women walked along the reef gathering shells and went out line fishing, either standing on the edge of the reef or sitting in their canoes in the lagoon. Men fished during the day, and also went out with a fishing rod and a pressure lamp or with their spear, goggles and a torch at night. Even old people who were too fragile to go further than the beach remained oriented towards the sea. Old people whose houses were located inland often relocated to the house of a relative directly on the beach.[2] Some told me that this was for reasons of easy access to the sea for bathing and toilet.[3] Others said that it was cooler, mosquitoes were fewer, and that they enjoyed sitting on the beach and watching canoes and boats come and go across the lagoon.

Notes for this section begin on page 49

Anywhere, Any Time, Anybody

Pororan Islanders emphasized that they could fish anywhere they chose around their island [laik blong mi yet]. They used markers on land and at sea for orientation, as well as for describing their outings back at the village and telling others where fishing was good (see also Hviding 1996; Sharp 2002). These markers included ston [reef outcrops], pasis [passages], shallow reef areas and, for instance, a coconut palm with yellow fronds. Some of these markers had names and ancestral stories of particular *pinaposa* attached to them whose details were known only to members of the *pinaposa*. Others were personal, informal, and shared only, say, between two men who often went fishing together. These markers, however, did not constitute boundaries of clan territories (see esp. Sharp 2002). 'Boundaries? That's a bush habit', Tsireh explained. 'The fish roam around freely. The mud-crabs roam around freely, popping up from holes here and there on the beach. How would we make boundaries that would keep the fish and everything else inside?' Furthermore, the Pororans did not string the markers up into conventionalized 'paths' used for going to particular fishing sites, in order to fish for a certain species in a certain season (see esp. Hviding 1996). Instead, they emphasized that 'we just try'. As Kil once said, 'I go and think of one spot, and I try and see if there are fish there. If not, I move on to the next. My decision.'

An exception to the absence of boundaries and prescriptions of where to go at sea were the bans that the *tsunon* sometimes placed on a particular area of the reef, in preparation for a feast or in order to allow this area to recover just before the holiday seasons of Easter and Christmas, when many islanders working away return home. These, however, were not described as boundaries, but as 'leaving the place alone to rest' temporarily [lusim hap na bai malolo pastaim]. Particular species, too, were 'left alone', that is, protected by a ban imposed by the *tsunon*, usually on the advice of a Pororan Islander trained and working away from the island as a marine biologist. In 2004–05, these species were dugongs, turtles and dolphins. When a turtle or dugong did go into their net occasionally, however, people felt free to consume it, arguing that it had 'come on its own' [em yet em ikam, *ngilanou*], without being 'called' through the use of spells [pulpul].

People from other villages, who would not know of the bans imposed by Pororan *tsunon*, were expected to inform their relatives on Pororan beforehand when they intended to fish in reef areas associated with Pororan, and vice versa. Such venturing into other people's areas was rare in 2004–05, however. Villages were too far apart for making fishing journeys between them by canoe, and the high price of petrol prevented the islanders from using fibreglass boats for fishing, except for trolling on their way to Buka Town. The only location that is so close to Pororan that formal arrangements were necessary is Petats. A formal sea boundary between Pororan and Petats has been agreed upon.[4] It is marked by a small passage called *kukubei* between Pororan and the uninhabited island of Yaming.[5]

The islanders claimed that they could go fishing any time they wanted to, as well as anywhere they choose to go. 'When I want to go, I go', they said. Of course, there are better times and worse times in the year or day for catching particular species, or for using particular methods. The Pororans distinguish two seasons, *halat* [October–March] and *hiningal* [April–September]. *Halat* is characterized as the season when the tide is low during the night. During *hiningal*, the tide is low during daytime. Therefore *halat* gives plenty of occasion for line-fishing in the day and gathering mud-crabs with bamboo frond torches in the mangroves at night, while during *hiningal*, many people go line-fishing during the night, and gather shells on the reef during the daytime. Some older couples with adult children or young couples with children below school-age might set up camp on Manuan, an uninhabited island close to Pororan during *hiningal*, for a few days or for more than a month, in order to make use of the rich fishing grounds there. However, fishing activities were not entirely constrained by the seasons, and this point was important to the Pororans. It was possible to go night fishing when the tide was low, too, and some people did it even though it was less convenient.

The exact timing of the tides and periods of high and low tides are determined by the moon, which the islanders observe and from which they deduce what species are likely to be plentiful at a given time. Wind, rain and a particular condition of the sea, when it is 'dirty' with fauna carried by the current from the Gagan River, also influence the islanders' decisions about fishing times. It will be important to my argument below, however, that the islanders do not claim expert knowledge on these matters. Several old and experienced fishermen firmly insisted, in this or similar wording: 'We do not know what will happen at sea, if there will be many fish or perhaps no fish at all. We just try it out. Sometimes fish are plentiful, sometimes they are not. Who knows about them?' Correspondingly, Pororan fishermen who boasted about a large catch did not praise their own foresight or skill, but dwelled at length on their own surprise at running into so many fish just when they were least expecting it.[6]

Aside from seasonal changes, Buka mainlanders' demands for fish, too, impinged on the timing of Pororan fishing activities. Members of a particular *pinaposa* might gather shellfish and perhaps go spear-fishing at night in preparation for a feast that *pinaposa* relatives on the mainland had asked them to help with. Furthermore, many men and some married couples usually spent Tuesday and Friday nights line-fishing in the lagoon in preparation for the market the next day, where the islanders exchange fish for starch food. These markets were held at Kessa and Karoola in 2004, and at Karoola and sometimes at Kessa and Kohiso in 2005. They are said to have been an important feature of island life ever since the island was settled, briefly interrupted only during the early 1990s, when the Bougainville Crisis made sea-travel dangerous. The village schedule, a remainder from German colonial times that the *tsunon* continue to encourage villagers to follow, assigns fishing to entire days just before the markets.

However, this schedule, rendered to me verbally by Pororan women, is most interesting for the ways in which island life diverged from it during my fieldwork. The islanders spent more time at sea than the schedule would suggest. Moreover, they felt free to go fishing any time, on any weekday.[7] 'Fishing is not work. It's not like gardening, something you have to do if you want something to grow. You can go fishing any time you want, or you can leave it', Salu's daughter Jennifer told me. Often, she wanted to go fishing when the children at the hamlet were getting too much for her. Once, for instance, we had spent half an hour trying to calm down two of her children and two of her sister's children, whose game had turned very rough. When Jennifer saw Salu returning to the hamlet after a visit to the garden, she told me: 'You and Salu can look after them for a while. I am fed up with them, I am going to the sea.' She quickly changed into an old <u>laplap</u>, picked up a basket and a paddle and walked down toward the beach. Her four year-old son Hangot followed her, tugged at her <u>laplap</u> and said quietly: '<u>Mama</u>, I want to go, too.'

Table 1 • Weekly Schedule, Pororan Village

Weekday	Activity
Monday (<u>Manrai</u>)	gardening
Tuesday (*Hulu*)	fishing
Wednesday (*Hohopis*)	market; chiefs' meeting
Thursday (*Hanina*)	'Government day': assembly and community work; once monthly: village court
Friday (*Hatolim*)	fishing
Saturday (<u>Sararai</u>)	market; preparing food for Sunday
Sunday (<u>Sande</u>)	church; soccer matches; visiting; resting (on the beach)

Jennifer shook him off and shouted angrily: 'You especially! Your crying especially I wanted not to hear for a while!' His sobbing left her unimpressed as she pushed the canoe into the water. Salu quickly put down her basket full of sweet potatoes, went to pick Hangot up from the beach and explained to him: 'your mother is fed up with you. Let her go now, and later she will come back, and you will eat the fish she will bring.' Later in the evening, probably picking up on my surprised face when she had left Hangot behind, Jennifer explained to me: 'If I could not go fishing any time I wanted to, I would go crazy here. Everybody would go crazy. You see, this island is packed with people; this hamlet is full of children. I need to leave the place behind sometimes for a rest. At sea, I can be on my own, nobody is directing my movements (<u>nogat man ibosim wokabaut blong mi</u>), I can go around wherever I want, and nobody can make me come back. It's all up to me. I am free.' Other islanders expressed similar sentiments about fishing and the freedom it afforded them. They admired people who anticipated difficult situations, and especially situations where they would be on the shorter end, and left for the sea before they could get caught up in them. Some older women told me—at the same time verbally distancing themselves from such behaviour and chuckling with admiration—that some village court cases had to be postponed infinitely because the accused 'went missing at sea' [<u>em igo lus long solwara</u>] each time the case was scheduled.

Finally, the Pororans claimed that anybody could go and fish any time and anywhere they liked. This included women. On the one hand, there is an association of men with fishing and women with gardening, on Pororan just as on the mainland and in many other saltwater locations in Melanesia. Providing fish is the task of men, not women. There is no better way for a Pororan woman to insult her husband than to demonstratively pick up his fishing spear and goggles, go out in the family canoe he built, return with a large fish 'of the kind that only men catch' in the deep passages in the lagoon and share the fish with others, excluding him. Kil's daughter Denise did this once, loosing her temper after a week of hearing rumours of her husband's latest affair. Her husband was staying with her at her brother's house at Kil's hamlet, Kobkobul. After being excluded from the consumption of her fish, he went to stay with his own relatives at Mulul, drank homebrew for several days and suddenly re-appeared at Kobkobul a week later, carrying three large fish by the tail. He casually put them down by the fire, and when Denise picked them up to clean and cook them, he quietly settled back into the hamlet.

On the other hand, many Pororan women spend a lot of time at sea and contribute a lot of fish to the family's diet without ever making a point of it. As long as they do not claim their catch as theirs but cook it along with their husband's, this is perfectly acceptable, and some women are held in high esteem for supporting their families in this way. However, their role as fishing people, like rather than unlike men, made Pororan women suspect to mainlanders. Many young women I knew on the mainland envied me, on the one hand, for staying on Pororan, where they themselves would love to go and find a husband 'who will catch lots of fish for me'.[8] However, they were deeply ambivalent about Pororan women. They told me that they would never want to be like 'those island women, who go fishing, just like the men, *tsomi*'. Perhaps that was why they never took me up on the offer of hosting them on Pororan, despite the strong attraction that the fish and Pororan men's reputation for cheerfulness and great joking skills held out. Mainland men, meanwhile, told me that they would never be so stupid as to marry a Pororan woman (although some do). 'They are saltwater women. They only think of going around at sea. They don't work, and it is hard to control their movements [bosim wokabaut blong ol]. When they get tired of staying somewhere, they just take off. Who would want to marry a woman who goes around like that, wherever she wants, whenever she wants?'

Gardening and Fishing

While Pororan fishing is 'free' in time and space and for anybody, mainland gardening is 'emplaced', at least ideally regulated by schedules, and conducted with one's own people [*eri*, us] and in clear physical separation from others [*eru*, them]. On the north coast, the women and men of a *ngorer* planning to go to the gardens that day usually set off together in the morning, in one big group or in several small ones of close relatives. Ideally, they are the senior women of the *ngorer* owning the hamlet and the garden area they are going to, their sons and the sons' wives, who live at their husband's place. Numbers in the hamlets I am familiar with vary, depending on who is currently employed in Buka Town, on who may have gone to the coconut plantations to make copra for some extra cash, and who might be resting in the hamlet. Usually, there are more women than men, as more men are employed in Buka Town and as men are only responsible for the clearing of new gardens and other heavy work—although some enjoy doing planting, weeding and harvesting, too.

When they turn from the footpath in their own hamlet into the Buka main road, the women of a group walk in the middle, shielded by men (if there are any). They may greet other groups walking along the road, but usually they keep conversations within their own group. Then, they turn into the branch road that leads to their *pinaposa*'s garden area, and from there into secondary branch roads that lead into their *ngorer*'s area. Although everybody works their own plot, they usually try to stay close to others and maintain lively conversations. The women plant, weed and harvest mostly sweet potatoes, but some have taro gardens, too. Most grow vegetables and bananas, either along the side of the gardens or in separate plots. They work near the ground, in non-expansive, down-ward-oriented movements. They crouch, kneel and work with bent backs, often only with a knife and their hands up to the arms covered in soil. Every now and then, a small group stops to chew betel together and gossip. In the mid to late afternoon, the women place tubers they have dug up for dinner into large baskets made of coconut fronds, close the baskets securely with banana leaves—'I don't want other people to look inside!'—and tie them to their backs with ropes of banana fibre. Women only are allowed to carry tubers in baskets on their backs, while the men carry hoes and bush knives. Together, they return along the road they came to their hamlet.

In the past, gardening was organized by the *tsunon* of the group. He assigned plots to different men and women, made decisions on fallow periods and on when the clearing of new gardens, planting and harvest-ing should begin. Nowadays, the *tsunon* still assign garden plots, but no longer control the timing of the activities. Nevertheless, day-to-day work in the gardens remains a cooperative affair of the people belonging to a *ngorer*, including the in-laws, and at least ideally, the appearance of the gardens should be one of co-ordination and unity. All the gardens in a *ngorer*'s garden area together, and not just each separately should look 'neat' and 'smart'.

Like gardening, hamlet life on the mainland is characterized by an ideal of inward co-operation and clear demarcation from 'other people'. Families should eat together in the morning and evening and offer close relatives food if they come by around meal times. Men were relatively mobile during the week, as many of them worked in Buka Town. Wives, however, were expected to stay at their hamlets, with their mothers-in-law, and not 'go around' elsewhere. On Sundays, all *ngorer* members ought to relax at the hamlet, including those who were away working in Town during the week. 'Going around' at other people's places is not encouraged, although visiting is permissible, as long as there is a reason for it. Saturday markets at Kessa, at which mainlanders exchange starch food for fish with Pororan Islanders, are one of the moments when main-land life is oriented outward. Other occasions are marriage and mortuary rites, when members from different *pinaposa* cooperate and compete in gathering food for distribution at large feasts. These are exceptional events, however. In everyday life, as already noted, mainlanders greatly value the privacy and sense of security that their gardens, hamlets and the co-operation with their kin on land that is controlled by their group afford them. When their land was encroached upon, or when other conflicts appeared with other groups, I found my mainland hosts quick to react. They put the matter to their *tsunon*, who would settle the problem with the *tsunon* of the transgressor group.

The Pororans got bored and unhappy easily, they said, when they stayed with mainland relatives. Being used to going fishing any time and anywhere they wanted, and being used to walking around the island freely and at their own time, they found gardening difficult and the relatively regulated, inward-oriented lifestyle that comes with it disconcerting.[9] From the Pororans' point of view, there was a close connection between gardens [*kui*], hard work [*tokui*], broken backs [baksait ibruk] and 'hard bellies' and anger [belhat] among mainlanders. 'They are stuck to their own people, and they never get along with other people', the Pororans said about the mainlanders. On the island, by contrast, fishing [*roror itasi*, lit.: going around at sea] was associated with rest [*mamaluh*] or freedom [in English], with happy people roaming around at sea and yet more happy people eating 'sweet' fish, which they ask off 'other people' as well as their own kin, as we shall see. I was often assured that 'there is no work on the island'. Kil explained: 'This is why so many mainland women want to be married on Pororan. No work, they can go around a little, too, there is plenty of fish, and life is sweet.' Although she was right, those mainland women who did indeed marry Pororan Islanders found the Pororans' lifestyle as disconcerting as the Pororans found life 'in the bush'. Besides not even thinking of going fishing, which they considered inappropriate for women, many of them used to complain about the lack of privacy on the island. Kil's daughter-in-law Helen, a mainlander, told me how she felt physically insecure at first as 'other people kept walking through our hamlet, just past the table we were eating at. I didn't even know who they were, but the old lady here [Kil] did not seem to mind'.

These Pororan and mainland descriptions of Pororan as a fishing place and the Pororans as fishing people, in contrast to Buka mainlanders as gardeners point to a contrast in people's dealings with space and time, as well as a contrast in gender expectations. These are linked locally through a single term, *roror*, going around, which is central to descriptions of the Pororans' saltwater life, but not to that of mainlanders. I begin exploring this term in this chapter by focusing on the particular kind of *roror* that the Pororans used most commonly in their self-descriptions: *roror itasi*, going around at sea or fishing. In the following section, I will explore what exactly makes fishing 'going around', and what makes 'going around' so valuable, giving consideration to space, time and gender in particular. First, however, it is worth looking at fishing in a little more detail, to understand what exactly *roror itasi* refers to.

Fishing Methods

I begin with an introduction to the different fishing methods employed on Pororan or remembered by older people in 2004–05. The aim is to give a clearer impression of the range of activities that may be described as *roror itasi*.

Gathering Shellfish on the Reef

Visitors often praise the abundance of shellfish on the reef around Pororan, whose area is much larger here than around Petats or along the Buka north and east coast. During *hiningal* in 2004–05, when the tide was low during daytime, the reef around Pororan was usually sprinkled during the day with women and children who slowly wandered about and occasionally bent down to pick up shellfish. Women went on their own, with a female relative or friend, or with a group of their own or a relative's children. Sometimes children got together in a group after school to collect shellfish. Some people dragged a canoe behind them for easy transport back to the village at the onset of high tide. But many simply walked along the dry reef or in shallow water with a basket in one hand into which they placed the shells they picked up. Most of the shellfish gathered were immediately boiled, wrapped in leaves and given or sold to mainlanders at the next market. In contrast to the mainlanders, who are said to truly relish it, the Pororans themselves eat shellfish only rarely. When longer-term residents on the island begin to reject shellfish offered to them and instead ask for permission to gather shellfish themselves for their own relatives on the mainland, people say that they are becoming islanders.

A kind of shellfish that is not subsumed under the generic term, *kessa*, is clamshells [*mamop*]. Only the bigger ones are removed from their shells and boiled. Smaller ones are taken to clamshell gardens, usually located on the reef off their owners' hamlets. The Pororans started making clamshell gardens during the past few years at the suggestions of a local marine biologist and a priest, as a potential resource for sale to external buyers. Although no buyers had arrived yet, the Pororans appreciated these gardens in 2004–05 because they provided quick and easy access to larger amounts of shells in preparation for a visit by or to mainland relatives. However, during a spell of hot and dry weather in March–April 2005 the clamshells began to rot in their gardens on the exposed reef. Many islanders, who just then required clamshells for feeding Easter visitors, were speaking of abandoning their clamshell gardens.

Outings to the reef to gather shellfish often yielded other kinds of food, as well. Usually, women carried a sharp and heavy iron pole with them with which to break *matats*, an edible kind of sponge, off the reef. A smaller sharp iron stick was used for spearing various species of reef fish that were usually roasted on the fire and eaten by family members. They were said to be too small to be given away. Children gathered edible seaweed along their way.

Line-Fishing off the Reef's Edge

Women and children used store-bought iron hooks of various sizes and nylon strings of different strength, rolled up on a bottle or a round, smoothened piece of wood, to catch various kinds of small fish on the reef when the tide was regressing, and more commonly off the reef's edge at low tide. Sometimes a bamboo rod was used. They began their trips by disentangling their fishing lines, sticking some hooks into their hair, taking a basket for the fish, a knife with a cork floater, and a small plastic bag that, tied to their clothes, served as a container for bait. In the past, I was told that women used hollowed out coconut shells, worn on a string around their neck, for storing bait, and long, vertical fishing baskets called *bona*, two of which were tied around their hips for storing their catch. For bait, the women collected small shellfish called *gum* at locations on the reef where they were known to be plentiful before walking to the reef's edge where they threw out their lines. Women often stayed on the reef for an afternoon, enjoying a bath every now and then.

Shooting Fish at Low Tide on the Reef

In the past, men used to get up early during *hiningal* and catch fish on the reef as the tide regressed. Old people described to me how they shot fish with bow and arrow, with a spear or simply a knife. During *halat*, when the reef is exposed during the night, the same was done in the late evening, in the light of large torches made of coconut fronds. Married couples walked along the reef together, taking older children with them. The men walked ahead of the women and threw backwards to them the fish they killed. The women stored these fish in *bona* tied around their hips, and carried tied-up coconut fronds on their backs as a supply for further torches. Today, the islanders say that too many people live on the island, and the fish no longer come all the way up to the beach because they are scared.

Fishing with Fish Traps

Another fishing method that I was told of on Pororan as a matter of the past is trapping fish in a narrow cane trap, up to about one metre long. These were left on the ground of the sea on the lagoon-side of the island, held down by reef stones. Some old people were still holding such traps, but were not to my knowledge using them in 2004–05.

Kite Fishing

Kite fishing, too, is a method no longer used but remembered on Pororan. In the Buka area, only Petats and Pororan Islanders used to employ this technique. Attached to the kite made of pandanus leaves was one string that the fisher held, and another one to which a ball of cobwebs was attached. The kite, I was told, made the ball of cobwebs dance on the surface of the sea. Fish would come, attracted by its movement, and the cobweb ball would get stuck in their mouths.

Net Fishing

Fishing by net was the most common fishing method of the past, and is said to have yielded much larger catches than the islanders make using other methods nowadays. A net, made from a vine that was rolled into a string, was spanned between a bent bamboo rod and a straight piece of bamboo attached to both ends. Fishing nets were made in four sizes. The smallest one, about a metre and a half long, is still made and used on the island, mostly by children, for catching small baitfish on the reef at low tide. Nets of two larger sizes, one about three metres and the other about five metres long, were used in the past primarily by young people, who practised with them before they began to use the largest kind of net. Nets of the three larger sizes were lowered from canoes, mostly beyond the reef's edge. The fisher held two nets, one in each hand, and his helpers, often his children, drove the fish towards his canoe, hitting the side of their canoes and making noise. If the correct magical procedures had been applied to the net, the net would soon be heavy with fish, said the islanders. In order to take his catch into his canoe, the fisher kicked the far-away end of the net with his foot and then lifted the net with his knee. This fishing method was abandoned sometime in the 1970s.

In 2004–05, the islanders sometimes used large, store-bought nets. These were owned jointly by the members of a *ngorer*, and were usually managed by the *ngorer's tsunon*. Fishing with these nets required a large number of people, who all shared the catch. The only occasions at which I saw the nets in use was when a *pinaposa* prepared a feast for which large amounts of fish were needed, or when they caught fish as a contribution to a feast prepared by mainland relatives.

Particular *pinaposa* on the island used to make nets, bespelled with magic, in which two different turtle species and sea cows were caught. The *tsunon* had banned fishing for these species in 2004–05.

Dynamite

The *tsunon* mentioned that in the recent past, dynamite was sometimes used if a large catch was required for a feast. They banned the use of dynamite, however, at the recommendation of the trained marine biologist.

Line-Fishing from a Canoe

In 2004–05 the use of hook and line from a canoe at high tide was the most commonly employed fishing method, especially during the night in hiningal. Two men, or a married couple, might go out to the reef and into the lagoon in a canoe with a pressure lamp on it, wearing raincoats against the cold. They might return in the middle of the night or, if the fish were biting well, in the early hours of the morning. They usually smoked some of their catch and boiled one or two fish for immediate consumption. The busiest nights were Tuesday and Friday, just before the markets on Wednesday and Saturday mornings.

During the day, people visited <u>ston</u> and <u>pasis</u> that they knew were good fishing spots. People also found new spots all the time. In addition, some men and fewer women went line fishing on the open sea, or just off the reef's edge. They both hoped and feared that a shark would bite there. Sharks sold especially well at the markets, and the catch of a shark always made for a good story.

Diving with Spear-Guns

A recently introduced fishing method mostly associated with young people (mostly males but also females) is diving in the deep passages on the reef with fins, goggles and a spear gun. This method was popular in 2004–05, but spear guns were expensive and their use needs some skill. Many young people therefore dived with sharp iron poles instead, and children practised with cheap goggles and smaller iron poles closer to the island. Catches from individual spear fishing outings were usually smoked and sold at the next market. Often a group of boys [boi, hitots, as all men were called on such occasions] belonging to the same pinaposa went go out spear-fishing in preparation for a feast, ideally with torches at night, when the best catches were made.

Trolling for Bonito

One of the most exciting activities of island life in the Buka area was, by general agreement in 2004–05, trolling for bonito. The elder men on Pororan were usually happy to tell and enact stories of past days' trolling from mon.[10] When trolling, one man on each of the mon's five seats would paddle, and the other would hold a string. On the seat behind, the side of paddling and string holding would be reversed, and so on, so that each man could help the one in front of him to take the fish off the hook, and could be helped by the man in his back. Traditionally, bonito were caught with hooks the base of which was made of dolphin bone or the jawbone of the sea cow.[11] The barb, tied to it with a string running through holes in it, was made of turtle shell. Magic was 'put on' to ensure a good catch. These hooks are no longer made on the island, although some of the old men hold some among their possessions.[12] They were tied to a strong fishing line made of vine, which was attached to a bamboo rod attached in turn to a piece of wood at an angle of ninety degrees. On this piece of wood, the fisher would place his foot, so as to have his hands free if needed. No bait was used, as people pointed out to me. Instead, the movements of the hook trolling behind the mon at about 30 to 50 metres distance, and in the final instance the movements of the mon itself and the fishermen on it, attract the fish. The emphasis in stories about trolling on mon is on the speed of these movements. Ten young men would paddle the mon, given strength by the magic of the tsunon who went out with them. The men on the mon would 'follow' the birds that indicated the presence of a shoal of bonito, and would paddle at full speed when the hooks would be running along the surface of the sea just above the fish.[13]

In the past, Put, one of the pinaposa on the island 'knew how' to attract bonito to the fishing grounds around the island.[14] They did so with the help of fish carved from river stone, one of which was hidden on the beach with his 'owner' staying nearby and asking the bonito to come, and the other of which was used for a fire sacrifice (*hahats*). Under the direction of the holder of this knowledge, one Put man at any one time, 'everyone' would go out to troll, and the Pororans emphasized that the catch used to be enormous.

When the Pororans went trolling in 2004–05, they did so without *hahats*, in fibreglass boats powered by an outboard motor and with store-bought lures instead of the old hooks. The most common occasions for trolling were trips to Town. Strings and lures were kept ready in the back of most boats, and boat owners transporting family or passengers would usually take a detour if someone on the boat spotted the birds that indicate the presence of bonito. A trip to Town then turned into a race after the birds that could take the Pororans far off their usual route—when the petrol lasted, even out of the lagoon and onto the open sea. I never heard passengers complain about the delay this caused, or about arriving in town wet and with the blood of fish on their clothes. To the contrary, everyone on the boat used to join in the excitement of watching out for birds and for the movements of fish close to the surface of the water, and of shouting directions to the skipper. Two or three men sitting or standing in the back of the boat each used to hold a string of about 30 metres' length, and when one or more of them felt the weight of a fish, they called out to the skipper to stop the boat. The catch was then hauled in, and everyone cheered over the fish that the men took off the hooks and threw into the back of the boat.

Going Around at Sea

The diverse fishing methods introduced above made, of course, for a variety of bodily movements, and of movements of canoes, hooks and line and other equipment. However, the Pororans consistently focused in 2004–05 on a particular style of moving that characterized fishing irrespective of the method used: *roror*, an indeterminate 'going around' unbound by conventions of time and space.

Musong, a woman who took me out fishing sometimes, used to surprise her relatives by getting up all of a sudden, dropping the sweet potatoes she had been cleaning or leaving the group of women she had been chatting with and setting off for the sea without any further delay or explanation. She also had a reputation for coming back from afternoon line-fishing outings long after dark. Occasionally, her husband asked her to come back earlier and save him some worries. Musong would nod, but she kept coming back late. On one occasion, she justified herself: 'I was throwing out my line, and the fish were biting and biting and biting. I caught so many fish, and then I still wanted to go to that other place and get some more, I forgot about time and so I am late, sorry.' On outings we took together, Musong would move from fishing spot to fishing spot in zig-zag lines across the lagoon, getting more and more excited as the fish were biting well. Once, she threw a look back at the village over her shoulder and said to me: 'Let's go a little further yet. Let's stay out a little longer. *We* don't have worries.' Women enjoying an afternoon gathering shells on the reef, too, often spoke about being in no hurry to get back to the village. 'Let's see if there are some more shells that way', Taliau, Salu's niece, said once as we were walking along the reef, pointing further south on the seaward side of the island. 'When I gather shells, I never feel hungry. I just walk and walk and walk, and I don't need food, I don't need a rest, I can stay out for many hours. I could stay out for days', she added.

With regard to its potential for opening up space, in addition to time, the most highly valued fishing method was trolling for bonito, because 'then you can really go far away, and fast!' However, even in their canoes or when fishing off the reef's edge, people created movements farther and faster than what their relatively minor shifts in position would suggest. Musong, for instance, employed sudden changes in direction that made her head spin, as she said, for creating an impression of 'free' movements. When moving from one fishing spot to the next, she used to say 'let's go there, no there, no there', giving her canoe a little push in a different direction on each 'there' before deciding for one of them. 'We are free to go wherever we want! Who would boss us around here?' Kil, similarly zig-zagging across the lagoon from fishing spot to fishing spot in her canoe, had a different way of turning her relatively spatially limited movements into more expansive ones. 'We paddle, we paddle, we paddle', she hummed, repeating over and over the beginning of an old Pororan song about women's fishing activities, in the rhythm of her paddle dipping into and out of the water. After a while, she began talking to me, continuing the song with allusions to movements far beyond the lagoon, deep in the ancestral past: 'We paddle, we paddle, we paddle all the way to Petats, no, to the Christmas Islands, no, to Torokina, no, to Buin!' This was the list of places to the south of Pororan, ending at the southern tip of Bougainville Island that Tsireh used to recall when talking about headhunting raids of the ancestors in pre-colonial times.

Once, when Kil and I went out fishing with a rod and line off the reef's edge, Kil made the tiny outward and inward movement of her wrist when throwing out and pulling in her string, amplified by the rod and the string on it, a starting point for exploring movements that roamed situations, and thus places and times of considerable distance. She did what Pororan women do during *hahur*, a session of singing and dancing after the death of a person of rank. Throwing the line out and pulling it in rapidly, not giving any time for fish to bite, she suddenly caught hold of the end of the string, tied it to the rod and began using the fishing rod as a broom of the reef. She imitated herself sweeping her hamlet in the mornings. She started humming mourning songs. Two grandchildren, obviously anticipating what would follow, started dancing on the reef. Kil's singing grew louder and she hit her grandchildren with the tip of the rod, as women hit the closest female relatives of a deceased of rank with sticks during *hahur*. Her grandchildren shrieked. Kil suddenly turned her fishing rod into a paddle and imitated being on a canoe, and her grandchildren lined up behind her, paddling in rhythm, one with a fishing knife in her hand, the others with their hands holding imaginary paddles. '*Tasi te posanam*', began Makots, seven years old, trying to get her grandmother to sing her favourite fishing song that begins, 'the sea is high'. Kil did her the favour, and all of them paddled along and did the movements for the song, which speaks of women looking for shells at high sea. Eventually, Kil ended with a laugh and a shrill 'ehee', and Makots plunged into the sea just beyond the reef to cool off. Then we resumed catching reef fish. Through this little diversion from the ordinary, lasting no longer than five minutes, Kil had opened up the repetitive movements of throwing a rod out and pulling it in, and had taken her grandchildren onto a journey across disparate everyday activities and ritual occasions that was propelled forward by changes in relatively small bodily movements, amplified by the fishing rod.

What makes fishing exciting, and what opens up time and space at sea, then, is not a spatial or temporal expansion that activities take, measurable in metres or hours, but people's expansion of space and time by their own methods, unpredictable to others and sometimes surprising to themselves, it seemed. They dwelled on moments in which they did not know what would happen next, where they would go next [Musong], when one would get back [Musong and Taliau], or what directionality the movement of a fishing rod turned dancing prop might take on and where it would take one's thoughts [Kil]. The excitement of those moments was felt keenly not only by the people who deliberately created and experienced them at sea, but also by the people who were waiting for them back at the village. Watching Denise take yet another unexpected turn in her canoe out in the lagoon from the village, Kil exclaimed, with something between concern, envy and admiration: 'Hey! Where is she going again? Does she not want to come back at all? Does she want to go all the way to Hitou? Has she forgotten all about her relatives on Pororan?'

The Pororans give three different reasons for the open-endedness of fishing movements. The first is the fisher's 'will' [*ngil*], which is recognized as shifting rapidly at sea, and which apparently works to some extent apart from the person, overriding his or her usual interests and concerns (see also Harrison 1993). 'I wanted to go to that elevated reef part, but then I thought of a passage nearby and I changed my mind. And then I caught so many fish, I forgot about everything', Jennifer said once, apologizing for returning much later than her family had expected her from an outing to the lagoon.

Alternatively, the unexpected turns of fishing routes were sometimes attributed to the tide, sudden wind or rain, and in the case of fishing in the lagoon to currents from the Gagan River that are said to lift up plankton and to thereby 'make the sea dirty' and fishing at certain locations difficult. All of these are said to be beyond the ordinary control of either people at sea or those who await them and their catch on the island. They may, however, have been 'called' by people with the capacity to hinder or help others' ventures with non-human help, through spells, ritual actions and calling upon the power of the ancestors.

A third cause for fishers changing their mind about where to go and how long to stay at sea is said to be the inclinations of the spirits of the dead [tevil, *nomnomi*]. These spirits are said to send fish to the hooks, or to withhold them. When fishing with line and hook from a canoe,[15] many islanders call out aloud to the spirits all the while. Others only mumble between their teeth. They may address 'them', the spirits, in general. Kil, for instance, used to shout intermittently for the entire duration of an outing: 'Yupela! Mi laik bai yupela givim mipela planti pis! Bai kanu blong mipela pulap! *Elomi ema haleiem a ts'ien a parpara!*' [You! I want you to give us many fish! Our canoe will be full [of fish]! Give many fish!]. Other islanders address specific ancestors of theirs. The old man Hotu told me that he used to take the base of the hook with which his grandfather used to catch bonito whenever he went trolling. He claimed that the hook and his grandfather, who was a very successful fisherman while alive and whom he called out to while trolling, helped him.[16] But although the islanders call out to the spirits for help, they also state that, in the end, the spirits' inclinations can neither be predicted nor can they always be changed. While certain kinds of behaviour are known to cause the spirits to withhold fish—for example, when someone is badly prepared and goes fishing without a knife for killing the fish, chopping up bait or cutting the line if necessary—the spirits may also withhold fish for no apparent reason, or may give a large catch without any apparent motivation.

Return from the Sea

Roror ends very suddenly, space falls back into place, social relations come back to mind and time becomes a factor of those relations when a fisher feels the weight of a fish on the line, pulls it up into the canoe or boat and takes it off the hook. This sudden transformation of space and time is most noticeable in trolling for bonito. Men who feel a fish on the line call out to the skipper to stop the engine so that it can be hauled in. After an often substantial time of 'going around' with their eyes just on the surface of the water, on the bird that indicates the presence of a shoal of fish or on the movements of fish just below, fishers will now align their posture and attention vertically. They jump up and bend down over the water, trying to make out the shape and size of the fish below. This is a moment of great anticipation. Not only may the fish on the hook attract sharks, which make it necessary to haul it in very quickly, but it may also be a shark itself. As men put it when speaking about this moment after their return: 'Will I eat this fish, or will it eat me?' A second man often stands ready with a piece of wood to fend off sharks.[17]

When the fish is safely on board, the men will lean back and look around. After rounds and rounds of 'going around', they will have lost their orientation. When islands fall back into place as the boat comes to a halt, they often do so in directions and distances that surprise the fishers. At the same time as islands re-appear, social relations come back to mind. A fish on board appears to invariably trigger thoughts of those who want to eat it. For example, after a long spell of just enjoying a 'rest' at sea while their lures were trolling behind the boat, the men on a boat who began trolling once on their way to Town started deliberating, after the first fish had been heaved aboard, about whom they would give it to. As they turned the engine on again to continue trolling, these considerations slipped from mind. But with each fish that they hauled in, the fishers initiated a new round of calculations, each more complex than the preceding one, as they jointly adjusted the number of fish due to the owner of the boat, and as each of them revised his own plans for the distribution of his share. Eventually, time, too turned from an open expanse in their mind into a factor of the relations they 're-perceived' in the fish (Wagner 2001): 'Will we continue a little and catch another fish for your in-laws, too? Or should we go back now, so that my wife can cook this fish on the fire for dinner?' one man asked the other. At other occasions, and not only in trolling, I have noticed fishers similarly plan and revise the distribution of the fish every time they took a fish off their hook.

Others at a hamlet, especially close relatives such as mothers, fathers, sons, daughters, spouses, will eagerly await the return of a person who went out to fish. Usually a fire will be ready to smoke the fish on, and perhaps to boil one for immediate consumption. Upon a fisher's return, often precisely those relations and persons that he or she was keen to leave behind when going out will be acknowledged as highly valued. For instance, when Salu's daughter Jennifer at Lulutsi returned from her outing that she embarked on when she was fed up with her own and her sisters' children, she handed her fishing basket to her son Hangot, who cautiously approached her together with some siblings and cousins. Hangot proudly carried the basket to the fire and laid out the fish for smoking.

Moments of handing over and receiving fish are often very tense. The quality of social relations is highly indeterminate in such moments, when they appear anew after a 'rest' at sea. For instance, Hangot's cautious movements towards his mother upon her return from the sea made it obvious that he was half-expecting her to shout at him or push him away again. He was pleasantly surprised when she gave him her basket instead, thus privileging him over his cousins. When Denise's husband returned, after his absence from Kobkobul for a week, with three fish for her, he moved similarly cautiously, uncertain of what would happen. Denise took the fish, to his obvious relief. However, her slow movements and careless handling of the fish made it clear to him that his presence at the hamlet was acceptable to her, but not particularly welcome. Kil's son Lawrence, finally, with plenty of experience and a quick mind did not leave others much of a chance to object to his plans for his fish and them. 'Mama, a ts'ien terelo' [mother, your fish] he would call cheerfully as soon as he was within shouting range, move over fast, put the fish carelessly onto Kil's kitchen table and start doing or talking about other things. With other people, he proceeded likewise. Many people appreciated him for being generous while avoiding 'putting other people down below', that is, making the recipients of his fish look and feel inferior. Others, however, recognized his ways as merely a particularly cunning way of establishing himself in a position of superiority. Salu's relatives, for instance, carefully avoided Lawrence, especially when he was coming from the sea.

The tension of moments of handing over fish is greatest, and people's faces often express strong anxiety or anger when fishers do not return to their own hamlet, but land on a beach either belonging to 'other people' or frequented by various people in the village. They might do so because they live in inland hamlets, or perhaps because they intend to give some fish to a person outside their own hamlet. Passers-by then loudly admire the fish. In Tok Pisin and Hapororan, they say that they 'like' [laik, mangil] or 'like to eat' [katsin nin] the fish they 'see' [ngot]. By extension, they express their admiration for and willingness to enter into relations with the person who caught the fish. People are highly ambivalent about moments of 'looking' or 'being looked at', of which returns from the sea are only one instance (see also chapter 5). There is a small but significant difference between *ngot ne* as an ordinary form of looking at, looking after or attending to other people or things, and the more immediate, stronger form of *ngot* used in this context: looking or staring at someone or something. The latter contains vague references to envy and the use of sorcery, or to great admiration and the use of love magic.

It is worth considering in more detail here the mechanisms of attracting fish and making them stick employed in various Pororan fishing methods, and the mechanisms of attracting people and making relations appear anew with fish. Specifically, I am interested in the role of 'looking' [ngot]. The islanders spoke to me with fascination of kite fishing as it was practised in the past. They told me vividly how fish would see the cobweb ball suspended from the kite dance on the surface of the water, and how they would think: 'Ah, my food is over there'. When swimming up to the surface and 'eating', they would have their mouth 'stuck and altogether stuck' in the cobwebs. 'This fish saw this thing and thought it would eat now. But no, the fisherman made soup of the fish.' Similar observations about the attractiveness of buoyant movements to fish (and about resolving the issue of who would eat whom to the advantage of human beings) were made with regard to trolling for bonito. Here, the hook running fast across the surface of the water, and by extension the fishermen's movements of *roror* alone attract the fish. Fish, in turn, attract other people, who see and admire them upon a fisherman's return from the sea.

Judging from people's faces in such moments and from their explanations afterwards, most felt highly uncertain over the question of who would 'eat' whom. Would the fisher attract looks, admiration and future returns (food to eat) from the recipient of his fish? Or would the recipient obtain the fish, as well as a debt that would allow him to establish future relations with the fisher? This uncertainty is described as an indeterminacy of the directionality of movements. Will the fish respectfully be handed 'up' to a person, or condescendingly thrown 'down'? Will it be drawn 'upward' as a form of tribute, or politely requested as 'help' from a person thereby assuming a position 'below'? Much depended on mimics, body language and verbal elaborations, and much depended simply on who was faster in giving their own preferred shape to the newly emergent relation.

The translation of such tense moments into less ambivalent, more determinate and calculable and properly acknowledged relations is often achieved through the intervention of a go-between. For instance, Salu once loudly admired a neighbour's catch, apparently not thinking much about it, and was immediately handed a fish from the neighbour's baskets, respectfully, with the words: 'Here, you are my good neighbour, this is for you'. Later in the evening, when enjoying the fish, she commented ruefully that perhaps Tabo was now short in fish for her many children. The next day, she sent her granddaughter Roni to Tabo's house with a basket full of smoked fish. 'Tell her: Salu sends this, for your fish. That is all you have to say', Salu instructed her. Children are often used on such occasions, and will repeat their message word by word, as Roni did in this instance. Tabo looked pleased, and some days later sent her small daughter over with a bundle of ripe bananas from her garden that she respectfully put down by Salu's house. '<u>Mama</u> sends this, for the fish', the shy little girl finally managed to say her line. Over time, what was an accidental 'bumping into you with your fish', as Salu later commented to Tabo, turned into a strong relation of mutually respectful support between neighbours.

Unlike children, adults sometimes act as go-betweens with intentions of their own, and may even act without the knowledge of the donor. For example, the old man Hotu once told me that he used to catch so many fish when he was young that 'the women came to put their heads under my feet'. His adopted mother eventually turned this—perhaps flattering, but ambivalent for the danger of envy, fighting or sorcery—admiration into productive relations with Sian, one of most senior *tsunon* on the island. Without Hotu's knowledge, she took all the fish he caught to Sian. Sian reciprocated with a hook for trolling that he made and bespelled for Hotu. His mother continued to take the fish that Hotu caught to Sian. Eventually, Hotu married Sian's daughter Ninio.

It is for the new, open-ended relations that a fish on the line holds out as a potential that Pororan Islanders return from going around at sea. It is for 'seeing' these novel relations emerge, too, and perhaps for participating in them that Kil and a group of female relatives used to stay up on moonlit nights when the men were out at sea, singing fishing songs while keeping the fires going on which the catch would be smoked. When she saw the canoes approaching the island, however, Kil used to send all young women around into the house to sleep. 'You go and hide', she commanded, 'who knows what will happen if you see their fish?' She would grab each of us by the arm, shove us into the house, shut the door with a clang and threaten: 'I will beat you with my broom if I see you going around out there!' What was Kil telling us to 'hide' from, knowing fully well that we would come out again the moment she had left?

Sia and Hulu

Drawing on James Leach's (2003a) strategy of looking to 'origin' stories as accounts of contemporary relations of gender, power and a particular mode of creativity, I present below a Pororan origin story of two siblings going around at sea. This story evokes a mode of life at a time before the emergence of gendered human relations, as we know them today. It relates how those came about as the highly contingent outcome of two siblings gathering shellfish, and as a result of painful interventions that one made on the other. In 2004–05, this story was more important to the islanders than any other I learned of.

The protagonists of the story are called Sia and Hulu, 'one' and 'two' in Hapororan. Numbering story characters whose names are so important that their surrender would require the killing of a pig is a common strategy on Pororan. However, with regard to these two, no one claimed to know their secret names in front of others. This story was only told to me in full once, but was often alluded to. The islanders assumed that I knew the story, as indeed I did from the notebooks of Beatrice Black-wood (n.d.), who learned it from Gordon Thomas, a Buka west coast planter who had undergone male initiation on Pororan. The story is rendered below, pieced together from the one full account and the many allusions I heard on Pororan:

> Sia and Hulu were gathering shellfish on the reef. Sia picked up a shellfish [some people say it was an octopus] and placed it between her thighs, in order to have her hands free for collecting more. The shellfish got stuck there, and Sia was unable to remove it. Hulu tried to help Sia, but Sia told Hulu to stop because it hurt too much. Eventually, Hulu pulled the shellfish out from between Sia's thighs when Sia was asleep. Sia turned into the first woman. She gave birth to the sibling pair's first child, whom they killed. They buried the skull, and from it grew the first coconut. All human beings descend from the later-born children of Sia and Hulu.

We may perceive Pororan Islanders' movements at sea as a re-creation of the original state of the human world as described in this story, and the transformation of *roror* into ordinary and properly acknowledged relations as a re-enactment of the story of Sia and Hulu. The parallel is closest where young people are transformed, often through their fishing activities, through giving fish and the relations that evolve from that, into married men and women. Those who *roror* the most, both at sea and on land, are said to be *hitots*, young people. The term *hitots* is applied to both men and women. Men retain this label, and often carry it into middle age especially when they are active fishermen or when they otherwise spend much time away from their wife and family, for example when engaged in wage labour. Women, however, gradually turn from *hitots* into *kukubei*, young marriageable women, and are then expected to soon turn into mothers [*tsina* and eventually *tobuan*, senior woman; mama]. When Kil told us to go and hide in the house rather than watching the men return in their canoes, she addressed us as *kukubei*.

Like Sia in the story, young women are said to be transformed by having something 'stuck' [pas] to them that changes their movements. This 'something' is sometimes said to be love magic, and is sometimes said to be the woman's first child (see also Gillison 1993). The islanders very often attribute both the effects of love magic—which is usually fatigue, sometimes falling down, sometimes a lack of mobility due to a hurting leg—and pregnancy to a woman's 'seeing' and 'liking' a man who returned from the sea with a large catch, and of 'eating' his fish. More generally, however, anyone (including men, women and small children) who feels the weight of a fish on the hook, and who later attracts the attention of other people with this fish, has something 'stuck' to him- or herself that transforms movements of *roror* and brings relations to mind. This something then gives occasion for acts of 'pulling', like Hulu's, in which men become defined as men, women as women, and through which particular relations become apparent.

If, as I argue, in every fishing outing and return, Pororan Islanders re-enact the story of Sia and Hulu, and thus the emergence of human gendered relations out of an original state in which gender did not matter, then this clarifies, firstly, the double-role of Pororan women as those who receive their husband's fish (in ordinary social life) and those who fish themselves. When they fish, they are not women, just as men at sea are not men. Relations, including relations of gender, only emerge when a fish bites, and when the fisher then returns to the village. Only then is one's own will impinged on by that of other people and one's awareness of what they want: fish. The 'return from the sea' I have described above appears, in the light of the story of Sia and Hulu, as a saltwater version of the processes of gendering that have been observed widely and in various forms in Melanesia (see esp. M. Strathern 1988).

Secondly, the bumpiness of the processes of gendering—which the story of Sia and Hulu leaves no doubt about—throws a novel light on the

Pororans' habit of taking to the sea when relations turn difficult, which Buka mainlanders did not appreciate. Taking to the sea is not escapism, or an attempt to forget one's own marginality relative to others, such as mainlanders at the markets or the magistrates at the village court. Instead, in setting off in their canoes and leaving behind relations that they consider dissatisfying, in going around at sea and then returning and re-creating relations, the islanders claim 'power *over*' (Wagner 2001: 46) social relations *within* which they perceive themselves to be constrained by others. This holds both for relations between particular persons on the island and for relations between Pororan Islanders and Buka mainlanders. They do not claim anything resembling individual authorship (see, e.g. Woodmansee and Jaszi 1994) of these relations. Nevertheless, they 'own' the processes of the emergence of social relations through their capacity of indeterminate 'going around', and of attracting fish, the media through which gendered bodies and relations emerge.

Here is a saltwater answer, then, to a question that many anthropologists working in Melanesia have been concerned with, and that James Weiner has put succinctly: 'How do social relations acquire their outline?' (2001a: 77). He argues that relationships can only appear if fore-grounded against something that is not relational (78). But what is it, and how might one describe it? Adam Reed, in his ethnography of inmates at Bomana gaol in Port Moresby, has argued that these inmates make the outline and limitations of Melanesian sociality appear by switching positions between ordinary relations and novel ones, likened to those of white people. These include, for example, friendship (see esp. Reed 2003: 159–61). Their ability to switch between these two modes of relationality, Melanesian and white, or new, gives the inmates a certain edge. They make the contingency of each mode of relationality appear by drawing on the other (170). One might draw a parallel between 'friends' at Bomana and Pororan fishers engaged in *roror*. Both friendship and *roror* offer positions from which to foreground 'given' Melanesian relationality, and to make it appear contingent by drawing out its limits. However, Pororan *roror* differs from friendship at Bomana insofar as the islanders only rarely draw connections between fishing and modern life.[18] Instead, the story of Sia and Hulu suggests that Pororan Islanders consider *roror* very much their own style of movement, and their own capacity of rendering relations indeterminate.

In the following chapters, it will become apparent that Pororan Islanders *roror* not only at sea, but also on their island and on the Buka mainland. It will be shown how all Pororan relations oscillate between disappearing into *roror* and re-emerging, in the eye of the observer, when the relational significance of a person's movements has been detected.

With verbal allusions and sometimes gestures, however, the Pororans usually link people's apparently unpredictable movements around the village and the wider area, and the indeterminacy of relations that they perceive in them, to fishing. Fishing, then, is not only the islanders' predominant subsistence activity. It is also the activity in which the key quality of island sociality becomes most clearly apparent.

NOTES

1. See Blackwood (1935: 359–69) for a detailed account of materials used, building process, and terms used in connection with canoes (*tsinih*) by Petats Islanders in 1929, many of which were still in use on Pororan during my fieldwork.
2. I was told that at Malasang Village, on the Buka east coast, old people live in a 'village' of their own directly on the narrow beach between the sea and the steep cliff that lines the coast. They leave the village on top of the cliff when they become too weak to climb the cliff every morning and evening to wash in the sea.
3. Pit toilets existed on Pororan, but few people used them.
4. A similar pattern of inter-island boundaries only has been reported from small islands in Milne Bay (Kinch 2003; Foale 2005).
5. *Kukubei* = young woman/women. The passage is named after a raid in the pre-colonial past in which Pororan headhunters, disguised by pandanus leaf capes as worn by women, killed a group of young Petats women who were fishing there. The passage is mostly used as a loose reference point rather than a strict boundary. Only those gathering sea cucumbers, a source of large cash incomes, are supposed to remain strictly on their own side.
6. For further ethnographic examples of fishing people's capacity for and enjoyment of surprise, see Astuti (1995), and Rutherford (2003).
7. Sunday is an exception. Many young boys especially used to go fishing early on Sunday morning, so that the family would have fresh fish to eat after church. In late 2004, one of them died on such an outing (see also chapter 5). Some people suggested that his death was no surprise, given that he had broken the Sunday rest. Other boys who used to fish at the same time in the same area were terrified and stopped fishing on Sundays.
8. In her unpublished field notebooks, Beatrice Blackwood expressed her difficulties at eliciting standards of beauty from young women. My Buka acquaintances, too, were very vague on physical attributes they admired, but were very clear about their criteria for choosing a husband: 'Mi laikim bai man blong mi painim planti pis blong mi.' [I want my husband to catch many fish for me.] That there is more to this statement than economic considerations should become apparent in the course of this chapter.
9. Could it be that anthropologists looking for 'society', by contrast, saw no value in expansive and solitary 'going around' at sea and focused instead on gardening, where people were working in kin groups, on land they owned and where 'social structure' therefore appeared more immediately observable? In some cases, people were even explicitly concerned with the re-creation of their

own social structure among the food they grew, as on Dobu (Fortune 1963). I am thankful to James Leach for the suggestion that this may be a reason why Melanesian ethnographers have tended to focus on gardening rather than fishing in settings where both occurred.

10. See Blackwood 1935: 369–81 for a description of *mon* and how they were built. *Mon* are outriggerless vessels with a high and often decorated stern and prow, seating two to ten men, plus a skipper. They were used for trading, warfare and fishing. They were traded from the Buka north coast for pigs. Women could travel in them, but did not own them. Unlike *tsinih*, which were left on the beach, *mon* were kept in special sheds on the beach close to today's hamlet of Puein, four *mon* per shed, one on top of the other on racks running along each long wall. *Mon* were not in use on the island in 2004–05, but were considered an important element of life in the past (see also chapter 6).

11. According to Gordon Thomas, cited by Blackwood (1935: 338), it was a clamshell.

12. I was told that the hooks are still in use on the Buka east coast.

13. See Blackwood (1935: 327–41) for methods, equipment and magic for catching bonito. Pororan was the centre of bonito fishing and bonito magic in the Buka and northern Bougainville region at her time of fieldwork.

14. Gordon Thomas reports that Keketin held this magic (Blackwood 1935: 339). There needn't be a contradiction to my findings, as Put and Keketin are closely linked and are sometimes both called Keketin, although their exact relation was debated in 2004–05. Thomas (ibid.) notes that a Naboen man held this magic, too. I cannot confirm this, perhaps because my knowledge of Naboen is limited. Keketin and Naboen I intermarry frequently. The Naboen man might thus have learned the magic from his Keketin father.

15. When women stand at the reef's edge, they seem to be less intensely engaged with the spirits. I have never been fishing with a spear gun and therefore cannot comment on this.

16. Hotu had unearthed the hook when he dug out his grandfather's bones at the suggestion of the Japanese in World War II, who encouraged the Pororans to wear the bones of deceased relatives around their necks as a protection against American bombs.

17. Unlike other fish, which one hits on the back of the head to kill, a shark has to be hit on its snout, because this is where its life force is.

18. And if they do, for example when they speak of shopping as *roror iTaun* [going around in Town], they model modern life on fishing and not the other way around.

CHAPTER 2

Kin on the Move

One afternoon in Buka Town, in the shade on the veranda at the hotel owned by his uncle Albert, the Pororan workman Kevin was conversing, mostly in Tok Pisin, with his baby daughter Roberta, two months old, who was sitting on his lap: 'Roberta! When you arrived here this morning, where did you come from? Eh? Where had you gone?' On Roberta's behalf, her mother, sitting on a chair some metres away answered: 'Roberta was at Ieta [Ieta Village, close to Buka Town], she was with her relatives there, with her grandfather [MF] and her grannies [MFZs] and aunties [MZs].' Kevin continued:

Ah, you went to Ieta? To your mother's place, where she grew up? Father did not come. You know, father never comes when you and your mother go to Ieta. The Ieta people, they are your relatives, your and your mother's relatives only. Your father has no relatives there. What would he do there, at his in-laws place? So he stays back. He does not come, either, when you follow your mother to Nova. You remember that time you went to Nova, to see your grandmother [MM]? It is good that you went back there. It is good for you to know your mother's relatives there. Your *pinaposa* is there, at Nova. But your father cannot go; he cannot go and stay with his in-laws. . . . Your father is not from Nova. He is from Pororan. Will you come to Pororan, too? Now you are too small. But soon, father will take you to Pororan, your home. You will stay there with his people, you and your mother. Both of you will stay there and eat plenty of fish. You will grow fat and strong on Pororan; you will become a strong woman of Pororan. Perhaps you will get married on Pororan, too. Or perhaps not, perhaps you will like to get married at Ieta, where your mother grew up. Eh, Roberta? Did you like any of those boys you met at Ieta?

In Kevin's conversation with his daughter, two issues stood out clearly that are important to relations between parents and their children on

Notes for this section begin on page 79

Pororan. The first is the apparently close link between, if not the conceptual conflation of a person's physical movements and her kin relations. Kevin explained Roberta's travels—those she had already performed and those he imagined she would perform in the future—to the little baby as a matter of attending to [*ngot ne*] particular kin relations. Kevin mentioned those thought to be most important by Pororan Islanders: those to one's mother's paternal and maternal relatives, and those to one's father and father's maternal (less commonly, paternal) relatives, with whom a person usually grows up. Kevin envisaged that Roberta would grow up with his relatives on Pororan. From there, she would set off from time to time with her mother to visit her mother's paternal relatives at Ieta, and, most importantly, to visit her mother's maternal relatives at Nova.

Secondly, Kevin's tone of voice oscillated between that of a formal lecture on the movements he was expecting her to perform, and that of a set of suggestions that he teasingly put to his little daughter, as if challenging her to grapple with them. Roberta is to grow up at her father's place and respect her father's relatives. She is to follow her mother on travels to her maternal relatives, whose *pinaposa* or 'line' [lain] she will continue. Those are her 'roads', as the Pororans call conventionalized movements that people perform relative to particular others, and through which they render relations of kinship visible. But Kevin's occasional lapses from a strict and determined into a teasing, very gentle but also almost ironic tone of voice indicated a rather different understanding of these movements. They appeared to put his daughter's future movements into question the moment they were made explicit. Knowing Kevin, a Pororan Islander with a keen sense for the unpredictable and humorous sides of everyday life and a 'fishing boy' like most of his peers, I suggest that he was also apprehending his daughter's movements as *roror*.

Watching, Discussing and Eliciting Movements

Pororan Islanders take an enormous interest in discerning a purpose and relational significance in the physical movements of others, and in manipulating these movements on occasion so as to turn them to their own advantage. For instance, one hot afternoon in April 2005, I took a walk across Pororan Village with Helen—Kil's daughter-in-law—and two of her children. Helen is from the Buka east coast village of Gogohei. She and her children, the girls Makots and Talisa, seven and six years old, and the boy Hence, three, were living at her husband's place, Kobkobul, for part of my time on Pororan. One particularly hot afternoon during a long dry spell, Helen, Talisa, Hence and I set off to take our evening bath on the lagoon-side of the island, where the water was deeper and cooler than on the reef off Kobkobul. Because we were wearing only old laplap 'for the sea', Helen suggested that we should not take the shortest, busy and exposed path along the soccer field, but follow smaller paths through the hamlets of Konamun and Rawa, where we would be less widely visible. However, our attempts to 'hide', as Helen put it, met with no success. As we walked along some houses belonging to Lawrence's paternal relatives and along others to whose inhabitants he traces no relations, various people called out to us: 'Where are you going?' or 'Are you going to wash now?' 'Who is there?' Latsil, Lawrence's FZ, shouted from inside her house, where she must have heard the neighbours' greetings to us. 'Those two from over there', a passer-by whom neither Helen nor I recognized informed her loudly, 'Mrs Beleh [another name of Helen's husband Lawrence's] and Katharina, and two of the small ones, Talisa and Hence, they are going to wash.' Helen was uncomfortable with the attention we attracted. She pointed out that at her village, Gogohei on the Buka east coast, only her close relatives would ask her where she was going. Other people would mind their own business. 'But Pororan is different', she added with a shrug.

In the evening, Marta, Lawrence's FZD, visited Helen to ask about Makots, whose absence she had noticed when we passed by her mother's house. Helen dispersed Marta's worries that Makots might be ill by telling her that Makots had had another one of her frequent arguments with her sister Talisa in the afternoon and had preferred to spend the evening with her paternal cousins at Kil's house. Marta immediately incorporated the information into her more general apprehension of the two sisters' relations, and put these to Helen and me for comments. Looking at Talisa, who had fallen asleep next to Helen on the bench under the house, Marta observed: 'She is really stuck with you, eh? Follows her mother all the time. Comes with you, leaves again with you, returns with you to your people every time you go. Makots is different. So, she once again stayed with the old woman [Kil] this afternoon . . . entirely happy with her people here, right? That woman of Pororan.' Helen nodded. For my sake, Marta added that Makots, unlike Talisa, had spent some time on the island as a toddler. 'She enjoys staying with her grandmother and going around with her cousins. It does not matter if her parents are not here; she will turn up on her own. But Talisa, she never comes on her own. And the moment she arrives, she is leaving again to visit her grandmother at Gogohei.' Turning to Helen again, Marta stated: 'I am sure Talisa will get married over there, at Gogohei. But Makots will marry here on Pororan.'

There was a striking proliferation of highly specific verbs of movements in the conversations in which people analysed one another's movements on Pororan. For instance, Talisa comes [*lam*], leaves [*la*] and returns [*la puets*] to her mother's relatives while Makots arrives [*sot*] on Pororan on her own, enjoys staying [*ka, kaka*] with her grandmother and going around [*roror*] with her cousins. Other verbs of movements that Pororan Islanders use in highly specific ways include go up [*la nias*], come down [*kobi*], go over there [*la nehe*], stay here [*ka nien*], walk [*tatal*], paddle [*lis*, among others] and follow the road [*kura maror*]. Using one or the other made a big difference. For instance, people were usually said to 'go' somewhere from their own hamlet, and to 'return' to their own house afterwards. However, women living with their husbands (like Helen) and visiting their own relatives were said to 'return' to them. In addition, men and women of a matrilineal group 'return for the death' to the house of a deceased relative, even if it is the first time they go there. Finally, of people going to Town on important business, it is asked if they would 'follow the bush road' [*kura maror ilatu*] or 'follow the ocean highway' [*kura maror itasi*]. Both were inappropriate descriptions in cases where people were planning to 'just go around to/ in Town' [*rorotun iTaun*], which they might do either by truck [*ni kar*] or by boat [*turu bot*].

In contrast to the sheer number and the specificity of terms that the Pororans used to describe movements, they used very few and very vague terms for describing the persons whose movements they were watching or discussing. For example, the neighbour informed Latsil about our walk to the sea by saying that 'those two from over there' were going to wash, adding our names. 'Those two', a commonly used reference in such situations, could be husband and wife, in-laws, siblings, cousins or two neighbours who conceived of themselves as unrelated 'other persons'. Similarly, the islanders often referred to a person they observed walking on a footpath vaguely as 'our person', indicating some sort of connection between the observer and the person observed, or 'their person', indicating a lack of such connections (or their irrelevance in this particular moment). Another commonly used expression was 'X, Y's person' (slightly more specific, but still leaving the relation between X and Y unspecified). Marta, for instance, did not bother to distinguish Makots's people on Pororan as her 'father's people', and did not bother pointing out that her cousins she was going around with were her *hinas*, her cross-cousins, as opposed to her parallel cousins. Haku speakers on the Buka mainland were much more careful in their use of kin terms, by comparison with the Pororans. They told me, for instance, to beware of the loss of 'meaning', as they called it, that occurred when Buka vernacular and Tok Pisin kin categories were mixed up in everyday conversations. The Pororans, of course, mixed the two sets of terms without any apparent concern.[1]

Movements, and careful descriptions of movements, did the work on Pororan that kin terms did elsewhere in Buka, as will become apparent below. They were sufficient to the islanders for knowing [atei] relationships. Kin terms could be added to observations of movements, but were neither necessary nor sufficient alone. 'What if I lie to you', Josepha said when I asked her how many children she had. 'Some are married on the mainland. They never come to visit. I think they have forgotten all about their old mother. So how would I know if they are still my children? How would I know how many children I have?' This sceptical attitude towards verbal information—here specifically kin terms—not immediately anchored in visual perception resonates with that of the Usen Barok in neighbouring New Ireland: '[T]alk, the Barok say, is cheap' (Wagner 1986b: xiv). The Barok turn to what Wagner investigates as 'images' instead. Pororan Islanders, by contrast, seek knowledge and power in observations of movements.

Kin terms, and more generally, talk not grounded in the observation of movements have one additional role to play on Pororan, however. They may be used to elicit the movements in which relations are then apprehended. Kevin's conversation with Roberta had an aspect of that, as he was not just describing the movements she had already performed, but was also projecting those he was hoping her to perform relative to particular people in the future. A stronger example of elicitory talk was provided by a girl called Sem, about ten years old, who appeared at Kobkobul one afternoon, saw Kil sitting in front of her house chewing betel nuts, and called (in Tok Pisin): 'One for me—grandmother!' Kil shouted back at her: 'How now "grandmother"! You do not ever help me at all!' Then she pulled a betel nut out of her bag and threw it to Sem. It is worth noting that Kil did not question Sem's claim on genealogical terms. The islanders argue that most children at the village can somehow trace relations to most of those two generations above them (Kil is Sem's MMZ). Relevant to Kil's response was, instead, the absence of a longer-term relation of help, which is the content of relations of matrilineal kinship on Pororan as it is elsewhere in the area (see esp. Crook 2007). The help of grandchildren may take various forms. Kil's youngest daughter's children, who live with her at Kobkobul, run errands and help her with everyday tasks. Makots and Talisa made themselves grandchildren to Kil while staying in Town by occasionally sending (or having sent on their behalf by Helen) baskets of sweet potatoes from Helen's garden at Gogohei, with written notes saying: 'From Makots/Talisa, for grandmother'. Kil used to proudly remark to others: 'My little grand-children from Gogohei are thinking of their old grandmother.' Sem, however, had not provided any such help when she claimed the status of a grandchild. Nevertheless, along with her verbal denial of an exist-ing relation Kil threw a betel nut to Sem. One might understand this movement as confirming Sem's claim to grandchild status 'in advance', with a view to drawing her firmly into a relation of 'help' in the future. This seems to have appeared more profitable to Kil than insisting on the absence of such a relation in the past.

Sem's claim was unusually bold. Adults usually make such direct and explicit claims to relations only at specific events set somewhat apart from ordinary village life, especially at village court hearings. Cases heard by the village court include issues of land rights and, most frequently in 2004–05, of adultery, in which groups of in-laws confronted one another. At the village court, statements of accusation and of defence were commonly peppered with kin terms. Their use drew attention to the discrepancy between the ideal behaviour expected of relatives and their actual behaviour, and to elicit the ideal behaviour instead of the observed one. Most impressively, the *tsunon* used Hapororan kin terms when they announced their judgement, as part of a process of 'straight-ening' relations that had gone astray.

There is a risk to this talk that elicits movements and appropriate behaviour more generally, however: 'What if I lie to you?' What if no movements will be carried out afterwards that confirm the talk, and that render visible the relation that the talk aimed to bring into being? If not followed by observable movements, talk will remain 'just talk', 'a lie' and an embarrassment to the person who uttered it. Thus, people try to avoid such talk. Usually, only the *tsunon*, whose task it is to 'straighten' relations, use talk to elicit particular movements and behaviour, for instance at the village court. However, the highest-ranking *tsunon* of a *pinaposa* will not engage in such talk himself. This will be the task of the second in rank, the <u>mausman</u> or messenger, who thereby deflects from the man highest in rank any possible accusation of 'lying'.

The Pororans' assertion that in talking, they might 'lie' to me, and that I had to 'see for myself' who was related to whom on the island at first caused me considerable difficulties. It took time to 'see' movements, and I would never have been able to see very well without the help of people who explained movements and relations to me, even at the risk of 'lying'. In the following section, I will re-produce some of their verbal renderings of the ideal shape of kinship on Pororan, which helped me to see, bit by bit, particular kin relations and their limits in the everyday movements of people on the island. I begin with the most important in matrilineal Buka: bihainim mama, 'following one's mother'.

Mothers and Children

Here is what Tsireh had to say about matrilineal kinship, bihainim mama [following one's mother], or the relationship between women and their children:

> Matrilineal kinship is just that: following your mother. In the beginning, the child goes around during the day, and then comes back to the mother every night [arm movement downward-outward and inward-upward]. When they grow up, children leave their mothers [arm movement downward-outward]. A girl will go to stay with her husband [arm movement downward-outward]. She will stay at his place, and her mother-in-law will look after her. At first, she will just stay, she will not come back. Once she has settled in, she can come back and visit her own people. She visits her mother, who is living at her father's place, and all her relatives there [arm movement inward-upward]. She will bring food for them, or a little something from her husband's place. When she has children, she will bring her children, to show them to her relatives [arm movement inward-upward]. Now, when her father dies, her mother will return to her own place, her mother's place, the place of her *pinaposa* [arm movement inward-upward, higher up and in towards Tsireh's face than the first]. The daughter will then go to visit her there, to support her, maybe by bringing sweet potatoes or making firewood for the mother. This is good; this is showing respect to the mother and to the ways of our ancestors. When the daughter grows old and her husband dies, she will follow her mother [arm movement inward-upward] to her mother's place, along with all the other women of the same *pinaposa*. *Pinaposa*—their children are stuck together, that is the meaning. That is it. That is matrilineal kinship.

The words that Tsireh used to describe the relations between women and their children—most importantly, leaving or going, returning and following—are the same in which mothers on Pororan tell their children what to do. His arm movements, too, are reproduced by mothers in their dealings with their babies. In my first week on the island, I watched Jennifer's little daughter Tarasih, who had just begun to walk, being encouraged to 'go now, go to grandmother', 'go now, go to your brother', but most importantly, after every excursion to another person, to 'come back now, come back to mother'. Once, a few weeks later, Jennifer put Tarasih, whom she had been holding in her arms, down onto the ground while picking up a basket of sweet potatoes that she was going to take to her FZ in the neighbouring house. Tarasih shakily wandered off on her own. 'Hey! Where are you going?' asked Jennifer. 'You cannot go about like this. You go with your mother, stay with your mother. Where mother goes, you go. You must hear your mother's talk. You must always follow your mother.' She lifted Tarasih up and swung her inward-upward fast, so that Tarasih performed in the air just the same movement that Tsireh had made with his arms when speaking about a woman's 'return' to her mother. Charles Stafford has observed the importance of 'going' and 'coming' in Chinese relations, including relations of kinship (2000). On Pororan, however, this movement was particular to, and constitutive of one very special relation: that between children and their mothers, and by extension that between the members of a *pinaposa* to the group's *hahini*, the most senior of the *tobuan*, the senior women or 'mothers' of the group.

Over the half a year or a little more that I lived with Salu's people at Lulutsi, I had occasion to observe children, both young and adult, leave and return to their mother, and to listen to others' comments and explanations of these movements. Jennifer kept her children—three at the time, as her firstborn was living with his uncle—carefully together. They were free to leave after breakfast and 'go around' the village, merging into the groups of *masal*, children roaming around the village and the reef around in their little canoes. However, she admonished them to always 'return to your mother' for food and for the night. In the evening, her children sat with her and their grandmother around the fire. She would ask what they had been doing, where they had been going, and would encourage them to play with some people's children but not others, on the grounds of particular relations of mutual help or absence thereof between the parents. Jennifer often complained that Sagi, her sister, did not do likewise with her children. Roni and Takeli, seven and four, often left the hamlet before breakfast, uncertain as to whether or not their mother would get up to cook, and only came back late. Jennifer worried that Sagi had no influence whatsoever over her daughters' 'going around', their movements and the relations they developed with other people, and that later on, Roni and Takeli might cause real trouble because 'they won't know whom they belong to'.

At the hamlet of Kobkobul, meanwhile, Kil was in a quandary over what to do with a little grandchild of hers, Chris's son Holyweek.

Holyweek, three years old, was dutifully 'returning' every night and was a good child otherwise, too, but he was not 'returning' to his mother, who was staying with his father in Buka Town. They had left Holyweek in the care of his grandmother and his aunt Talmits. Holyweek became increasingly attached to Talmits. In the first week of his parents' absence, he slept sometimes at Kobkobul and sometimes at Talmits' house at Hutjen. From the second week onwards, however, he went to sleep at Hutjen every night and refused his grandmother's and Denise's increasingly urgent invitations to Kobkobul. He ate with Talmits, he 'followed her everywhere', as Kil observed in the third week of his stay, and sure enough, in the fourth week, he began to call her <u>mama</u>. Talmits did not mind. In fact, she seemed pleased. She had no small children to look after at that time, enjoyed Holyweek's company, and told me that she herself had had another mother than Kil for many years, from the age of four until she was in her thirties. The other mother had been a paternal aunt, too, with no daughters of her own. She had taken Talmits on, as Kil was busy looking after too many children, her own and her late sister's. Talmits had stayed with her aunt, had supported the aunt when she fell ill and had been known to villagers as that aunt's child, until the aunt died and Talmits returned to Kil. Perhaps because of her own history with another mother, Talmits felt sympathy for Holyweek. She would have been happy to take him on. Kil, however, was concerned. Talmits was pregnant, and Kil was worried that she might over-burden herself by taking on another small child. So the next day, when Holyweek was hanging at his '<u>mama</u>' Talmits's arm as she was peeling sweet potatoes, Kil walked over resolutely, pulled him away and shouted: 'Where is your mother? Has she left you again with auntie Talmits? That is not right! Look, auntie Talmits is pregnant. Can't you see that her belly is growing already? Is she going to carry you, too, with a big belly? Is she going to wash your trousers, too, when she has another baby? You better go and look for your mother! Where is she?' Holyweek sat down on the ground and cried. In the evening, he asked his uncle Albert to take him to Town the next morning, so that he could be with his mother. Holyweek's case shows the flexibility of relations between mothers and children—the closest and most important ones that there are, according to the islanders. At the same time, it shows the limits imposed upon a person's capacity to 'follow' the mother he had selected, by others' close observation of everyday movements and the relations that emerged in them, and by the intervention of those whose opinions mattered. In this case it was Kil, the senior woman at Kobkobul, who decided whose child Holyweek could be.

Adults, too, 'return' to their mothers, and ought to perform in their everyday lives movements of the shape of Tsireh's hand movement:

leaving and returning, downward-outward and inward-upward. Talmits, after her other mother died, re-established relations with Kil by 'returning' almost daily to her, bringing her sweet potatoes that she placed respectfully next to Kil's kitchen house, bringing firewood that her husband had cut, or 'giving a little bit of help' otherwise, for instance by helping Kil look after Denise's baby while Denise was out at sea. Whether or not those 'returns' would indeed come about on any particular day, however, always remained uncertain. In what was a particularly bad week, from the perspective of Talmits wanting to 'bring a little bit of help' to her mother, Talmits made three attempts at delivering a basket of sweet potatoes to Kil, and all of them failed. On the first day, Denise's daughters Honik and Teha came over just as Talmits was about to leave her house with Kil's sweet potatoes and indicated that they were hungry—their mother hadn't made breakfast. That was Talmits's sweet potatoes gone to another purpose, and she didn't want to turn up at Kobkobul empty-handed. The next day, Talmits ran into Tsireh on the way, and he demanded the sweet potatoes. As Talmits owed him respect as her *tsunon*, she gave him the sweet potatoes. Again, she did not 'return' to Kil on that day. On the third day, Talmits, having almost made it to Kobkobul, furiously 'threw away' her sweet potatoes to a cousin who was lacking food again and was wandering about waiting to be invited for breakfast by someone. Talmits feared that the cousin might bother Kil and decided that she needed a lesson: she put the sweet potatoes down in front of the cousin and complained loudly about her habit of 'going around looking for food here and there'. Her 'lowering' of that cousin, who had long needed a lesson according to other relatives, gained her respect from neighbours looking on, but again, it meant no 'return' to Kil. When she finally did return—after the next market day, when she could stock up on sweet potatoes again—Kil pretended to be busy with something else. Finally, she looked at Talmits and said: 'Look who is there—you? I didn't know if I had a child over there [nodding in the direction of Talmits's house] any more.' In the light of Talmits's history with another mother, this statement can be taken at face value.

Often, Talmits's 'return' to Kil failed not because Talmits didn't make it, but because Kil wasn't around. Talmits used to swear under her breath on the many occasions when she brought sweet potatoes to Kil at Kobkobul, and Honik or Teha informed her that Kil had a) gone fishing, b) gone to chew betel nuts at her sister's, c) gone to Town, for how long, nobody knew, d) decided to take a little walk, e) walked over to Tsireh's for a serious discussion of *pinaposa* affairs, f) was out on the reef gathering shells, g) had gone to see Anna at Francis's [the highest-ranking *hahini* of Plisoh], or h) was attending a mortuary feast on the mainland that some relatives had picked her up for in the morning. The list could be continued. On no occasion did Talmits consider her mission accomplished by leaving her sweet potatoes at Kobkobul, for Kil to eat when she got back. 'Someone might take them. Or they might rot until <u>mama</u> gets back. No way', she used to say, pick her basket up again and either hunt Kil down—if she was reportedly somewhere on the island—or go back to her own house. Sometimes, however, she would go around a little on her way back, chew betel nut and possibly 'lose some sweet potatoes on the road', that is, give them to relatives.

At Lulutsi, Jennifer and Sagi had another problem in 'returning' to their mother: they already lived in the same house. Many people on the island criticized the arrangement. 'It isn't straight', they said. Salu, however, justified her daughters' premature return to live with her, and pointed to smaller movements of departure and return that they nevertheless performed in the present:

> This house, Hulagam [her husband] built when we came back from Arawa [the provincial capital of Bougainville until 1988]. At first, this place was very empty. I stayed, and Hulagam when he wasn't working in Town, and Tsunon [her youngest son] built this little house here for Jocelyn [Tsunon's wife], and they stayed with their children. That was all right. Then, Sagi [her eldest daughter] came back. She had been staying with her father's sister [in another hamlet], but then she and Uari [her husband] came to stay here. You know, Uari is from East New Britain. Land over there is scarce, so he cannot take Sagi back to stay with his people. It is good he is here; he is a good <u>tambu</u> [in-law]. Then, Jennifer returned, because at her <u>tambu</u>'s place, too, there was no space for her husband to build a house for Jennifer. So she came back, and she and Henry stay, as well. It isn't straight, they say, all right, but we are doing fine here. I like having my daughters here to help me. Sagi goes out in the mornings, I don't see her, and then she comes back with lots of firewood. Jennifer leaves, and I know I don't have to worry about dinner, because she will come back with plenty of fish.

One daughter was missing from Salu's account entirely, her youngest, Helen. 'I don't know now about her', Salu had said and changed topics when I asked in 2004, having learned from Jennifer beforehand that she had another sister besides Sagi. Jennifer eventually told me that Helen had left Pororan many years ago and had not visited them since. She was living in Kimbe, West New Britain with a son. That was all I knew about Helen, until in November 2004, Helen sent word that she was thinking about coming back. In December, a message came through a Pororan

Islander working in Town for Salu's son Charles to pick her and her boy Lionel up there with his boat—they were 'returning' for Christmas. They ended up staying until the end of my fieldwork in June 2005, and had no intentions of leaving again at that time. Helen told me what had happened, and why her mother might not have mentioned her to me: 'I left the island because something bad happened. A man came up onto the veranda of <u>mama</u>'s house when I was sleeping there. We never found out who it was. I didn't want to stay on Pororan any more. I left, and I told <u>mama</u> I wasn't sure if I would return. I stayed over there, at Kimbe, for many years, but then I started being sick all the time. I wanted to come back. I was missing my mother. I was thinking of her saying now, "Maybe my child is dead; maybe my child is no longer thinking of me; maybe I have no child over there any more." I didn't want that, so I came back.' Again, as in Kil's statement about Talmits's belated re-appearance, the real possibility that a child may not return, and that without returns, she is lost to the mother for good is expressed clearly in Helen's account.

There was one woman at Lulutsi who often came and went, but who never 'returned' to Salu and her people: Jocelyn, Tsunon's wife, who lived in a small house of her own just behind Salu's house. Although a valued member of the hamlet and good friends with Jennifer in particular, Jocelyn retained the restrained behaviour in front of Salu that is proper for a daughter-in-law. She did not join the others at Lulutsi for meals, but cooked food for her own children in her own kitchen house and spent most of her evenings on her own veranda, with her daughter Hesa and her youngest son, Goman [the older one, Sirim, was going through an adventurous phase and often stayed out overnight]. Every now and then, Jocelyn and Hesa left for an extended visit to Jocelyn's favourite sister at the place where she had grown up, Hahalis Village on the Buka east coast. Less frequently, they returned to Jocelyn's mother at Nova Village, in western Buka. Sirim and Goman usually stayed back on the island on such occasions, being looked after by their paternal aunts. Hesa, by contrast, always accompanied her mother. In addition to her emotionally close relation to Hesa, Jocelyn explained that Hesa ought to 'follow' her because 'Buka people are matrilineal'. Where would Hesa go in old age, asked Jocelyn, who would help her after her father's people on Pororan would have sent her away, if not her mother's relatives at Nova? And who would 'continue the line' of Jocelyn and her ancestors, if not Hesa? Hesa's brothers, whose children would follow their own mothers, were less important in this respect. Hesa, however, should ideally visit Nova as well as Hahalis, where Jocelyn had grown up and where she hoped that Hesa would marry, because she already had relatives there whom she could co-operate with. When Jocelyn and

Hesa returned from their returns to the mainland, the Lulutsi children used to run and greet them on the beach, just as they would greet everyone else. But when four-year-old Takeli in her excitement once told her mother and aunt that Jocelyn had 'returned', they both corrected her sharply. Jocelyn had arrived, but not returned. They ridiculed Takeli for being *mata kut, talinga tup*—eyes closed, ears closed—that is, a little dull.

Pinaposa Gatherings

Takeli was so small that her being *mata kut, talinga tup* about Jocelyn's 'return' was nothing to worry about. However, when the 2005 school year began, the *tsunon* on the island decided that something had to be done about what they described as school children being *mata kut, talinga tup* about their *pinaposa*, their matrilineal group. And so the *tsunon* announced in the week before school started that school children would have their lunch no longer randomly sitting around anywhere they liked on the school compound, but together with the members of their *pinaposa*. On the first day of school, lunch was a mess. The teachers had read out the names of their *pinaposa* to the children beforehand: Mulul, Put, Keketin, Takap, Plisoh, Holu, Naboen, and had announced where each group would have their lunch. However, when they saw their 'brothers and sisters' (parallel cousins on their fathers side, with whom they ideally lived at the same hamlet) move to other spots (because their mothers belonged to a different *pinaposa*), the younger students especially became confused. Several protested loudly when a teacher separated them from whom they knew as their nearest kin, and explained to them that they must go and eat with their *pinaposa*: 'their children are stuck together', as Tsireh translated the term. On this occasion, the Lulutsi children, and through them Salu, gained much praise. They knew exactly that they were Takap, and who would be there with them in their group: the children who 'returned' to Salu at Lulutsi every Sunday after church and played with them, while their mothers were gathering to chat and to discuss matters pertaining to all of them jointly. The children of the men who attended the gathering, as Salu had long explained to them, were not Takap. They were the Takap's father's children [*pian hatuhan*]. The Lulutsi children had the privilege, here, of living at the hamlet of a *hahini* who was very active in gathering her kin for meetings. Children growing up in larger *pinaposa* whose members interacted less closely had greater difficulties in appreciating the company in which they were suddenly asked to eat their lunch.

Among the people who 'returned' on Sundays to Lulutsi and whose children the Lulutsi children were therefore familiar with was Soaka, a parallel cousin of Salu's who lived with her husband on Hitou. In addition, a large group of Takap came walking over from Yaparu, the village on the southern tip of Pororan. One of them was a man who looked different, never spoke Hapororan and was known as an enthusiastic gardener—the only one I heard of on the island. The Lulutsi children called him 'Uncle Benni'. Jennifer told me, when I asked, that Salu had 'picked him up' at Arawa, the provincial capital, where Salu and her husband had lived form the late 1960s to 1987. When they returned to Pororan, he 'followed' them there. With the financial support of the Takap, he married a Pororan woman. Now he was one of them, Jennifer said. 'We are not many in our *pinaposa*', she added. 'So we were happy when he followed us, returned with us here.' Another man who used to join the Takap on Sundays without being 'anybody's immediate business', as Jennifer put it, was called Tom, from Haku. Tom lived with his wife's relatives in another hamlet. He had arrived on the island as a young man and had attached himself to the Takap because they were relatives of his own relatives in Haku, although no one could quite specify the relation. What holds for the relation between women and children, then, holds for *pinaposa* membership, too. It is not determined by birth, but is created in movements that people perform, and in which they let other people know whom they belong to. Limits are imposed upon their movements by others welcoming them for particular reasons—in the case of the Takap, their own lack of people—or not.

It seems only plausible, then, that Salu refused to give me a definite list of the members of their *pinaposa*. She pointed out that it changed all the time. Jennifer, like me, though for reasons that had nothing to do with the idea of cross-checking population figures, recording clan membership and the like, was impatient with these constant changes. Sometimes, she prepared large amounts of food on a Sunday morning and nobody came after church to eat it; at other times, the hamlet was awash with people with hungry faces and she was unprepared. 'Something isn't working over here', she used to mumble on such occasions. 'This *pinaposa* something of ours is in a mess'. Salu used to laugh at her: 'Their will. Their decision to come; their decision not to come. We cannot command them around. You want to be their boss? You will get sick of it!' [Laik blong ol. Ol yet, ol ikam o ol ino kam. Mipela ino inap long bossim wokabaut blong ol. Yu laikim na yu yet bai bossim ol? Bai yu les!] Instead of 'bossing' them, if someone appeared one Sunday who had not turned up for many weeks beforehand, Salu would make a big show of her surprise, like Kil did when Talmits re-appeared at Kobkobul but less seriously: 'Look who is here? Is it really you? I thought you might have gone missing altogether. I thought you were stuck altogether with your in-laws over there, giving all your help to them, every little piece of fish, all your money, all your good thinking. Now what, you come back to us, really? And did you bring a little something for your mother's people, too?' Usually, the person had dropped 'a little something' off with Sagi, Jennifer or one of their children at the kitchen house.

The unpredictability of 'returns', however, was not only due to the movements of people 'returning', but also to the high degree of mobility of the person they were returning to. Just as Talmits often had to pursue Kil across the island with her sweet potatoes, so Jennifer often had to fetch Salu for *pinaposa* meetings—and sometimes she failed, because Salu had decided to 'take a little break'. Two such 'little breaks' had recently made Salu famous around the village as a 'real saltwater woman, unsurpassable [*mei lul*]'. First, in 2003, Salu had left Pororan at very short notice in order to see her son in the neighbouring province of New Ireland. She had put Jennifer in charge of her house for what she said would not be more than a couple of weeks. She had ended up staying away for almost half a year. Since her return, many people had popped in at Lulutsi in order to hear of her adventures. 'Come on, Salu! You must have been going around absolutely everywhere in that time! You must know every single village in New Ireland now! Or perhaps you went around other places on the way? Tell us now!' Salu used to smile, said that it was 'nothing, just a little bit of going around', but did not deny that she might have gone places she wasn't telling people about. She took with dignity her daughters' part angry, part laughing and part respectful remarks every now and then about the time when she had taken 'a big holiday, really—we did not know if she would come back. We thought she might have drifted from New Ireland to Rabaul, and then all the way to the Philippines! We did not know if we still had a mother!' The Takap, during that period, had not met a single time, according to Jennifer, not knowing what to meet for in the absence of their *hahini*. The second event that had made Salu a 'real saltwater woman' in the eyes of other villagers was an outing in her canoe one Sunday. Salu had left in the morning with no particular intention—or none that she had bothered to mention to us. She had returned in the afternoon with no fewer than 48 octopuses in her canoe, breaking the village record within living memory. She had prepared some for the next market and had distributed the rest freely around the village, some already fried in oyster sauce. Most Takap had already left when Salu returned. After about two hours of waiting, they had departed, saying that there was nothing they could do if their *hahini* had decided to 'go around at sea again'. Soaka was the only one left when Salu returned, and she was happy to take some of the octopus and stories of Salu's catch along to Hitou.

This, then, was <u>bihainim mama</u> on Pororan in 2004–05: people, children and adults, 'returned' to, helped and sought the support of their mother, or the senior woman of their *pinaposa* on a regular basis. Young children were expected to return every night and for every meal; adult children sometimes 'went missing' and returned unexpectedly after many years during which a mother could not be certain if she still had a child in them; and *pinaposa* members return on Sundays after church for a meal, though one never knew in advance who would come on any particular occasion. All these movements were described verbally through the same verbs of movement: retuning, coming, seeing/visiting, and with gestures resembling exactly the hand movement that Tsireh drew into the air when he explained <u>bihainim mama</u>. The Pororans were interested in this movement, not as a foregone conclusion, but as a contingent emergence out of people's will and 'going around': children sometimes failed to return; a mother went around at sea instead of providing a stable point in space for their return.

Fathers, or 'Making Grow'

Men are said to 'pull' women into marriage [inward-upward hand movement]. One way of doing this is through love magic, which can be bought from experts at a particular village on the Buka west coast. However, the Pororans claim that they need no magic but can 'pull women' just with their thoughts, or alternatively, with their fish. 'The women used to come and put their heads under my feet', as Hotu put it, and it was indeed because of his large catches, channelled to a high-ranking *tsunon* by his mother, that Hotu came to marry this *tsunon*'s daughter (see chapter 1). Marriage on Pororan in 2004–05 was highly informal.[2] It simply meant that a woman took her personal belongings to the house of a man, usually one whom she had gone to visit frequently before, and usually after discussing the matter with her relatives, while he discussed it with his. This was not always the case, however. Hatuna, for instance, informed her mother Talmits rather casually one day that she had just moved in with a man from Hitou, whom she had been seeing for about two weeks. In order for a marriage to be 'straight', a man should pay bride price, or should at least show efforts of accumulating the bride price. However, the ceremony in which the bride price is handed over, *sinahan* [bride price] (see chapter 5) is usually held long after a couple has started living together. It takes some time to accumulate a sum considered appropriate, which in 2004 was an equivalent of about GBP 500 and some *beroan* [shell money] for a woman who did not have the status of a *hahini*. Furthermore, something else is of much more immediate concern than the bride price: a house.

Since he has 'pulled' the woman, her relatives will demand of her new husband that he 'put her somewhere'. A man must negotiate with the *tsunon* of his *pinaposa* for a house site, which may be difficult to find because 'there are too many people on this little island', and then he must build a house. Ideally, the new couple should live at the man's mother's hamlet, where his mother will 'look after' the new wife and 'make her stay well'. House-building itself is usually done by a group of men, often by the young man who will own the house, his father or an experienced carpenter who oversees the activities and performs specialist tasks, and his brothers and cousins. First of all, the building materials are cut and transported, inward-upward in the Pororans' accounts, to the house site. This may take only a few days in the case of a small house of 'traditional' material brought from the Buka mainland, and several years in the case of a permanent house, whose components are expensive. Once all materials are assembled, house poles are cut, and the floor of the house is made, ideally of plywood. Alternatively, the house is built directly on the ground. Sago leaves for thatching are sewn together if no corrugated iron is available. Walls may be made of mats of sago or pandanus, or of plywood. Finally, the various house parts are nailed or tied together with vine. Windows and doorframes are often left open at first, and may be completed later with a door and fly wire. Large houses are opened with a small feast, called 'smoking the house'. Small houses are merely completed with an especially large meal for the work crew, which may be expanded to include others at the hamlet and casual visitors. The arm movements that accompany accounts of house-building complete what those accompanying accounts of 'pulling a woman' begin: a forceful movement running inward-upward, followed by a slower downward-outward one.

In the absence of a house, children may refuse their fathers the respect normally due to them. This link between fatherhood, house-building and respect became especially apparent in the events that evolved around Easter 2005 from the failure of Gisa to build a house for his wife Solohi, Kil's ZD, and their children. Gisa's children were already between twelve and twenty-four years old, a house site had long been marked for them at Solohi's relatives' hamlet, and Kil's eldest son had sent money for house poles. Nevertheless, as people pointed out, 'they have no house' [*emei ta luma tereru*]. They were living instead in the large permanent house of Kil's son Chris. One night in early 2005, Solohi's eldest son Ken drank homebrew and confronted his father Gisa at Chris's house.

He accused Gisa of making him feel ashamed in front of his mother's people because he had been too lazy to build a house for Ken's mother. When Ken threatened aloud to beat his father and to physically throw him out of Chris's house, onlookers found themselves in a difficult situation. On the one hand, they shared Ken's perception that Gisa's failure to build a house was disgraceful. On the other hand, they were not prepared to allow Ken to beat his father, whom he owed respect. The tension was defused, although not permanently, by Kil's son Lawrence, Ken's *sungut* [male member of Ken's *pinaposa* in the generation above him] whom Ken respected. Lawrence took Ken to his own house, where Ken aired all his concerns and his shame at his father's failure to build a house for the family. Gisa went to sleep that night at the new house site, in recognition of the validity of Ken's accusations. Solohi sat down at the bottom of the stairs to Chris's house crying over the difficulties of the situation.[3]

When Lawrence, Kil, Ken and some other Plisoh discussed the problem that night and pointed out what Gisa should have done a long time ago—build a house, so that his children could look up to him—they performed over and over a particular hand movement. This was an abrupt inward-upward movement, indicating the 'pulling' of a wife, and a smooth downward-outward one, indicating the release and 'return' of a woman and her children for visits to their maternal relatives. This movement constitutes an 'opposite version' to the downward-outward and inward-upward one by which women and *tsunon* accompany conventionalized accounts of matrilineal kinship, bihainim mama. When Tsireh explained this movement once, he said it meant men's capacity to 'make grow' [*hatuhan*]. Although women are known to grow on their own—they do not need to have a husband; 'going around with men' every now and then is enough—it is far preferable for the children if they are 'made to grow' by a father. Tsireh said:

> He holds them, he looks after them, he builds a house for them and makes sure they don't wander off on their own and encounter trouble; he wipes their noses and cleans up their faeces. Therefore they look like him. When they grow older, he brings them fish to eat. He pays their school fees.[4] In return, his children will show his father respect [*hatsitsi*] by bringing him their 'first fruit' [in English]: the first mud crab they catch, the first sweet potato they dig out in the garden, the first plate of the first meal that a little girl cooks on her own, the first fish that a boy catches. When the father dies, the father's relatives will always want to see his children, and they will continue to support them, because on the children, they can see the father's face.

Tsireh's account of the tasks of Pororan fathers, and of their children resembling them, resonates strongly with accounts of Trobriand fathers (Malinowski 1929: 207; see also E. Leach 1961; A. Weiner 1976). There, fathers feed and form children (see also Mosko 1995). On Pororan, however, the hand movements that accompanied Tsireh's account, as well as the Plisoh's discussions of Gisa's failure, indicated that all the intimate, multiple acts of looking after children were part of a capacity, not to give substance and form to a human body, but to shape movements. This capacity is objectified in the arm movement indicating a pull and release, and more importantly, in the physical movements of women and their children relative to particular men—their husbands and fathers— in this particular pattern.

Houses—places where they could be 'put'—were an important tool for men to steer the movements of their wives and children, but were not a one-off solution for men to have their capacity to 'make grow' recognized by others. Of Kil's four sons, for instance all had built houses, but none lived in their own house with their family. Kil watched, discussed with Talmits and Denise and other relatives and evaluated her sons' movements with their families carefully, judging them by the degrees to which they could be described in a particular kind of hand movement. Jerry, according to Kil, was doing fine. He was working in the PNG Highlands. His wife and children were with him. Kil had visited them there, had seen their house and found it appropriate, and approved of the fact that Jerry sent his wife and children over to his wife's place in Manus twice a year and took them to Pororan once a year. (Jerry's salary was far above that of ordinary Pororan Islanders.) Albert, as will be shown later, was in deep trouble. Chris was not doing well. His house, of course, was occupied by Solohi. He himself was moving between one wife in Rabaul and another who lived with him partly in Buka Town, partly at Lawrence's house on Pororan, and partly at her relatives' place on the mainland in 2004–05. When Kil learned that Chris and Georgina were staying at Georgina's place at the time, she let out a scream of dismay: 'Iii! What is he doing again? Does he have no good thinking at all? What will it look like? Doesn't he want to bring her here, put her here safely, look after her and the children, instead of going around at his in-laws' place?' Kil's hand movements, inward-upward and downward-outward, said more clearly than her words what she was expecting of Chris.

In comparison to Chris, Kil praised Lawrence. Lawrence and his family spent most of their time in Buka Town, where he ran a hotel and restaurant and where Helen worked as a teacher at a highly regarded primary school, on Sohano, a small island inhabited by rich Buka and some foreigners. Helen's school had given them a house to stay in. From there,

Helen occasionally returned with Makots, Talisa and Hence—though sometimes only with Talisa and Hence—to Helen's mother and brother at Gogohei. If they wanted to—though usually, only Makots wanted to—the family could spend time with Kil on Pororan, at Lawrence's own house. What looked like a stable arrangement at the time, however, and what could indeed be summed up as a neat movement of a woman to her husband and occasionally back to her own kin with her children was a recent and fragile achievement. Lawrence told me that he had first stayed on the island with Helen after they got married, eight years earlier. However, since he was working in Town, she was alone with his mother on Pororan all the time, and this caused problems:

> It's never easy if you stay with your in-laws, but for Helen, it must have been very hard. <u>Mama</u> didn't like her. Who knows now about <u>mama</u>. So Helen wasn't happy there. She asked me to take her to Town to stay there, her and Makots. I did, but it was too expensive. We had a tiny house, not good for a family. So Helen suggested that we move to her place, Gogohei, where her brother was. I didn't want to, but I had no better suggestion. So I commuted every day from Gogohei to Town. All the dust on that road made me cough. And it wasn't right. I wanted Helen and the kids to stay with me, in a house of our own, not with her people. Makots and Talisa should grow up with their father, not their mother's people. So we went back to Town. Now, Helen teaches at Sohano Primary School. I pulled some strings, and Helen is a very good teacher, so it wasn't hard for her to get the job. Last year now, the school gave us a house. Since then, we are staying very well.

All the obstacles that Lawrence mentioned re-appeared in other island men's accounts of their own difficulties at 'making things look straight'. These were dislikes between their mother and their wife (in almost every case), financial constraints and the cost and unreliability of transport between Town and Pororan that made it difficult to look after one's wife while earning money, most importantly for paying children's school fees. Under those conditions, the movement of 'pulling' a wife, 'putting' her somewhere and occasionally releasing her and her children for 'return' visits to her relatives was not a one-off affair, but resembled more the hand-by-hand pulling in of a fishing line. It was piecework, and it wasn't made easier, as Charles at Lulutsi once complained, by the fact that everyone was watching all the time and was 'saying this and saying that'.

However, there is an additional problem: in the context of marriage, the passion for 'going around' that the Pororans—both men and women—are known for becomes problematic. Lawrence, for instance, had to negotiate with Helen his habit of 'going around', which in his case included not only several hours a day or night spent at sea (*roror itasi*), but also 'going around with women'. Helen had been a fool, her mainland relatives told me, for marrying a saltwater man, who would be 'going around' all the time. More problematic was the case of Lawrence's brother Albert, which will be discussed below. His wife's 'going around' prevented the appearance of movements of a shape that would have proved his capacity to 'make grow'.

The Ninja

Albert was married to Hogun, a woman from Yaparu, the village on the southern tip of the island. In 2004–05, Hogun was rumoured to be going around with Hanun, a man from the hamlet next to Kobkobul. The two of them had had an affair, on and off, for more than twenty years. When rumours about Hogun's 'going around with that man, Hanun' reached a peak in early 2005, others at the village began to draw attention to the fact that Albert felt tired all the time and had a pain in his legs that sometimes prevented him from walking. Albert's brothers were dismayed, his mother deeply concerned. She suspected that his state was due to magic that Hanun worked, perhaps with Hogun's help, to prevent Albert from divorcing her. If Albert divorced Hogun, Kil argued, he would no longer give rice to her, which she was long used to giving not to her children, but to Hanun. By feeding Albert magic, Hanun made sure his own source of rice did not dry up. Kil used to lament the state of affairs by attempting to calculate the number of rice bags that had been diverted from their proper route, from a father to the children whom he intended to 'make grow', over the 20 years of Hanun and Hogun's affair.

Besides Kil, another person was deeply affected emotionally by gossip about the affair. This person was Albert's daughter Audilia, seventeen at the time. Talmits, Kil and I heard one night that she had left the island, stayed in the room shared by the female helpers at Albert's hotel in Town and refused to come out or talk to anyone. On our next trip to Town, we went to see her, and Talmits eventually convinced her to tell us what had distressed her: 'They said I don't have Albert's face. What will happen to me now? Will Albert throw me out?' In light of the Pororans' assumptions that all children resemble their fathers, it seemed reasonable that Audi was worried that her 'wrong' face would make her unwelcome with her paternal relatives. Talmits, however, calmed her down: 'Who is talking about your face? Let them talk! Who looked after you when you were small? Who wiped your nose, have you forgotten? Your father's people! That was I, remember? Who cleaned up after you? Look at the old lady, here she is, Kil! And who built a house for you? That was Albert, or who else. Who gave you this job in Town, so that you could bring money to your mother every now and then? Albert.' With each sentence, Talmits moved her wrist vigorously inward-upward and downward-outward. 'Who is talking about faces? It is not your fault that your mother is going around with this man.' Audi could not be convinced to return to the island with us, but at least she left the room from then on and made herself useful at her father's hotel.

When Talmits, Kil and I returned to Pororan, Kil's granddaughter Honik came running out to the boat to tell us the latest rumour: a ninja, a 'man in black' with Rasta-locks had been seen and had pursued women and children in the garden area. Talmits dismissed Honik's talk, but the Plisoh women told us the same, and the ninja was the main topic of conversation, too, when I went to visit Ardie at the school and then the Lulutsi that night. The ninja was said to be moving incredibly fast. Some claimed he was flying. He was said to be 'going around' along the road between Pororan and Yaparu. A few days later, the ninja's black clothes were found buried at one of the Stations of the Cross along this road. For a few more days, people working in the gardens or travelling this road had ninja appearances. The ninja rumour fascinated the islanders more than any other during my time on the island. Although everyone dismissed the possibility of a ninja roaming the island outright, most people were also shaken with nervous laughter, and others lurched into imitations of the ninja's movements of flying, rushing, running and going in circles. Others again gazed expectantly towards the sky, suggesting that where there was a ninja, there might also be UFOs.

Jennifer eventually made the link between Hanun and the ninja explicit in a conversation with her relatives at Lulutsi: Hanun alone had Rasta-locks on Pororan.[5] Furthermore, he presumably had to move along the road between his house at Pororan and Hogun's at Yaparu very fast, unless he wanted to be caught by either Albert's or Hogun's brothers. Jennifer's explanation that Hanun used his ninja-dress as a disguise on the road between Pororan and Yaparu did not seem convincing. All the more convincing, however, was the image of radically different and complementary kinds of movements that she wove out of the gossip of Albert's shaken-up marriage and bad health and the rumours about the ninja. She made relational sense of the inexplicable, fascinating, fast and witch-like (see Munn 1986) movements of a 'man in black' by establishing a connection to Albert's slow, closely circum-scribed and energy-less movements, reported at the same time. These two in conjunction must have provided the strongest possible image, to Pororan Islanders who apprehend kin relations in movements, of the strange state of relations among Hogun, Hanun, Albert and his chil-dren, after twenty years of a mother's 'going around', twenty years of diverted rice bags, and twenty years of the use of magic that had even-tually almost immobilized Albert.

The rumours about the ninja, along with gossip about Hogun, Hanun and Albert ebbed off after a group of Hogun's and Albert's male mater-nal relatives immobilized Hanun, at least temporarily. As in-laws with a shared interest in this marriage (which was one of several currently linking these two matrilineal groups), they jointly stood watch several nights around Hogun's house, eventually caught Hanun and beat him unconscious, according to eyewitnesses. Hanun, who was carried back to his own house by his relatives whom the Plisoh informed, did not leave his house for about a week. Albert recovered more slowly. Hogun, as Kil reported upon her return from a visit to Yaparu and consultations with the women there, took to 'just staying' and made sure she fed her chil-dren and her husband well. When more ordinary movements and rela-tions could be observed again, the islanders' attention turned elsewhere.

In talking about, and in imitating so vividly the movements of the ninja, the islanders were drawing attention to the state of relations whose proper shape—downward-outward and inward-upward, inward-upward and downward-outward—had disintegrated over the years of a troubled marriage and an apparently interminable love affair. I needed Jennifer to point out the connection before I saw it; the Pororans did not.

In 2009, I learned that Albert had died. Roselyn, who sent me the message, added, 'You know how he used to not be able to walk well.'

The subversion of Albert's movements by Hogun's 'going around' indicates clearly the strong dependence of men on their wives and chil-dren, not for their sexual identity (M. Strathern 1988: 63), but for their capacity to 'make grow' to become apparent. Men needed their wives and children to move inward-upward and downward-outward, from the father's perspective. From the woman's relatives' perspective, something else became apparent in this movement: matrilineal kinship, a woman leaving and later returning to her relatives, followed by her children. The woman's relatives owe the fathers of their group's children respect for making this relation apparent. 'Following your mother is the most important thing on Buka. But showing respect to your father is impor-tant, too', said Tsireh.

Fishermen and Gardeners

There is both a parallel and a contrast here to descriptions of the role of fathers on the Buka mainland. Tsireh told me, and my hosts at Tegese later confirmed what mainlanders said about fathers as gardeners:

> A woman is like a banana growing in a garden. A man comes and sees her now, and thinks that this banana is tall and strong. He asks the owner of the banana if he can cut a sapling. He cuts a sapling off the banana, and he takes it to his own garden to grow there. He waters it and looks after it well, so the banana grows tall and bears many fruit [*pian*, fruit or child]. The man takes the fruit and sends them back to the owner of the mother banana, because that is where his banana came from.

The women I knew from Lontis, Gagan and Gogohei, were all very proud of the large number of banana species found in the area, and of the quality of the banana fruit that grew in their own gardens. They made manifold connections between the qualities of bananas and the qualities of women. For instance, only women are strong like the rope of banana fibres, with which they tie their baskets to their backs. Most importantly, however, women, and not men, can be moved to a new place and will grow there, like bananas in Buka, like a special kind of hardy nettle on Ambae, in Vanuatu (Bolton 1999), and like sweet potatoes whose vines women pass on among relatives in Tambul in the PNG highlands (A. Schneider, pers. comm.).[6]

There are resonances between mainland accounts of banana growth and Pororan accounts of fathers or *tsunon* 'pulling' people and settling them down. However, there is also an important difference. Bananas, and mainland women if we take the parallel literally are 'cut' off a place: a hamlet or a garden, in which the mother plant is firmly rooted. They are then firmly implanted as a new plant. Mainland women are expected to stay and spend their time with their husband's people, working their husband's land. Pororan women, by contrast, are 'pulled' by men with fish in moments when they 'go around'. This is not a one-off achievement, but a movement that has to be effected again and again because saltwater women, like men, are inherently mobile. They render invisible in their 'going around' their relations to particular others. Unlike Buka mainlanders and other Melanesian gardeners (Leach 2003a), the Pororans do not emphasize the separation and extraction of a person from another person and a place, and her transportation to another place. Instead, they draw attention to the creation of a movement of a particular shape out of indeterminate *roror*. This is done through the particular entanglement of looks and wants described in chapter 1—that is, it is a matter of attraction rather than extraction.[7] Emotionally, there may not be much of a difference, but in terms of aesthetics, there is. Separations are not made between people, but between different kinds of movements.

Matrilineal Kinship: A View from Pororan

In an article about Central Bantu systems of kinship and marriage in 1950, Audrey Richards formulated the 'matrilineal puzzle', which arose from the 'difficulty of combining recognition of descent through the woman with the rule of exogamous marriage' (Richards 1950: 246). She formulated the problem primarily in terms of authority and control over children and the group's landed resources. Fortes (1950) made a similar argument for the Ashanti, pointing out matrilineal descent was an arrangement of polar relations that forced each individual to face two ways, towards his or her mother and his or her father. The matrilineal puzzle has been re-stated (e.g. Schneider and Gough 1961) and expanded upon by various authors. For example, it was debated whether matrilineal systems are less flexible than patrilineal ones in situations of rapid economic and social change (e.g. Murdock 1949). The puzzle has also been debated. Keesing (1975) has suggested that matrilineal descent in the Trobriands, as described by Malinowski (1922), is both stable and flexible. In Bougainvillean enthnography, Jill Nash's (1974) monograph on the Nagovisi has aimed to illustrate the endurance and in fact re-invigoration of a matrilineal system in a situation of rapid economic and social change.

At first sight, Pororan Islanders' interests in hand movements of two shapes, one objectifying the relations between mothers and their children and the other the capacity of fathers to make children grow appear like a local expression of the matrilineal puzzle. However, unlike in Richards's argument and subsequent debates, the tension inherent in the relations between mothers, fathers, children and the two sets of in-laws do not arise on Pororan from conflicts over the control or authority over a woman, her children and a group's resources. Instead, they arise from the question of whether or not this woman and her children will perform movements of the appropriate shape, downward-outward and inward-upward from the perspective of their own relatives and inward-upward and downward-outward from that of their husband/father. The two sets of in-laws share an interest in those movements, for whose proper appearance each side depends on the other, rather than tugging at the woman and her children from opposite ends. This is a different kind of puzzle from that described by Richards.

Researchers working in Papua New Guinea have long pointed out the difficulty of importing into Melanesia African descent theory, of which Richard's formulation of the matrilineal puzzle is a part.[8] Early ethnographic findings from the PNG Highlands challenged some of descent theory's key theoretical tenets (see, e.g. Barnes 1962; Feil 1984; Langness 1964; Salisbury 1964; A. Strathern 1973). Not from the highlands, but no less challenging was Peter Lawrence's Garia ethnography, which presented a society disturbingly fluid and constituted by relations without clearly defined limits (Lawrence 1984; see also Leach 2003a; M. Strathern 1992b). Out of these ethnographic challenges, anthropologists working in Melanesia have developed alternative understandings of kinship. These have emerged partly in conjunction with broader changes in anthropological theorizing, most prominently David Schneider's ethnographic and theoretical critique of the study of kinship (Schneider 1965, 1968, 1984) and the literature on kinship and 'relatedness' (Carsten 2000) since then.

In his monograph on Daribi kinship, Roy Wagner (1967) takes on Schneider's suggestion of avoiding both 'total system' comparisons and the comparison of randomly selected institutions by exploring instead what defines and what relates persons and groups in different ethnographic settings. Wagner suggests that Daribi persons and groups are all related to each other by maternal and paternal bodily substance, which he refers to as 'consanguinity'. Parallel flows of this substance are differentiated, and persons and groups thus defined, through reciprocity or exchange. More recently, James Leach's work on kinship among Nekgini speakers on the Rai Coast in Madang has built on Wagner's suggestions (Leach 2003a). Leach agrees that groups and persons are defined in moments of exchange, specifically marriage exchange when a man from one place extracts a woman from another. In contradistinction to Wagner, however, Leach argues that Reite people do not consider themselves related by the sharing of genealogical substance. The question of an alternative substance of relationship is answered with an ethnography of gardening, of the processes of growing taro at one's place with the help of spirits and the knowledge of stories, all of which are enfolded in the land. As people grow taro from this land-story-spirit substance, so they also grow children. Their nurturance, with its source directly in the land, relates persons who grow up at the same place.

On Pororan, movements define and relate people. Regarding definition, on the basis of the ethnography presented above, we can begin to 'see' persons, relations and matrilineal groups emerge as distinct from others as people perform, or try to make other people perform movements of particular shapes, suitable for being summed up in hand movements. Downward-outward and inward-upward movements 'define' matrilineal relations. Children make themselves children of a particular mother by consciously and deliberately performing movements of this particular shape relative to her. The members of Takap came to be defined as Takap by their return to the *hahini* on Sundays. Jocelyn came to be differentiated from the other inhabitants of Lulutsi by her movements of return to her own people on the Buka mainland, and by the careful linguistic differentiation that the adults at the hamlet taught the children to draw between her movements and those of Salu's children. The matrilineal groups on the island came to be defined, though in a 'beginners' fashion', through the *tsunon*'s efforts at orchestrating the movements of school children. We will see more sophisticated processes of *pinaposa* definition in the following chapters.

Inward-upward and downward-outward movements of the 'pulling' shape define persons with a capacity to make others grow. On Pororan, this is the capacity of giving shape to movements. It was first exercised by Hulu. He pulled off what had previously got stuck on Sia as they were going around on the reef. Fathers exercise this capacity in relation to their wives and children. They pull, put them somewhere and release them, grown. Houses are important as places where wives can be put, but more importantly, men make relations appear, or fail to do so, against a saltwater interest they share with their wives: going around. What in the context of fishing appears as the most valuable aspect of island life, the freedom to go fishing, and by implication to go wherever and whenever one wants, plays a more ambivalent role from the perspective of fathers efforts at defining relations among themselves, their wives and their children.

Regarding the question of how movements relate people, I note the movements of persons back and forth between fathers and mothers, or between Town and Pororan and Gogohei, as Makots and Talisa were performing them. Each did so in her own way, according to her own preferences, with occasional prompting from their parents not to neglect one or the other side completely. When the girls had not visited Kil for some time, Helen sent baskets of sweet potatoes on their behalf. The movements of the baskets 'stood in', as Kil once observed, for a visit by her grandchildren. They were an alternative way of extending 'good thinking' to a grandmother, and of providing the 'help' by which one becomes related to a senior person (see also Crook 2007). 'Giving a little bit of help' was deemed appropriate among matrilineal kin in particular. However, persons beyond the scope of one another's *pinaposa*, and with no intention of entering it (judging from their movements on occasions such as *pinaposa* meetings) would extend help to each other, too.

If movements both relate and define people, then how does one know what a particular movement is about? The answer, in Kil's words, is 'you will stay a little and see for yourself who is who'. For me, staying a little and seeing involved watching movements and asking others about the history of a particular movement and the meaning that they perceived in it. Often, both history and meaning are contested, as will be shown. What appears as a 'defining' movement to some people may appear as a 'relating' movement to others, while others again, lacking knowledge of past movements that might help them understand the one at issue, may only perceive a random 'going around'. Giving form to movements and opening this form up again for discussion, with regard to both their own movements and those of others, and by performing as well as by discussing them, is the art of kinship as Pororan Islanders practiced it in 2004–05.

With their attention focused so firmly on movements, Kil and others on Pororan showed a disregard for other media of relatedness that was astonishing, given their prominence elsewhere in Melanesia. On the background of anthropological writings on non-genealogical modes of 'relatedness' (Carsten 1997, 2000; see also Bamford 2004; Bamford and Leach 2009), the realization that matrilineal kinship on Pororan was not about genealogy did not appear surprising. However, given the strong interest in 'materiality' in current Melanesian anthropology (e.g. Bell and Geismar 2009), I was expecting a greater interest in the material qualities of objects. In the islands region, ethnographers have reported the prominence of human bodies and anthropomorphic objects (see esp. Battaglia 1983; Munn 1986) and, with regard to the role of fathers, the importance of faces (see esp. Malinowski 1929; E. Leach 1961; A. Weiner 1976). Concerns over faces did, indeed, appear at a certain moment described above, when Audi worried that she might no longer be welcome with her father's people because of her 'wrong' face. They appeared again at other moments, and will be revisited later. However, Talmits' forceful reply to Audi shows that movements top faces in Pororan kinship.

Similarly, movements top places in Pororan perceptions of the power of the *tsunon*, as will be shown in the following chapter.

NOTES

1. For a list of Hapororan and Tok Pisin kin terms, see appendix C.
2. This is especially remarkable given the early preparations for and the importance of marriage and marriage ceremonies in the past (see esp. Blackwood 1935; Sarei 1974).
3. This case was perceived to be especially problematic because Solohi has the status of a *hahini*, and should thus truly have had a house of her own. Furthermore, her eldest son Ken is a future *tsunon*. This complicated matters insofar as villagers of lesser status could not have physically prevented him from committing the outrage of beating his father without committing the more serious outrage themselves of laying hand on a *tsunon*.
4. See also Sykes (2001). School fees are the most significant item of household expenditure in Buka.
5. In post-Crisis Bougainville, Rasta-locks were usually considered a statement of support for the BRA. Given the intense fear that the islanders said they had felt of the BRA as recently as the early 1990s, this can hardly be dismissed, although Hanun himself was not, as far as I am aware, known to have been a BRA himself.
6. For writings on plant metaphors in the Austronesian context, see esp. Fox (1971). See also Fox and Sather (1996).
7. A comment on Hulu pulling off Sia what had previously got stuck on her is in order. The Pororans, with their hand movements, emphasize the action of pulling, and not the fact that something came off, and later something else [a child] came out of Sia. We may think of the actions of a fisherman extracting his hook from a fish. The removal of the hook takes place after the fact.
8. Her writings on the matrilineal Bemba, of course, are not (see esp. Richards 1939, 1956), and she voiced sharp criticism early on of what came to be a 'classic' in descent theory, Evans-Pritchard's *The Nuer* (Richards 1941). Her article in *African Political Systems*, however, is couched in the terms, and answers to the theoretical interests of descent theorists.

CHAPTER 3

Mobile Places

The previous chapter was concerned with the relations between mothers, fathers and their children and their objectification in movements. This chapter is concerned with places and the groups of people that inhabit them. The *tsunon*, the male hereditary leaders in Buka, are the persons responsible for 'looking after the place' [*pinapu*, ples] and the people who live there [*areban ipinapu*, lit.: people at the place]. What exactly this task of 'looking after the place' involves was demonstrated in a highly entertaining way once on a journey from Town by truck to the beach at Karoola and then by boat to Pororan. I went with a group of Pororan workmen who were going home on a Friday afternoon. One of the workmen, Bona, is a *tsunon* of Naboen. On this truck ride, the workmen [called 'boys', ol boi or *hitots*] jokingly elicited from Bona the behaviour of a *tsunon*, and he made a point of delivering it. Bona made sure that the cargo—mostly rice, flour and other store-bought goods for the workmen's families—was properly stored on the truck. He then ordered the boys to climb on and told them to make space in the centre front for the women in our party. Bona himself rode on the cabin of the truck, above everyone else's head. He greeted every truck we met along the road and passed bottles of homebrew, betel nuts and sticks of betel pepper back and forth on behalf of his workmen to the men on other trucks. Each transaction received a comment such as: 'X from Y is giving five betel nuts to his in-law Z on Pororan! Very good! Maybe Z will think of his chief [him, Bona], too, and leave a betel nut for him?' When the workmen became thirsty, they passed money from the back towards the front of the truck to Bona. Bona took it, jumped down to buy a carton of beer at a trade store, climbed back up onto the driver's cabin—not without admonishing the women to duck down so that they would not be above his head, and 'everything above the *tsunon*'s head is his'—and distributed the beer from there. Bona personally changed all six of our broken tyres, with some other men's support. He attacked every broken tyre with wild kicks of his worn boots and

Notes for this section begin on page 99

verbal abuses, under the cheers of the workmen: 'Fight that tyre! Fight it, chief!' The tyres delayed us, and night fell just as we reached the junction at Hanahan and turned into the unpaved road across Buka Island to Karoola. Bona turned his attention towards the 'big bush'. 'We are late! Sorry, we are coming at a bad time! All of you, hear me, we are not coming to cause trouble! We are sorry!' he called out. (He explained the next day that the islanders did not know the spirits who lived in the bush, and that it was not good to be on the road at night, although it happened often enough.) When we reached Karoola at about midnight, no boat was to be seen. Bona distributed some canvas he had taken along, first to the women whom he showed the driest spot on the beach, and then to the workmen. He went around with some bread and then told us: 'Sleep now, sleep. Your chief will look after you.' He stood up on a tree trunk that bent out over the reef and torched towards the island for a boat, which arrived to pick us up at about 3:00 A.M. Bona got on the boat last, making sure we all got on safely.

Various aspects of Bona's deliberately exaggerated performance of being *tsunon* evoked tasks, character traits and activities associated with *tsunon* in the past and in the present. His special concern for the women mirrored that of a *tsunon* for the women in his group and especially the *hahini*, who will 'continue the line'. In return, they must respect him, and must bend down low so as to stay lower than his head, the location of a *tsunon*'s power. In his mock attacks against the tyres, he evoked the fighting prowess for which Pororan *tsunon* were, according to the islanders, known in the pre-colonial past. When Bona acted as a physical mediator in transactions between the Pororans and others along the road, and when he distributed bread on the beach, he acted out the *tsunon*'s role in organizing formal exchanges and food distributions in the colonial past as well as in the present. His taking charge of spatial arrangements on the truck and his sharing out of canvas for sleeping on the beach called to mind the *tsunon*'s task of distributing house sites and garden land among his people. Bona, not just anyone, communicated with unknown spirits, taking on the dangers this involves. Finally, his position up on the driver's cabin (for which Buka police sometimes charge a fine) constituted a strong claim to the *tsunon*'s position of 'being above', 'going ahead' and deserving respect from those whom he 'looks after'.

When Bona described and explained his actions to me the next day as all part of 'looking after the place, and looking after my people', and when other *tsunon* described their role and their power, they draw the same movement with their arms into the air that are used to describe a father's capacity to 'make grow': inward-upward and downward-outward. This movement, as I argued with regard to fathers in the previous chapter, constitutes a claim to give shape to other people's movements. Fathers make this claim regarding their wives and children; they depend on their wives and children to validate their claim, and to objectify in their own, physical movements for all to see the capacity of a man to 'make grow'. Tsunon, however, claim the capacity to give shape to movements in relation to anyone who lives at their settlement—and what their settlement is, if it is only their hamlet or an entire village, depends on each particular case.[1]

Besides claiming—and, if all goes well, demonstrating—a capacity of eliciting movements, which sets themselves apart from those who move at their request, the *tsunon* create two types of units, or distinctions, in these processes of 'pulling' people and 'putting' them somewhere. In this chapter, I will concentrate on one of them: places at which people congregate, and around which their movements revolve. However, those places that are constituted by people's movements are not themselves immobile. They have changed location and form many times, according to Pororan Islanders' accounts of their settlements and their history. What remains stable across those accounts is the form of the movement by which the islanders objectify the process of place-making: inward-upward and downward-outward, 'pulling' people and 'putting' them somewhere.

Ancestral Settlement

As mentioned before, Pororan is a 'small spot' originally formed by rubbish drifting across the lagoon from the mouth of the Gagan River that got stuck on elevated parts of the reef [*remits*, lit.: stone]. The Pororans told me that their ancestors settled the newly emergent 'little thing' as soon as there was space enough for setting up small shelters. They came in small groups, from various locations across the Buka coast, and here is why they came, according to Tsireh:

> The people on the mainland, in the past, did not have protein. Our ancestors [those who migrated to Pororan] went to find fish for them. One or two from a *pinaposa* came to Pororan to fish, because fish were more plentiful here. They set up small camps, here and there, no houses, just small shelters in spots where the island was dry already. They stayed for some time and fished, and then they returned to the mainland with their fish. Eventually, they made houses here, but they made no gardens. They returned to the mainland with their fish, and their relatives there gave them starch food. That's how it was, at first,

and so we still return to the mainland today, and our relatives there give us starch food for our fish.

When talking about the emergence of the island and its first settlers once, Francis, the highest-ranking *tsunon* of Plisoh, stretched his arm out towards the inland side of his hamlet and added: 'You see that mountain there? That is the stone [*remits*] around which the island first grew.' After a meaningful pause, he continued and explained:

> This is the stone on which all the rubbish got stuck. This is the part of the island that fell dry first. Around it, everything was sea. But at this stone, rubbish got stuck and it became dry land. That is why this place is called Hapagas [to hold, to make hold]. Now, this place fell dry. When my ancestor first landed on the island [downward-outward hand movement], he landed over there [at the lagoon side of the island]. He rested a little and walked on inland. He was looking for a place to settle down on. He came to this mountain and it was dry. He settled on top of it. Later on, dry ground slowly emerged around the mountain. My ancestors climbed down the mountain. They hung on to it and they tested the ground below as it gradually fell dry, and they walked on it. [Pause] Plisoh, that means: We took everybody [inward-upward hand movement] and settled them here [downward-outward]. We pulled them, and there was no fight. The island was sea then. Only this little mountain was dry.

Francis was making a strong claim here. Hapagas is the spot most immediately and unambiguously associated with the Plisoh. Until the 1980s, it was covered in coconuts. But when he found that the village was becoming crowded, Francis 'followed the footsteps of the ancestors' and made a hamlet just below the small elevation that he referred to as a 'mountain'. With reference to this mountain, which he says fell dry before any other spot on the island, he is claiming that his ancestor 'came first', 'pulled everyone', assigned them the location at which they could settle, and maintained peace among them. That is, his ancestor directed the movements of other *pinaposa*'s ancestors to the island, and on it to particular locations. Those others depended on his ancestors for the maintenance of peace among people at the settlement.

Tsireh, who knew from Francis that I knew this story, told me the same story again at his own hamlet. Unlike Francis, who is characterized by others on the island as a 'stone', an 'old man, a man with great knowledge' and as one who ought to 'just sit, and others will do as he says', Tsireh is a lively storyteller. He is Francis' <u>mausman</u> [messenger], the second-in-rank in his *pinaposa*. It is his task to give orders and to tell ancestral stories, always on Francis' behalf and, according to him, never without obtaining permission from Francis. Tsireh began his account with a description of the lifestyle of the Pororan ancestors in the times of ancestral fighting [pait blong tumbuna] and headhunting [katim/ kaikaim man]. In those times, people from various groups lived scattered across the island in small camps and came together only briefly for raids that they carried out jointly, and that some islanders say took them as far as southern Bougainville. Upon their return, they cut up and divided the meat of their captives under a particular tree called Kutu-puets, of the species called *hitaku*.[2] They then dispersed quickly, fearing revenge raids. The *tsunon* of each group took his share of the captives' flesh to the *hitaku* that marked the meeting place for the men of his own group. He distributed it from there to the men of his group. 'Ehee, those were times. We went around everywhere, Pororan headhunters, at that time. You know that spot called *sirok ta neh*, on the Gagan River?' I knew this very popular one among Pororan headhunting stories, which are often told in the evening around the fire, especially to the entertainment of the children, but Tsireh could not be held up any more:

> One day, the *tsunon* met in the bush to deliberate: 'Where shall we go to fight? Shall we go and fight on Taiof [an island off the Bougainville coast]? On Petats? In Solos [the Solos language area on the Buka mainland]?' They decided to fight in Solos, and sent a messenger to the different settlements on the island to gather warriors. On the day marked by the *tsunon*, a group of Pororan warriors set out in their war canoes and paddled up the Gagan River. The Solos, however, had prepared a trap for them. They had blocked the river with their canoes at a narrow spot and were lying in wait for the Pororans under the bushes and trees along the river on both sides. When the Pororans had reached the barrier, the Solos jumped out of the bush and attacked them, shouting: '*sirok ta neh*' [(here comes our) soup for dinner]. The Pororans, however, fought back. The Solos fled. The Pororans captured some of them and took them back to the island in their *mon*. They killed them and distributed their flesh and skin to all the different *pinaposa* on the island, who made soup for dinner out of them at their respective camps, and took strength from it. The women hung up the skins of the enemies over the fires, and the fires were bright with the grease that dripped from the skins.

Having thus set the scene for what he had originally planned to tell me about, Tsireh jumped up from his bench and whispered conspiratorially:

'I pulled all of them here! Kuntali, this man, my ancestor!' He then re-told the story of Hapagas, acting out the 'short rest' and the walk of his ancestor from the lagoon-side to Hapagas, and the careful descent from the mountain to swampy ground underneath.[3] He then described the relation between the ancestors of Plisoh and those of others on the island through a set of specific contrasts. Most importantly, Kuntali 'came first' [kam pas] and 'went in front' [la nimumua], while others 'came later' [kam bihain], and went or hid in the back [la nimur, hamois nimur]. Kuntali told or ordered [rang] all others where to settle, and they heard [longon] his talk. Therefore Kuntali and the Plisoh are above [ka nias], and others are below [ka nikopu]. Because the Plisoh had given them a place to stay, therefore they deserved respect [hatsitsi]. Finally, Tsireh repeated his original claim, this time more loudly and almost triumphantly, that 'Kuntali pulled everyone here'. He accompanied this statement with a sudden, inward-upward movement of his arm. When he recounted, again, how he 'settled them all down' around him, he completed the movement by turning it downward-outward. After that, Tsireh added yet another headhunting story, this time a funny one, dissolving the power he had just spoken about into laughter among the audience of his children and grandchildren that had gathered around:

Once, the tsunon met and asked each other: 'Where shall we go fight this time?' They deliberated, and they decided that they would go to fight very far, in Torokina [western Bougainville]. That's it, everyone got ready. The women cooked lots of food for the men to take on the raid. The men prepared their spears, and the tsunon put some power on them, and they got the mon ready. It was a beautiful mon, very big, and they decorated it, too, and put spells on the paddles for going fast. That's it. The men are ready now. They all get on, with the tsunon in the middle. But there, you see [pointing out onto the reef]? The mon is shaking! It is shaking back and forth! The warriors, those warriors of Pororan, they do not know about mon! What is it? The mon shakes, and shakes, and shakes and . . . capsizes! Oh, and all the decorations, and the magic, all the paddles, all the warriors drift on the reef now! Reef! Not deep sea! Not far away, in Torokina, just here, off the shore of Pororan, they capsized and they drift in the sea, those strong warriors of Pororan!

It is not untypical on Pororan to take the sharp edge off a powerful story by telling a funny one afterwards, but this was a particular way of taking the edge off: the movement of pulling and release with which a tsunon demonstrates his power is dissolved here in aimless drifting. A clever grandchild of Tsireh's picked up on the point and asked: 'Grand-father, and Kuntali, their *tsunon*, did he drift, too?' I could not hear Tsireh's reply, because his audience burst into uproarious laughter.

Colonial Gathering

Tsireh continued the story of Kuntali, on another occasion, by describing the important position that his ancestors had held after the arrival of the Catholic missionaries and the German colonial government. The missionaries came to Pororan Island first, of all places in Buka. They set up three small chapels at different locations on the island, gathered the islanders there, showed them how to wear laplap and told them to stop fighting.[4] Then the police burned the small settlements that were scattered across the island, gathered the inhabitants at a single spot on the beach, and ordered them to clear the bush for an assembly àrea and then for a village around it. They asked about the number of clans on the island and assigned each clan one section of the village to settle in, Mulul, Put and Takap on one long side of the assembly area, and Naboen, Holu and Plisoh on the other [see Map 4].[5] The village was fenced with a wall of coral rubble to keep wild and domestic pigs out.

Tsireh often dwelled on the reported beauty of the 'nice and clean' colonial village, in which 'neat' houses faced 'straight' roads, and contrasted it positively to the small, scattered settlements in which people were hiding from enemies in pre-colonial times. Tsireh attributed the appearance of the village not to the missionaries, however, but to one of his ancestors. This was Sakuan, to whom the Germans gave the 'blue cap of the government', that is, whom they made tultul of Pororan under the system of indirect rule.[6] Sakuan had learned carpentry from the Germans while he was a member of the colonial forces, and when he returned to Pororan, put what he had learned into practice. This is how Sakuan single-handedly built all houses in the Plisoh section of the village:

> One day, Sakuan called together all the Plisoh men and sent them to gather building materials for him: tree posts, tree branches for the walls, sago fronds from the mainland for roof and walls. They brought these things. The next day, he sent them out fishing. He alone stayed in the village and built a house, on stilts and neatly square-shaped. When the men came back with their catch in the afternoon, the house was completed. They ate together to mark its completion. The next day, he asked the men to gather materials again. The day after, he built

another house while the men were fishing, just like the first one. When the men returned, the two houses stood in a straight line along the road. They ate together again to mark their completion. And so they continued, until enough houses were completed for all Plisoh.

Sakuan built not only ordinary houses, but also *tsuhan*. In their interactions with *pinaposa* relatives from the mainland, the islanders presented themselves as being without *tsuhan* of their own (see the introduction). At other times, however, they related a history of *tsuhan* on the island that eclipses mainland relations altogether. This history begins with the *hitaku* of the times of headhunting. The *hitaku*, as many islanders pointed out, were in many ways like the later *tsuhan*. Each group had one; the *tsunon* held meetings there; and food was distributed from them. The Pororans called the *hitaku* the sign of later *tsuhan* [mak blong tsuhan]. The first two 'real' *tsuhan* that emerged on the island were built to resemble the trading ships that the Pororans had seen in the lagoon, and that they first thought were islands drifting along. The first *tsuhan* was called Maywara, after one such ship. The Maywara, however, was only a trial version of another *tsuhan* in ship form, larger and more beautiful, that Tsireh's ancestor Sakuan built on Pororan:

> One day, Sakuan was walking along the beach. He found a piece of driftwood that was too good for letting it rot. He took it. He pulled it up the beach and built a platform for distributing food from it. Later he added the walls of a ship, a captain's house, a large rudder at the outside, and a steering wheel inside. The ship as a whole was called Drip [drift]. It was used for food distributions. It stood right over there, and its mast was as high as the highest tree. Close to it stood a tree of the kind that you see there next to the church. The one with the red flowers. There used to be many of this kind on the island, the entire island was red with their flowers. And the whites put an iron plate here, next to Drip. The iron came from Germany. Engraved on the plate, it said: 'Beautiful sun-rising flower—Pororan'. And some called Pororan Australia No. 2.

Once again, an inward-upward and downward-outward movement was prominent in Tsireh's narrative, and he underlined it with gestures. Sakuan pulled driftwood up the beach, fashioned from it a structure that resembled white people's ships, and distributed food from it. Secondly, various details indicate the transformation of indeterminate into determinate movements and relations. Sakuan fashioned Drip after ships that he had 'seen' and admired in the lagoon.[7] The name Drip resonates with the islanders' fantasies during fishing trips or boat rides about drifting off, and thus calls to mind open-ended movements and relations. By 'pulling' the driftwood and cutting it into shape, one might suggest that Sakuan 'pulled' the power that ships, white people and open-ended movements were seen to hold to the island. This movement was reversed downward-outward, the power of the assemblage was confirmed and more particular relations became apparent when food was first assembled at and then distributed from <u>Drip</u>. These relations included white people, too, as Tsireh's reference to the iron plate suggests. Sakuan engaged in these relations on behalf of others on the island, as a *tsunon* should.

At about the same time, the Pororans also built the first 'real *tsuhan*' in house form. Bishop Wade—the American bishop of Bougainville who underwent Pororan male initiation before World War II—is said to have initiated its construction and blessed it, and to have called it 'Saint Paul'. Saint Paul belonged to all *pinaposa* jointly. From Saint Paul, all six later Pororan *tsuhan* emerged, one belonging to Takap, Put, Mulul, Naboen, Holu and Plisoh each. Each was built with a sago leaf [*kal atoh*] from Saint Paul's roof in its own, facing the village clearing in its owners' village section. Here, the *tsunon* met, the young men of a *pinaposa* lived for some years and were trained by their elders in ancestral knowledge, and the *pinaposa*'s three slit-gongs [*tui*] of different sizes were kept, whose beats announced important events and accompanied dancing at feasts (see also Thomas 1931). From here, food was distributed to other villagers, as well as to members of other groups at feasts. These were powerful places, said Tsireh.

From the perspective of colonial studies, the gathering of the island's population at a single, large village in German colonial times would appear to be a local expression of a logic recognizable in a range of colonial settings (e.g. T. Mitchell 1988). Colonial states attempted to make relations among its subjects 'legible' and governable, often through the concentration and orderly distribution of the population in space (J. Scott 1998). Tsireh, however, described the 'neatness' of the village with its new, square-shaped houses not as externally-driven changes, but as particular acts of 'gathering' people and 'making them settle' by a particular ancestor of his. The inward-upward and downward-outward hand movements, with which he accompanied his story of how Sakuan 'gathered' the Plisoh and the building materials and then built neatly separated houses for them, was the same with which he accompanied his account of Kuntali 'settling down' other people who arrived after him on Pororan. In the process, Sakuan drew on particular skills learned from the German colonizers, but his gathering of people at the colonial village, as Tsireh recounted it, unmistakably resembled Kuntali's.

Danilyn Rutherford has analysed how West Papuans in Biak 'turn what looked like an act of submission into a raid' in various ways in their relations with the Indonesian state (2003: 19). The Pororans, too, were 'raiding' the colonizers, at least retrospectively, in their stories. They 'pulled' and turned to their own ends the colonial project of village building. As Tsireh's story indicates, they did so, specifically, by investing the physical movements that the colonial project depended upon— the gathering of building materials, for instance—with their very own meaning. This meaning oscillates between a forceful statement of a local *tsunon's* control of the movements of persons and things in the process of building houses and *tsuhan*, and a more open-ended, evocative claim of organizing movements in such a way as to make a firm place out of something as insignificant as a piece of driftwood.

Present-Day Pulling

However, all *tsuhan* were destroyed, along with the colonial village, when Japanese forces occupied the island in World War II. Relations with white people finished abruptly when the Australians left Buka, and left the Pororans behind disappointed. ('They just went away,' they told me. 'We alone stayed back'.) Older people on the island who remember the occupation speak with respect of the Japanese, who treated them as friends. However, they also remember the hardships they underwent. All houses on the island were destroyed. For most of the time of the occupation, the islanders lived in hidden shelters beneath overhanging parts of the cliff or under the aerial roots of large trees. Houses were rebuilt at the village site after the war, but no longer in neat rows along straight roads, and no longer on stilts. Instead, they were built randomly across the old village site. The wall of coral rubble that surrounded the colonial village was torn down and removed when the population grew after the war[8] and when additional house sites were cleared. In 2004–05, the old village sections were inhabited more densely than before, and by mixed-*pinaposa* groups because children continued to stay on their fathers' land. Furthermore, unlike Buka mainlanders, who made the rebuilding of their *tsuhan* a priority after the war (Rimoldi and Rimoldi 1992: 58), Pororan Islanders did not rebuild theirs. In 2004–05, only one *tsuhan* existed as a physical structure on the island, belonging to Holu but used by all *tsunon* jointly for their meetings.[9]

While physically, the village was a mess (according to the islanders themselves), activities of 'pulling' and releasing others continued in the context of feasting, especially after a death or at a marriage, when *tsunon* gathered their followers and feast contributions and when they distributed food to visitors at feasts. The Plisoh still used as gathering sites some places associated with their ancestors, although not all members of the *pinaposa* were aware of the significance of those sites. For example, when the Plisoh prepared for feasts in 2004–05, they began the planning process with a meeting of the entire *pinaposa* (ideally—not everyone attended on all occasions) at Hapagas. The Plisoh women used to gather their feast contributions, both for Plisoh feasts and for feasts to which the Plisoh as a group contributed, at their old *tsuhan* site at the colonial village. At this spot stood a trade store belonging to the Plisoh. It was inactive and nailed shut in 2004–05 but was active during my visit in 2006. The store was named Kuntali after the first Plisoh ancestor on Pororan. Tsireh himself saw to it that the women did not 'take shortcuts', that is, that they collected their feast contributions at Kuntali rather than anywhere else, even if it meant carrying their food baskets longer distances.

Other *pinaposa* did not use sites of pre-colonial and colonial importance to their *pinaposa* when preparing for feasts, but used the houses of their *tsunon* and *hahini*. Some of those, but not all, stood in the area of the village that the *pinaposa* used to inhabit in colonial times. For instance, the Takap gathered for their regular meetings at Lulutsi, the hamlet of their *hahini*, which had no significance to her *pinaposa*, according to Salu. All she knew, she said, was that her *tsunon* in the generation above had told her to move there because a Takap man had lived there in the generation above. Salu knew the spots of colonial and pre-colonial settlement of her *pinaposa*. Especially important to her was the location of the pre-colonial *tsuhan*—a *tsuhan*, she said, not a *hitaku*—at Keketin, the largest of the pre-colonial settlement sites. She took me there one day, along with Rokayo, a high-ranking *tsunon* on the island from the *pinaposa* that had been the most powerful at Keketin. He went ahead and spoke to the spirits at the abandoned site before calling out to Salu that it would be all right now for us to climb up the cliff from the beach. The spot had long been abandoned, but her *tsunon*, now deceased, had shown Salu exactly where their *tsuhan* had been located. Rokayo, too, had been shown the site of his *pinaposa's tsuhan* there, in the past. Salu looked at the spot in silence for a moment, then shrugged and said complacently, 'Here it stood, in the past.' Then we left, and the two of them pointed out other spots inhabited by different *pinaposa* in pre-colonial times along the seaward side of the island. When I asked the two if they or anyone else was considering re-opening the old sites, Salu told me: 'This place belongs to the past. If you come here and you are not careful, you will get sick [the spirits will make you sick]. Who would want to live in such a place? What, are our places now not good enough?' Rokayo agreed with her. In chapter 6, I will show how difficult it was for people like Salu and Rokayo to push for this agenda in the context of formal Bougainvillean politics at the time. For now, suffice it to note their calm and decisive statements that places of power in the past belonged to the past, not to the present.

As old places were left behind, new ones were opened up by leaders who 'pulled' people there, told them where to settle, co-ordinated their activities and gave food away at feasts. One of those new places of the Plisoh was Kuri Village Resort, one of the hotels belonging to the company initiated by Kil's husband and owned jointly by Kil's sons Albert, Chris and Lawrence in Town. In 2004–05, Lawrence was managing Kuri. Here, he hosted Bougainvillean politicians for some of the meetings of the Bougainville Peace Process. Kuri was a popular gathering and meeting place for Bougainvillean politicians, foreign donors and Bougainvilleans working for foreign aid agencies in Buka Town. In front of the reception stood, in 2004–05, the two larger ones of the Plisoh slit-gongs. (The smallest was kept and used by Francis and Tsireh on the island.) The walls of the Kuri's main building were made of sago that had belonged to the brother of Kil's late husband, Kitou, who gave it to his brother's sons when they asked for his help. Kitou's account of his gift of sago to 'the children I made grow' [*apian hatuhan tagoan*] emphasized the importance of the 'leaf of sago' [*kal atoh*] that another *tsunon*, usually the builder's father, gave as an opening gift for any *tsuhan* (see 'Saint Paul' above). Kil, together with other women, had plaited the sago in a pattern that visitors often admired. Furthermore, Lawrence and Chris had planted colourful and sweet-smelling shrubs around Kuri that were meant to make the place attractive to visitors. Kuri, then, like the *hitaku*, <u>Drip</u> and the trade store called Kuntali, is another 'mark of a *tsuhan*' belonging to the Plisoh.

The importance of Kuri was objectified in the particular ways in which Pororan Islanders approached it. The only islander aside from Kil's sons who walked 'up' to the veranda, referred to as 'above' [*ias*], freely was Kitou, their father's brother. 'It was me—or who else?—who made these children grow, and who gave them the sago for this house', as he remarked once. Kil approached Kuri cautiously, but her sons would always call her inside the moment they saw her, lead her to the veranda and sit her down at one of the tables with a bottle of coke. Other islanders did not usually venture beyond the outer gates (except for those who worked as barkeepers, receptionists and waiters). They preferred to stay 'at the backside' [*imur*], as the Pororan workers' quarters inland across the road from Kuri were called. Here, Pororan Islanders used to gather on their frequent trips to Town. They used the workmen's cooking fire and water tank when, once again, the change of mind of a skipper or boat owner forced the passengers to overnight in Town. At this more informal setting 'below' [*ikopu*], 'chief' Bona (and sometimes John, a carpenter of rank, from Natasi) took charge of the cooking and handing out of food. At Lawrence's request, Bona 'looked after people' there, especially Pororan women stranded in Town without a sleeping place. Lawrence himself came to check on people below occasionally, as well as sending food down from time to time.

Through his generosity in hosting people 'below', Lawrence, while he was managing Kuri, gained a position for himself 'above'. When he came to join people 'below', conversations used to cease to a trickle, and he was seated 'above' on a chair and served food (that he usually refused). Lawrence's gaining of status was a gradual and highly indeterminate process for much of 2004–05. Not all islanders were happy to accept hospitality 'below'. The Takap, for example, made a point of coming to Town on their own, on the boat owned by Salu's son Charles, landing not at Kuri's landing bridge but on the beach next to the market, which was not claimed by anyone in particular but was used by various Town visitors. They always left again before nightfall. They said that they did not want to squat at a place belonging to other people, the Plisoh.

However, Lawrence's position 'above' was 'witnessed' by the islanders at large, including Salu, in an event that will be described in more detail in chapter 6: When Lawrence proposed to the *tsunon* in early 2005 that he might compete for a seat on the new Autonomous Bougainville Government, the island's *tsunon* decided that women from all *pinaposa* would 'carry him up to the *hagung ni tsunon* [the meeting of the *tsunon*; here: the government]'. 'All the mothers' of Pororan Island would express their support of Lawrence's candidacy by paddling him, surrounded by the Pororan *tsunon*, in a mock *mon* from Kuri to the government offices for registering his candidacy. The night before the event, members of all *pinaposa* slept 'at the backside' of Kuri. After the event, Lawrence formally thanked all of them with a meal 'above' on the Kuri veranda. The *tsunon*'s decision to support Lawrence's candidacy thus ordered all those taking part in the event as select representatives of their *pinaposa* 'below' him. They 'carried him up' and he was expected to 'throw away' to them hospitality and, after his election, 'good leadership', which some understood to mean government services.

The thread that runs through Tsireh's account of the past and through the process by which Lawrence came to be positioned 'above' consists of actions of 'pulling' and 'settling down' persons. In the course of such movements, certain persons and the locations they frequent or build—the *hitaku*, *tsuhan* and Kuri—come to be 'above', and others come to be 'below'. Certain places emerge and disappear into insignificance again, and new ones appear that look different and occupy other locations. Examples mentioned here are the *hitaku* of the distant past, the *tsuhan* and the neat colonial village, Francis' hamlet of Hapagas and a trade store and Kuri. My strategy here has been to trace these changes—both of location and of appearance—by using for guidance the movements of pulling and release that run through the Pororans' accounts. Keeping the movement as stable as they do, the different kinds of places that it creates become visible as versions of each other.

Leitana and the Little Thing

The task of the *tsunon* of looking after a place is different on the Buka mainland. The islanders' own explicit distinctions between their 'little thing' and Leitana, the Buka mainland, are pertinent here. Leitana is described as stable, solid and immobile. There is a story—which the Pororans do not claim to know but sometimes mention—about a turtle that swam up from the sea, and whose solid but soft shell now forms the ground of Leitana. Mainland *tsunon* are said to 'hold' pieces of this ground, which they look after. Those places do not move, and the *nitsunon*, the power of the *tsunon* who hold them is firmly emplaced in those places and literally implanted in the ground. Most importantly, it is emplaced through the *tsuhan* built by a *tsunon*. *Tsuhan* building requires the killing of pigs, that is, feasting, at each step in the proceedings (see Rimoldi and Rimoldi 1992 for a detailed description). Furthermore, a *tsuhan* continues to grow even after its opening feast, the *kinalal*, which is the most expensive feast of all in the Buka area, according to the Pororans. In the past, the jawbones of pigs killed for feasts at the *tsuhan* were displayed in its beams, providing a physical record of a *tsunon*'s capacity of attracting others and visually embellishing the *tsuhan*. Although this is no longer done, people remember this practice and often speak about it when visiting a *tsuhan*, pointing out that 'this would be full of pigs' jaws now'. *Tsuhan* are also enlarged over time by additional posts, in a competitive process of feasting between different *tsuhan* and their *tsunon*.[10] The *tsuhan* has to be torn down when the highest-ranking *tsunon* of the group, the 'owner' of the *tsuhan*, dies. It ought to be re-built by his successor, however, in the same spot. In addition to *tsuhan*, mainland *tsunon* invest their power, and have it judged by others in the neatness of their *pinaposa*'s gardens (see chapter 1). The neat appearance of a group's garden area shows that their *tsunon* can 'boss the land, and boss the people to hear his talk about when to garden, and where'.

People show their respect to the *tsunon* of the place, and to those who held it before him, by carefully 'following the road' that link their hamlet and their garden to the main road. 'Going around' randomly and trespassing onto other people's land would be disrespectful. Their careful movement along those roads, which become wide and well-worn through those movements, as people point out, is another way of imprinting the power of the *tsunon* in the ground, besides their work in their gardens and their help with *tsuhan*-building.

Pororan, by contrast, is an assemblage of coral rubble, sand and 'rubbish' that adhere to each other temporarily only, and of people who come and go. Pororan *tsunon* do not claim to 'hold' places. They had *tsuhan* in the colonial past, but only have one, shared among all of them, in the present. While the mainlanders re-built their *tsuhan* immediately after their destruction in World War II (Rimoldi and Rimoldi 1992), the Pororans did not rebuild theirs. Instead, they draw their followers together, either at locations with a past significance or at their own houses. Aside from *tsuhan*, the Pororan tsunon do not control their *pinaposa*'s gardens in the present. Francis told me that in the past, they did control the small garden areas in the interior of the island. Those garden areas still existed, and the members of each *pinaposa* were concentrated in one of them dating back to colonial times. However, in 2004–05, there was no evidence that the *tsunon* took an active interest in their *pinaposa* members' gardening activities. They left people to deal with their own gardens as they saw fit. They did not regulate fallow periods—which were virtually non-existent on the island—and were only asked *pro forma* when a garden was transferred to someone outside the previous gardener's *pinaposa*. Instead of 'holding' places—investing their power in *tsuhan*, gardens and neat roads connecting them—the Pororan *tsunon* claimed the capacity to pull others, which was rendered visible by others' movements.

This contrast stands out more sharply if we consider a corresponding contrast between spirits on Pororan and on the mainland, respectively. The spirits at issue are <u>masalai</u>, which are associated with particular *pinaposa* and dwell in particular locations. <u>Masalai</u> on the mainland, often little snakes or lizards, have their 'house' in a particular spot in the interior, commonly in ponds. One must be careful to behave respectfully at those locations. On Pororan, the only clan spirits I know of are marine animals, including octopus, shark and little sea snakes. Some are said to be particular ancestors who took on animal forms, while others appear to have transformed from landed into marine animals in the course of their people's migration to the island. Some have 'houses', such as a deep passage or a deep spot in the sea, while others are only loosely associated with a particular area of the reef. However, unlike 'in the bush', the spirits on Pororan—especially those that take on the form of octopus or shark—are known to roam around a lot. Spirit accidents I learned of resulted from people 'bumping into' the spirit 'going around' at sea, rather than someone misbehaving near a spirit's house.

This contrast is significant in the light of arguments about *na tadak* [singular: *tadak*], spirits that change appearance and are associated with particular clans and locations in New Ireland. Jessep (1977) noted that at one particular village, identification of a clan with a particular *tadak* constituted claims to the piece of land surrounding the spot of the *tadak*. Much the same could be said about the identification of a particular *pinaposa* on the Buka mainland with a spirit, a spirit site and land, perhaps not exactly there, but in the vicinity. For Pororan, however, Wagner's arguments about *na tadak* and their importance to his hosts in New Ireland are more helpful. Wagner (1986b) traces a particular clan's *tadak*'s manifestations across space in a shark living in a particular bay, a submarine rock formation occasionally visited by the shark, a rock outcropping, and a cave containing pictures of animals, and historically, by noting that the clan also lays claim to the *tadak* of defunct clans. Emphasizing the impossibility of a complete account, Wagner argues that *na tadak* is a form of power that cannot be pinned down to a particular manifestation, 'for the transformational capability of the *tadak* is intrinsic to its power and being' (Wagner 1986b: 100). No equally lively landscape of spirits can be detected in the Pororans' accounts. Instead, we find places themselves displaying transformative power here. Like *na tadak*, they change sites and change form, for instance, from a *hitaku* into a *tsuhan* and then into a hotel and restaurant.[11]

Stones

The Pororans' lack of interest in immobile places and 'emplaced' power sits uneasily not only with the strong interest that their mainland relatives and neighbours take in the matter, but also with ethnographic findings of a contrast between stillness and mobility, centre and periphery, heaviness and buoyancy that fascinates people elsewhere in Melanesia and Southeast Asia. In the final part of this chapter, I aim to pin this contrast down by focusing, for a change, on material objects that may help bring it into focus. These objects are stones. I will contrast the Pororans' interest in stones, and the role that stones play in their accounts of the world, of places and of acts of 'pulling' people, to the role that stones play in Tanimbar, Eastern Indonesia, where the contrast between stillness and mobility, centre and periphery and heaviness and buoyancy is central to everyday life and cosmology.

Stones [remits] are one of the few material objects that fascinate the Pororans. They enjoy looking at and telling stories about stones. Stones I learned of during my stay include prominent outcrops on the reef that make good fishing spots; the stone around which the island grew; pairs of river stones cut into fish shapes that were used in the past in fire sacrifices for attracting bonito (see also Blackwood 1935); a smooth stone used in the past to attract dugong; some very old men who were called stone; and two stones of knee height standing on Yaming, an uninhabited island south of Pororan, whom Kitou claimed as his ancestors. A group of foolish young men from Petats transported one of those Yaming stones to Petats by boat several years before. The stone disappeared overnight and returned to its old spot, and sure enough, a series of deaths occurred on Petats soon afterwards. To these prominent stones, I add the reef stones laid out in regular intervals along the path leading to Kuri's veranda. 'For decoration only', one of the Pororan workmen whom I asked about those stones replied, just a little too quickly.

The theme of stones, standing and moving, is familiar from Island Melanesia and the wider Austronesian region. I shall take a little detour through Susan McKinnon's Eastern Indonesian ethnographic material in order to demonstrate the difference between Pororan and Tanimbarese interests in stones. The first stone that appears in McKinnon's (1991) account and that interests me here is the culture hero Atuf, who turned to stone after he created the world as we know it today by piercing the sun with his spear and thus 'decomposing' an unproductive original unity. By separating sun and moon, he set their movements in motion that mark time; by separating sky and earth, he created the flows of rain and water between them; by distinguishing brothers and sisters, he made bride wealth flow between houses that extracted persons from one another. Eventually, however, 'the creator of a world of complementary forms . . . himself was destined to find his end in the most self-contained and impenetrable of all forms—imprisoned by the fixity of stone' (54). His power was not lost, but only contained. People continued to make offerings at the site where he turned to stone up until colonial times. Secondly, McKinnon gives attention to the ritual stone boats that 'anchor' the people of a village. The ritual centre of each village is a stone platform, in some villages constructed and everywhere imagined as a stone boat. The stone boat is 'mobilized' in dances in boat formation. It is both a unity and one of a pair. Each village has two ritual boat names:

one of the stone boat, and one of the sailing boat in which its inhabitants travel out to interact with others. The stone boat provides a weighty anchor—made heavy through the gathering of people and wealth—that balances the mobility of the sailing boat. The contrast is gendered. In the past, each crew of men that went on a sailing expedition was 'anchored' by a crew of women, confined in the captain's house, each with her own ritual responsibilities on the 'boat'. The contrast between weight and lightness, immobility and mobility is a dynamic one, construed in more ways than just the pairing of boats, and is central to Tanimbarese thinking and action in the world, according to McKinnon.

The Pororan stones that I have mentioned above are not 'ritual centres' paired with mobile counterparts on the periphery, like the stone boats. Instead, some of these stones are points of attraction deployed strategically at particular moments in time and in particular locations. They facilitate actions of 'pulling'. The river stones used to attract bonito fall in this category. They are brought out 'when times are good' and are placed one on the beach and one on the fire, providing directions, we might say, for the fish that are to be caught. The dugong stone appears to have been used in a similar manner, although I could not learn about the details of the procedures. These stones are embellishments of the capacity to attract. They are not, however, at its source, and they are not even essential for achieving the desired effects. The bonito stones are said to be 'possibly still around' in someone's kitchen house, but they may also have gone missing—who knows, say the Pororans. They told me to 'leave them—they belong to the past'. People are now engaged in other activities of pulling. Pulling foreign advisors and Bougainvillean political dignitaries to Kuri is one of them. Here again, stones are used to facilitate their success. They are laid out alongside the path leading up to Kuri's main building, for decoration or, we might say, for making sure people do not lose their way and wander off elsewhere.

Old men and Kitou's ancestral stones are somewhat like the Atuf-turned-stone in Tanimbar. Like him, those actors 'opted out' of the hustle and bustle and the movements all around them, voluntarily or not.[12] Their immobility removes them from ordinary life and most acts of 'pulling', which on Pororan require moving around among people and at sea. However, they do compel others to move around them, and thus make an impact on their lives. Old men on Pororan 'pull' the attention and care of younger relatives with threats such as 'you could treat me a little better, now that I cannot walk around any more. If you don't, I will die soon, and then my spirit will bother you'.[13] The stones on Yaming, as I learned from conversations with people who remembered the event on Petats, similarly 'pulled' the young men with their immobility: they posed a challenge to people who wanted to prove their capacity to make others, persons and things, move. The group that tried most recently to move one of the stones was not the first to do so. The stones already had a history of stubbornly returning to their spot. Precisely because of that, the men set out to gain some fame by 'winning over' the stones. They failed. Here, then, we have a Pororan parallel to powerful, immobile centres in Tanimbar—but to those that are remnants of the past, not those that play a crucial role as 'anchors' in their everyday life at present.

Finally, what about the stone that we might suspect is the hidden centre of gravity of the entire island? The spot on the reef around which 'rubbish' gathered, and that Francis claimed was located just next to his hamlet? Philip, the current *tsunon* of Put, had made inquiries into the matter long before my arrival. Philip came to Pororan as a schoolteacher from Taiof, an island off northern Bougainville. He arrived on Pororan with a keen interest in its history and politics and affiliated himself with a prominent *tsunon*, whom he learned from and whose successor he eventually became. Once, he told me, he had asked this *tsunon*: 'What exactly is Pororan?' The *tsunon* had told him the story about rubbish getting stuck on the reef. Philipp had wanted to know where it was, the stone that the rubbish got stuck on, but the *tsunon* had stared at him blankly and said, 'Who would know that? Things come and go, they get stuck and drift off again. Why worry about that stone now?' Philip concluded that, if the *tsunon* of the past did not worry about the stone, he should not worry, either. My sense, too, is that this is simply not a question that interests the Pororans.

Why would one worry about stable, powerful centres, in any case? McKinnon's arguments about weight and stillness versus mobility being central to Tanimbarese ideas about human productivity both draw on Melanesian writings, especially Strathern's, and speak directly to Melanesian anthropological concerns. Perhaps the clearest formulation of these concerns is Bonnemaison's in his work on Tanna, Vanuatu (whose stones I leave until later): 'The contrast between . . . rootedness and journeying is at the heart of Tannese (and Melanesian) thought' (Bonnemaison 1994: 122). I have given attention to stones on Pororan in order to show that Pororan is an exception to this rule. The Pororans are primarily concerned with making particular kinds of movements appear against a background of indeterminate 'going around'. They are not primarily concerned—not even when handling or talking about stones— with contrasting mobility against roots, stillness, immobility, anchorage or centres. If they were, one might expect to find strong evidence of these concerns in their appreciation of stones, which are central to both Tanimbarese and Tannese ways of creating the contrast.

As I will show more fully in the second part of the following chapter, this exception to the Melanesian and Southeast Asian rule is a highly localized one. As soon as we shift attention from Pororan to Buka, there is a stable centre, a 'mountain'. However, this centre enters Pororan Islanders' field of attention 'from the outside', in their interactions with mainland relatives, and as we will see, most of them find the aesthetics of rootedness that mainland thinking hinges on difficult to understand.

NOTES

1. Mark Mosko (1995) has argued that Trobriand chiefs are 'metaphorical fathers'. Although the observation of an analogy between chiefs and fathers certainly holds for Pororan at an analytic level, the point of contrast here is not metaphor, but the range of people in relations to whom chiefs/fathers make claims to the power to direct their movements. It should also be noted that the islanders themselves do not make this analogy (see also Powell and Mosko 1997).
2. Identified by Blackwood (n.d.) as a Carophyllum species. Kutupuets is still standing, near the small market site on the lagoon side of the island. Most skulls were removed after the missionaries' arrival. But some old men remember that the rain sometimes washed skulls out of the ground underneath when they were small.
3. Tsireh explained the name Hapagas by citing the ancestors' warning one another as they descended: 'Hang on [to the mountain].'
4. The end of ancestral fighting in the Buka area was reportedly proposed by the missionaries, but was enforced by a prominent *tsunon* called Goman. While the Pororans claim Goman for themselves, others in the region say that he was originally from Solos, but was a warrior with many wives and children in many different places.
5. Naboen is a bird, not a *pinaposa*. However, because there are very few Naboen (of three different *pinaposa*) on Pororan, all of them used to settle together and share one *tsuhan* in colonial times.
6. The position of <u>luluai</u> shifted regularly between the Keketin and the Naboen.
7. It is likely that some Pororan men at least had been enlisted as labourers onto such ships and had disappeared and perhaps returned on them, although the Pororans did not remember this in 2004–05.
8. By 2004–05, it had approximately quadrupled from the 1945 patrol census (Archer 1945–1946).
9. One further exception exists: Mulul 4 tried to build a *tsuhan* of their own, which would signal their separation from other groups within Mulul (see chapter 4). However, they could not finish the building process for a lack of pigs, and no physical structure existed on the island in 2004–05 that was pointed out to me as their (incomplete) *tsuhan*.
10. See esp. Rimoldi and Rimoldi (1992) for details on *tsuhan* building and growth.
11. Some people say that there used to be more spirits, but they are forgotten now. This points to the possibility that talk of spirits was inconvenient for

the Pororans as practicing Catholics, while talk of mobile and changing places might have been less obviously conflicting with the demands first of German and then of local priests.

12. The association comes from another piece of writing on stones, Bonnemaison's (1994) from Tanna.

13. Old women are not called stones. They are mothers [*tobuan*], and unlike men, they remain at the centre of their children's attention and support even when immobile, and without making threats concerning their spirits.

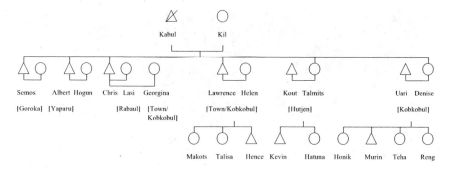

Figure 1 • Kil and her children, 2004

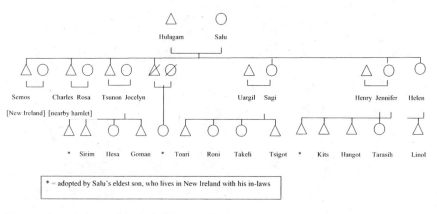

Figure 2 • Salu and her children, 2004

Illustration 1 • Kil

Illustration 2 • Tsireh

Illustration 3 • Salu [l.] and her neighbour Siatun [r.] with Salu's grand-children Roni [l.] and Tsigot [r.] at Lulutsi

Illustration 4 • The beach off Kobkobul at low tide

Illustration 5 • Trolling for bonito on the way to Town

Illustration 6 • The meeting room 'above' at Kuri Village Resort

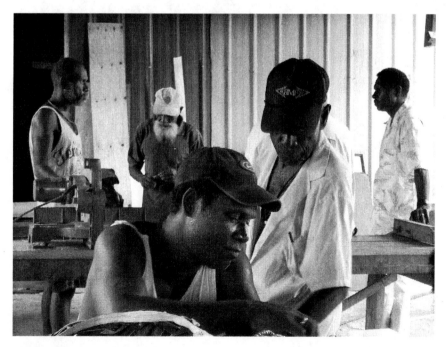

Illustration 7 • The workmen's area 'below'. Front: Kitou, tsunon of Natasi [standing] and one of the workmen. Back: Bona [l.] and Lawrence [r.], Tonio Silak, tsunon of Naboen III [center]

Illustration 8 • The *mon*

CHAPTER 4

Pinaposa

Matrilineages 'by the Hair'

The *tsunon*'s 'looking after the place' is at the same time a 'looking after' his *pinaposa*: by 'pulling' people and 'putting' them somewhere, he defines the boundaries of the *pinaposa* and cuts the multiple relations among women supporting each other off, depending on his own purposes. Nowadays he does so especially in the context of feasting, but also for business. Those whom the *tsunon* considers to be, or wants to come inside his *pinaposa* will be asked to contribute to the food and money given away by the *pinaposa* on a particular occasion. All those people are said to be *pinaposa* members 'by the hair'. This is a reference to the *tsunon*'s head, the location of his power.

Most Pororan *pinaposa* have members 'by the hair only', that is, people who have no connections to the *pinaposa* through their mothers, but who are supporting the same *tsunon* in the present. Among those were, in 2004–05, young men from East New Britain who came to Buka to marry there, because land was scarce in their own place. Another example of a supporter by the hair only was Benni, whom Salu and her family 'picked up' at Arawa. His movements, for instance to and from *pinaposa* meetings at Lulutsi, are explicitly attributed to Salu's original action of 'pulling him' to Pororan from Arawa. (When without *tsunon*, as Salu was at Arawa, a *hahini* may perform his functions.) This makes them no less valued as a member of the *pinaposa*.

More commonly, however, people try to discern relations through women—that is, a common ancestress—between people who support the same *tsunon* in the present. There is an assumption that sentiments of mutual help indicate that the people connected by them are 'of one mother'. 'She always helps me, so she must be my *pinaposa* relative', Salu observed once about a mainland woman with whom she used to exchange fish for starch food at the Karoola market on Wednesdays. 'She never haggles. She never comes without sweet potatoes. She always offers them to me first, before other women. I must ask her next time how we are related. We must be of the same mother.' Usually, some connection of matrilineal kinship can be found, and if not, is assumed to have existed in the distant past.

Besides attracting particular persons, *tsunon* of different *ngorer* have entered into alliances with others, and their groups thereby became one *pinaposa*: 'their children are stuck together', as Tsireh translated *pinaposa*, or 'I think their children are stuck together'. The 'I think' is significant here. *Pinaposa* connections between entire *ngorer* are traced through narratives of the past. The *tsunon* are open about the fact that these narratives are present-day renderings of events that 'maybe happened like this, who knows now'. Some accounts of past movements of 'pulling people' are based on highly idiosyncratic arguments with their roots in personal agendas. Many of these more idiosyncratic accounts of the past, and thus of island relations in the present are kept among close relatives only, for reasons that I shall discuss in chapter 6. Others, however, are common knowledge among those people on the island who take an interest, and some of them are recorded below.

It was Kil who first told me openly what others had long hinted at: that *pinaposa* members are not, in fact, related through 'one mother'. Speaking about Plisoh specifically, she said:

> This talk of one mother, that is what the *tsunon* say. We didn't come from one mother in the past. But the *tsunon*, in the times of ancestral fighting, decided that our two *ngorer*, that of Francis and ours here, should walk about together and support each other in warfare. So they told the young people: "I think we come from the same mother." That's it, that's how they did it. They told this about them being "one mother" so that their young people would not marry each other, because that would break the group. And it is still like that. We support each other, and we do not marry. And so we are one *pinaposa*: our children are stuck together.

Marriage, I learned later, would 'break the group' because, as Tsireh put it, at a marriage, relatives would 'line up' [in English] as supporters behind either the husband or the bride, depending on whom they felt more closely related to. If members of the two *ngorer* would marry each other, their 'lining up' would put them into a relation of competition and opposition, rather than of co-operation.[1] The same would happen on marriage and mortuary feasts of children of this marriage, where members of the same *pinaposa* would face each other as 'mothers' and 'fathers' of the child. Thus, marriages within a *pinaposa* would create an opposition, visible in people's physical movements of 'lining up' on opposite sides, which would render the talk of 'one mother' void. Kil was the first to tell me this openly, but once I indicated that I had heard about it, other *tsunon* followed suit in accounts of their own *pinaposa's'* histories. Upon my question if their young people knew, the usual reply was: 'They listen to their tsunon's talk.'

Just as *tsunon* could start to talk of 'one mother' and make people move and interact accordingly, so they could decide to 'finish this talk of one mother now'. This had been the decision of the *tsunon* of Mulul in 2004–05. Mulul was a large *pinaposa* of four *ngorer*, whose *tsunon* were known to be arguing fiercely over their relative rank. Hapot, the *tsunon* of Mulul II, told me the following story about Mulul's history and current relations between the different *ngorer* of Mulul:

> 'Mulul, that is four *ngorer*. The first of them came from the Buka mainland a long time ago to set up a fishing camp here. That is I, my ancestors. Eventually, they remained here for good. But because of the fighting in the times before the whites came, at one point they were about to die out. So they asked another group to join them, a group of people from Bei [a Buka mountain village]. That is Tsik [a Mulul *hahini*] and her people. They came and hid me. They are still hiding me now. You know, Tsik's people are called Mulul I. That is how they hide us, who really came first. And we are now Mulul II. All right, and then a group from Hahalis [a Buka east coast village] joined us here. They were called Mulul III. They have died out now. Finally, Mulul IV came from Hanahan [a Buka east coast village]. Now we are many. We are so many that the food is not enough, and the women started quarrelling. [The food portion assigned to Mulul at feasts is not enough for all Mulul *ngorer* to receive a sufficiently large share.] So we decided to throw out Mulul IV. We helped them, and they got ready to be on their own and build their own *tsuhan*. They killed 32 pigs. But then they ran out of pigs and could not finish it.[2]

Tsik's story was essentially the same, only in her case, the role of Mulul I and Mulul II were reversed. Note that Hapot, Tsik and other Mulul *tsunon* and *hahini* suggested that ordinary members of the *pinaposa* had started quarrelling and stopped supporting one another, and that the *tsunon* merely adjusted their own talk to match the new situation created by ordinary people's actions. Commentaries of other islanders suggested, by contrast, that the *tsunon* of Mulul themselves, rather than ordinary people, had begun quarrelling among each other over rank and ceased to co-operate as *tsunon* of one *pinaposa* should. People outside of Mulul remarked that Hapot and some other Mulul *tsunon*, each judging that they had the numbers to form a group of their own, had begun to 'pull people here and there', that is, to divide their movements and support between themselves. Whatever the case may have been, when movements ceased to display a single point of origin and return, Mulul ceased to exist as a *pinaposa*. What appeared instead was a division between groups of different rank, and arguments over who ranked higher.

In re-defining relations by 'changing accounts' of the past, the *tsunon* always took the risk, of course, that others would not hear their talk, that is, would not act accordingly. This was the case for Kitou, for instance. In 2004–05, Kitou, the current *tsunon* of Natasi, was often complaining about the lack of respect that people showed him, and the lack of attention they gave to what, according to him, was the island's 'true history':

> A brother and a sister were roaming the Buka area. The brother is called Hitas; the name of the sister is secret. Once they looked from the Buka mainland across the lagoon to the island of Petats. They decided to cross over. From Petats, they explored the other islands, especially Yaming[3] and Pororan. They settled down on Yaming. Because all other human beings were hiding out of fear of raids, every group in its own shelter, the brother and sister 'married back'. They had many daughters. Eventually, other people followed them to Yaming. Two Nakarip men arrived first. Their names were Kaper and Suaio. They were afraid to land at first. They knew of Hitas's power. But Hitas called them ashore and gave each of them one of his daughters as his wife, a particular spot of land to settle on, and a piece of sago thatching to build their *tsuhan* with. When he moved to Pororan, they followed him. He sat them down at those spots that they still inhabit today. Hitas, that is me [my ancestor]. He is the shark in the passage between Pororan and Yaming.[4] Kaper and Suaio are [the ancestors of the *pinaposa* called] Mulul and Put.

Kitou's talk was not effective in 2004–05, as the *tsunon* of Put and Mulul denied that he 'pulled' them and ignored his demands that they show him respect. Nevertheless, Kitou's story is a good example of the ways in which other Pororan *tsunon*, too—and some more successfully—made past movements appear in a particular shape for making claims to rank and establishing group boundaries in the present. When I suggested to Kitou that the Natasi, Mulul and Put had all 'come up from one mother', because Kaper and Suaio had married the daughters of the original Natasi ancestress, Kitou replied: 'How would that be?

Mulul and Put stay on their own. They are descended from Kaper and Suaio. I [my ancestor] put them here and there [nodding towards the site of the *hitaku* of Mulul and Put] and who stayed at their own place, with their own people [wife and children]. But I am descended from Hitas, who pulled them here. Therefore I am above them now.' Crucial to his argument was the point that Kaper and Suaio 'stayed with their own people' (or their people with them). That is, their wife and children did not 'return' to Hitas's wife/sister and her descendants, and thus no connection between them and their mother (Hitas's sister/wife) ever became apparent. What remains, in the absence of return movements that would have established matrilineal connections, is a relation between Kaper and Suaio's descendants and Hitas's, in which the former are subordinate to the latter, who gave them their mother and the place on which they lived.

While Kitou transformed in his account what could have become *pinaposa* relations (through the common ancestress of Natasi, Mulul and Put) into relations of rank between his *pinaposa* and the two others, the opposite happened in a different case, and one that the islanders found notoriously hard to grasp because it held elements of rank and *pinaposa* in tension. This was a kind of relation called 'basket' [*kohel*]. Although widely used to refer to any supporter of a *tsunon* at a feast, 'basket' more specifically refers to the descendants of a small girl whom a Pororan warrior captured in warfare and decided not to kill but to adopt. The girl would be adopted into the captor's *pinaposa*, and would subsequently marry a man from the same *pinaposa*, 'so as to tie her firmly to them'. The descendants of such a woman owe respect to the *tsunon* who spared their mother's life. The term basket refers to the loads they carry on his request, and to the food baskets that they must contribute when he hosts a feast. For example, the group of Salu's husband Hulagam are called Natasi, but are known to be the descendants of a [Nakarip] woman from Nova, who was caught by a Natasi warrior in the past. Hulagam is a member of the *hagung ni tsunon*, but the other *tsunon* make fun of him. Ideally, his group ought to be formally 'thrown out' by the Natasi, be given land and become a group in their own name once they are of a sufficiently large number. But until this is done, the group will 'come under' or 'go in the back of' the Natasi. In the case of baskets, then, a movement of pulling is turned into a movement of *pinaposa*, leaving from and returning to the captor's group. Relations nevertheless retain a hierarchical edge, and thus make for an interpersonal and a conceptual tension that the Pororans made explicit.

With the issue of baskets, I have reached an aspect of island relations that most Pororans are happy to leave to the *tsunon* to make sense of.

'Their talk', as the large majority of people used to say when I asked what they could tell me about baskets, 'the talk of the *tsunon*'. They thereby recognized a particular capacity, and a skill that the *tsunon* practiced in the course of their career, to 'talk into being' bounded groups of different rank where only particular, network-like relations of mutual help had existed beforehand (see Lederman 1986). They could combine people into groups, divide them again or, as in the case of baskets, create relations that were somewhere between mutual help and rank and located people somewhere between 'us' and 'them'. *Pinaposa*, like places, change appearance—boundaries, constituency and rank relative to others—over time, as an effect of the *tsunon*'s actions of definition.

As the example of Mulul in particular indicates, however, *tsunon* depend on the physical movements and acts of ordinary villagers in their efforts at defining groups, just as fathers depend on the movements of their wives and children for their capacity to 'make grow' to become apparent. The *tsunon* can 'throw away a piece of talk', as they like to say, but they cannot perform single-handedly the movements that make relations between entire groups of people apparent. The interaction between *tsunon* and members of their *pinaposa*, and the co-operative nature of making the shape of relations appear becomes most strongly apparent on ceremonial occasions, which are occasions at which relations are displayed, in mobile form, for everyone to see (see chapter 5).

At the same time, however, the *tsunon* must keep their 'talk' consistent with that of other *tsunon*: those on the mainland. Pororan *ngorer* and *pinaposa* do not exist in isolation, but derive their existence from histories of migration to the island that link them to others across the Buka area. I now turn to these connections.

Pinaposa Relations across Buka

'The clans do not stop here. They do not stop on Pororan', I was often told, and 'all of us [here in Buka] come from Punein'. Punein is a mountain in the Solos language area. It is uninhabited, and no one I spoke to had ever been there or had even considered going there. From the mountain, the ancestors migrated downward-outward to their present-day location along different 'roads' [*maror*]. They settled across Buka Island, on the Western Islands and later on the Carteret Islands, an atoll to the east. Northern Bougainville, although separate from Buka Island only by a narrow passage of deep sea, was settled by 'entirely different people' from another point of origin.[5]

In most cases, the *tsunon* of two *ngorer* decided to migrate together and form one *pinaposa*. They made settlements along their 'road', at which some people stayed behind while others moved on. Ancestral migration is not imagined as a walk across a fully formed landscape. Instead, people brought particular plant species along as they migrated, and places acquired their physical shape and significance through events that occurred as people settled the mainland. Elsewhere in Melanesia, ancestral stories describe the movement of the land itself, as it 'gave birth' to an island, incidentally in a circular motion that resembles the hand movements of Pororan Islanders when they speak of relations between mothers and children (Bonnemaison 1994: 115). Similarly, though not in terms of birth, the Pororans speak of a land in motion when they talk about 'rubbish' drifting across the lagoon, getting stuck on the reef and forming their island (see introduction).

Pororan is at the far end of Buka accounts of ancestral migration 'from mountain top to golden sea', as the Bougainvillean anthem has it. Its first, non-permanent settlers were men who had been sent out to catch fish for their group. They made small fishing camps only. Their relatives on the mainland supplied them with starch food in return for their catch. The fishing camps became permanent over time. Nevertheless, people on Pororan continue to return inward-upward every now and then, in order to obtain sweet potatoes for their fish, and in order to learn of their migration history from relatives along their road. They 'trace the footsteps of the ancestors', as they say. Most immediately responsible for doing so are the *tsunon* and *hahini* of a group. On behalf of their relatives, they maintain connections across the area that are vital for subsistence purposes and give people a highly valued sense of far-flung connections.

Two aspects of the Pororans' 'tracing the footsteps' are interesting and will be discussed separately below. The first is the particular processes of creating relations of value in the present, island style, out of relations to people on the mainland that are said to date back to the distant past. As we shall see, relations to mainland relatives are created and made to appear valuable just like relations among islanders. However, this time, the islanders are dealing with people who do not share their mode of making relations appear 'anew' by transforming highly indeterminate 'going around' into movements of particular shapes. Those people do not share the Pororans assumptions about, and interests in movements.

This becomes apparent when we look at the second interesting aspect of island-mainland relations, the stories of migration through which the two sides establish a partially shared sense of the origins of the relation that they are continuing in the present. The Pororans' and other Buka people's accounts and explanations of ancestral migration do not allow me to date migration, but they emphasized consistently that it took place <u>bipo bipo tru</u>, in the distant past, that is, before the arrival of white people. Records from colonial times confirm that the Western Islands were indeed inhabited by then, and apparently quite densely (Parkinson 1907). The migration that the Pororans talked about, then, was not one of the large-scale population movements that took place in Island Melanesia as an outcome of pacification, or of the colonizers' attempts to concentrate people in locations where they could administer them better (e.g. Hviding 1996; Küchler 1993). I shall investigate the migration stories that I heard on Pororan not as historical accounts, but as internal commentaries upon the processes of relating—tracing the footsteps of the ancestors'—in the presence. Pororan Islanders and Buka mainlanders interpreted these commentaries differently, and only some people were able to see through this difference and make sense of the interpretations of the respective other side.

The Pororans on Ancestral Roads

There are various good reasons for the Pororans to 'trace footsteps' and maintain matrilineal relations on the mainland. One concerns subsistence. In 2004–05, the Pororans depended heavily on sweet potatoes and other garden produce they obtained from mainland relatives, at the markets and on visits to mainland hamlets. Secondly, having many *pinaposa* relatives elsewhere was deemed both potentially useful and a mark of value in itself. For instance, Kil was delighted about each of the many invitations she received in 2004–05 to visit relatives on the mainland, informally or for a marriage or mortuary feast, because those invitations gave her a certain status on the island. 'Kil, where did you go again', other women would ask after her return. 'You went around in the bush for so long!' Kil would answer with dignity: 'My relatives over there always want me to come and visit, and then they don't want me to leave again. They really like me over there. And I have plenty of relatives like that.' She did, indeed. The following table shows the *pinaposa* relations that Kil was engaged in or told me about in 2004–05. Relations that I heard of but that were dormant during my fieldwork are marked by square brackets.

Not everyone entertained as many *pinaposa* relations on the mainland as Kil in 2004–05. Salu and her group, the Takap, entertained few, for instance, certainly partly because Salu and her family had been living in

Table 2 • Plisoh *Pinaposa* Relations

Village of *pinaposa* relatives' hamlet	Activities, 2004–05
Malasang	Mutual visiting; delayed exchanges of fish for garden produce; exchange of knowledge about *pinaposa* history.
Lonahan	A 20-year-old girl had been staying on Pororan for two months when I left. Her parents had sent her 'for a break', presumably to find a husband.
Hanahan	Mutual visiting; delayed exchanges of fish for garden produce; mutual support between workmen from both localities in Buka Town.
Tohatsi	Exchange of knowledge about *pinaposa* history; [use of truck for transporting copra to Town, past exchange of fish for starch food at Kessa market, until the Tohatsi's truck broke down].
Lumankoa	[A famous Plisoh rainmaker there sent rain to Pororan several years ago, at Francis's request.]
Karoola	Fish given in return for help and hospitality along the road; [gardens made on their land]; [some Karoola children brought up by Kil on Pororan], now employed by Kil's sons in Buka Town.
Bekut	[A Bekut girl brought up by Kil on Pororan], now employed by Pororans in Buka Town; hospitality to and gifts from her parents in Port Moresby.

Arawa for 20 years. After their return to Pororan in 1987, they had to pick up relations anew, which was only really possible when travel was safe again, after the Crisis. The following example may indicate how difficult it was to re-establish relations, especially for a woman like Salu who was used to being treated with respect. One day, a woman who claimed to be a relative of Salu's from Petats came to visit and told Salu that a prominent *tsunon* of their *pinaposa*, the Takap, had died at Lumankoa Village, in Haku. Those people of Lumankoa, they were the ones whose place Salu's first ancestors on Pororan had set off from, the visitor said urgently, so Salu had to go and help with the mortuary feast for the *tsunon*. Salu, although she said she was not clear about her exact relation to those people at Lumankoa, liked the idea of 'going around in Haku'. The Petats woman told her that a group of Takap from Lumankoa would come and pick her up for the feast by boat three days later, after picking up the group at Petats. Salu began preparing her contribution to the feast. She spent the better part of the day before the feast at sea catching octopus, which her children and grandchildren then cooked and packed into a huge basket for the relatives at Lumankoa. In the morning of the feast, Salu was up early, dressed smartly and then sat down with her basket and kept an eye on the lagoon. Several boats passed by in the distance, one almost certainly coming from Petats and continuing to Haku, judging from the direction of its sound. None, however, stopped at Pororan to pick up Salu. By lunchtime, Salu was mad. 'Ha! What kind of siblings are those over there? They are not my people! If they were my relatives, they would have picked me up! Those people, no way', she grumbled. She told Jennifer to distribute the octopus to people at the village, changed into an old laplap, picked up her fishing knife and her paddle and pushed her canoe into the water. Off she was for the remainder of the day. I met Salu's relatives in Lumankoa on a later occasion and asked them what had happened on that day. They did not think anything special had happened at all. Their boat had been full with visitors to the feast from Petats, and so they could not go and pick up the Pororans. They would invite them to come and visit another time. They did not know they had lost a relative on Pororan by not turning up on that particular day, and that it would be very difficult to make up for this.

Kil was more lucky in re-establishing relations with relatives she had lost touch with in 2005, after the Crisis had interrupted mutual visiting. Among those were the old women Rosa, who was running the *pinaposa's tsuhan* at Malasang (on her own after her brother's death), and her younger sister Lasi. Lasi had just moved from her husband's hamlet at Ieta Village to set up a new hamlet at an inland location not far from Buka Town belonging to the *pinaposa*, called Nova II. Contact between Lasi and the Pororan Plisoh was re-established at a chance encounter and conversation in Town between Kil's son Albert and Lasi's husband. Soon after this chance encounter, Kil asked Albert to arrange a date with Lasi's husband for her to visit Lasi's new hamlet. She stated two reasons. First of all, she was excited to see the hamlet and the large taro garden that Lasi's husband had mentioned to Albert. Secondly, Kil made references to a reconciliation ceremony with in-laws with whom the Plisoh had had arguments. Francis, the Plisoh's first in rank, had announced that he would host this ceremony two weeks later. For the feast, Francis required starch food, and Kil was hoping that the Malasang women, who were his *ngorer* relatives, might provide some. Two days later, Albert told Kil the date at which Lasi would be expecting her.

Two days before the scheduled visit to Lasi, Albert let Kil know that he had asked some of the young boys among his in-laws for some of the catch of a spearfishing outing that they were planning to go on the night before our visit to Lasi. Later that day, Kil indicated to Tsireh's daughter Maru that she would be pleased if Maru would give her a basket of shellfish to take along. Maru delivered two such baskets the following day. Denise and her children provided another basket. In the early morning of the visit, Albert took Kil, Talmits and me to Town on his boat, along with his son Ralph and Denise's daughter Teha. We stopped at Yaparu to pick up three baskets of smoked fish from Albert's in-laws. In Town, Albert and Kil discussed the details of the reconciliation feast to be held. After lunch, Albert talked Lawrence into giving him the brothers' company van for the day while Kil and Talmits took a bath and dressed up. Accompanied by one of the workmen, also of Plisoh, and by Ralph and Teha, Albert, Kil, Talmits and I set off on the van for Lasi's hamlet, consisting of three houses surrounded by some gardens at the end of a long and bumpy bush track that branched off the Buka east coast road.

Kil made admiring comments on the bananas along the bush track as we approached the hamlet, and then she praised loudly the large gardens around Lasi's house. 'Eh, these are real gardeners! Look how neat', she exclaimed. As she cut a papaya for us, Lasi explained whom the houses at the hamlet belonged to: herself and her married daughter, the third just being a kitchen house. Kil quietly instructed the Plisoh workman to get the baskets of fish and shells from the van and place them at the entrance of this house. Lasi nodded appreciatively. Kil then ventured inside the kitchen house and loudly admired some cassava roots in a basket there, which she identified as being of the species called Pomio. Kil and Lasi then exchanged news about their children and other relatives. The conversation was interspersed with Kil's statements of admiration for the small ducks and chickens around the hamlet. Francis's reconciliation feast was also briefly discussed. Lasi offered to send two large baskets of sweet potatoes. Her taro, unfortunately, would not be ready. Lasi then mentioned that her sister Rosa had expressed the wish of visiting Francis on Pororan. Kil and Albert suggested that she might come for a visit over Easter. They then asked Lasi about the migration histories that Kil and Albert had only been partly able to work out in the morning. Lasi admitted that she, too, had only partial knowledge of these, but that Rosa knew and would explain them during her visit.

When the conversation ran dry, Kil stated that she wanted to 'go around a little' and wandered off towards the gardens. Lasi quickly followed her. Kil admired all gardens greatly, but especially the large taro garden. She started plucking edible greens growing along its edges, and then pointed towards some nearly ready bananas. Lasi promised to send those when they would be ripe. On the way back, Kil went off to gather some flowers that she told me did not grow on the island and whose seeds she wanted to plant. When we finally left, about an hour later, we took away two baskets of sweet potato that Lasi's daughter had dug up for us, some roots of the cassava that Kil had identified as Pomio and some of its stalks for planting, three banana saplings, two bundles of edible greens that Lasi and Kil had gathered around the taro garden, various flowers in Kil's hair and hands, and the promise, not only of help with Francis's feast, but also of more bananas, two ducks and one chicken, and taro. Albert promised Lasi more fish from the catch of his in-laws at Yaparu.

Back on the island, Kil sent Honik and Teha to Maru's house with one of the banana saplings and a small basket of sweet potatoes. 'Tell her: this is the return for your help', she said. One of Albert's daughters came to 'return' another basket of sweet potatoes to the fishermen who had supplied us with fish for Lasi. Kil and I went to plant the remaining two bananas and the cassava at her garden. The cassava roots disappeared quickly, shared by Kil, her daughter Denise, Talmits, and two of Kil's sister's daughters, Solohi and Pinil, who came to inquire about our visit to Lasi. Kil spent a lot of time over the coming week regaling visitors to Kobkobul with stories of her 'going around in the bush':

> Albert took me, by car. We took this little branch road. Albert knew the road. Lasi's husband had told him. We went deep into the bush; the car was bumping and shaking. We thought we might go missing in the bush. We thought the car would capsize. But then, we saw those huge bananas, giant bananas, *mei lul* [an expression of admiration]. And then we entered their hamlet, and we saw a large papaya and they cut it open for us, and we talked and talked. I went around their gardens, and I looked and was startled by all the things inside, especially the taro, only it wasn't ready yet. I roamed around their garden, and then we went back to the houses, and they had already dug something out for us to take, and there was food and bananas and cassava to take back to the island. They gave everything for free, I just looked at it and they gave. And then we left, and the car was heavy with all their things.

In time for Francis' reconciliation feast, Albert arrived on Pororan with two large baskets of sweet potatoes from Lasi, along with another one, coming from Rosa's garden at Malasang.

Reconnecting with Mainland Relatives

Characteristically, both Salu's failed attempt at re-establishing relations with her relatives in Haku and Kil's successful one of re-establishing relations with Lasi and Rosa began with a—to them surprising—encounter with people claiming to be their relatives, who invited them over to their places. Both women were excited about the possibility of re-connecting with relatives they must have forgotten about, as they said. Both occasions for the surprise encounter were typical for island-mainland relations in 2004–05. In Salu's case, a relative from another island came to visit in order to report the death of a prominent *tsunon* of the group elsewhere. After deaths of important *tsunon* in Buka in 2004–05, the relatives usually sent out messengers to inform relatives all over the area, running, by car or by boat. Those asked the relatives they knew and could get a hold of to pass the message on among the people they could remember belonging to the same *pinaposa* in other locations. I had accompanied Roselyn's sister on a messenger tour in her jeep once, and had seen her strategies of spreading the word and the urgency with which she admonished relatives to pass the message on further. Therefore I was not surprised that a messenger turned up even on Pororan—one of the most 'out-of-the-way places' (Tsing 1995) within Buka—on the occasion of an important death.

In the Plisoh's case, the encounter took place not after a death, but among men doing business in Buka Town. This was another common way in which relations between distant relatives re-emerged in 2004–05. Town, shared among people from all over the area and from Bougainville Island, was a social hub. Here, it was not only possible, but very likely that two men doing business, as Albert and Lasi's husband were, established in the course of a friendly conversation that they were related. Town had not been playing this role for very long in 2004–05. According to the Pororans, during the Crisis, one was far more likely to run into serious trouble [bungim bagarap] than to run into relatives there. Usually, trouble took the form of armed men of the BRA [Bougainville Revolutionary Army], who detained a group of Pororan men once who had come to look for medicine for their community health centre, and who questioned and beat them severely before letting them go. Already by 2000, however, Buka Town was a sociable place, at least during daytime (R. Feinberg, pers. comm.), and in 2004–05, people from all over the area went there in order to re-establish contact, or initiate reconciliation with relatives who had 'gone missing' during the Crisis.[6]

After the surprise encounters, both Salu and Kil took to the sea, or asked relatives to provide fish. Mainlanders are known to relish fish, shellfish and other marine produce, which they have none or very little of themselves, and therefore the Pororans usually show their 'good thinking' for their relatives by bringing fish when they visit them. Salu went to catch octopus herself, firstly because she was good at it and enjoyed it, and secondly because she merely had to bring a small, distant relative's contribution to a mortuary feast. Kil, on the other hand, who was hoping to put the newly established relations to use for Francis' reconciliation ceremony, needed larger amounts of fish and marine produce, for which her relatives would give a return. She drew on Albert's in-laws, on Maru and Denise. Denise 'returned' the baskets to her mother as a daughter should; Maru could be asked on this occasion because she owed respect to Kil as her father's classificatory sister, and Albert's in-laws included a number of young men with an excellent reputation as fishing boys. Several marriages existed already between their *pinaposa* and Kil's, and most of them were far more satisfying than Albert's (see chapter 3). It was therefore in their best interest to remind Kil, the senior woman of Plisoh, of their fishing skills, and of themselves as potential future husbands for women of her group.

For Salu, her engagement with mainland relatives on this particular occasion ended with the preparations (there were other, more successful occasions). For Kil, it continued 'into the bush', to the hamlet of her mainland relatives. Albert took care of the practical arrangements for her movements. He provided the boat and talked Lawrence into letting him use the company van for her trip 'deep into the bush'. He had planned things ahead 'so that <u>mama</u> would look good returning to her relatives; so that they would send plenty of food for Uncle Francis's reconciliation', as he told me later. Kil was aware of, and appreciated his 'hard work', as she implied to others back on the island by saying that Albert 'knew the road', and which she spoke of in more detail privately. More importantly, however, Kil indulged in a description of her trip as *roror*, highly indeterminate going around. According to her account, she did in Lasi's gardens what the islanders do when fishing, or when staying up and watching the fishermen return to the beach. Skipping over her conversation with Lasi about Francis's reconciliation and about the whereabouts of various relatives, she told her visitors at Kobkobul how she went around, looked at things and received them 'for free' [nating]. Kil was glossing over the fact that we had, of course, brought fish. Instead, she stylized herself as someone who could attract cassava, bananas, sweet potatoes and other things just by looking at them. Once all those things were on the car, of course, the car was 'heavy', just as a boat becomes heavy with fish on a successful fishing outing. Kil reverted to a more ordinary relational mode. She 'returned' what she had acquired 'for free' to those who had contributed fish for the trip.

It may be worth repeating here the claim by some Pororan men that they do not need to buy love magic, which is expensive, but that they attract women by 'just looks', or sometimes even 'just thinking'. Kil was making a very similar claim here, only that she attracted garden produce rather than a woman. From my observations, playing off her attractive capacities was the single most important aspect of her *roror ilatu*, 'going around in the bush' to Kil herself. Having relatives there to tell other people on the island about mattered, helping Francis with the preparations for his feast mattered, and establishing relations that might prove invaluable at a time of food shortages was important, too. But most importantly, we may say that Kil was 'fishing' over there in the bush. Out of highly indeterminate movements and relations, she made highly valued movements of coming and going, setting off and returning appear. She 'pulled' garden produce (inward-upward from her own perspective) and gave it to others (downward-outward), thus recognizing them as relatives on the one hand and positioning herself 'above' them at the same time.

When her mainland relatives returned her visit and came to Pororan, however, the mainlanders used the occasion to present their own views of their relations to the Pororans, through accounts of the history of migration that linked them to particular people on the island. Those had nothing to do with fishing, and in them, the Pororans collectively came to be located 'below' the mainlanders. Some islanders, Kil among them, understood and appreciated the logic of the mainlanders' migration stories. Others, however, found it very difficult to make sense of what the mainlanders were telling them about the *pinaposa* history they shared. In the following section, mainland accounts of migration and the Pororans' reactions to them will be presented.

Migration Stories

At Easter 2005, Lasi's sister Rosa, the *hahini* of her *ngorer* at Malasang, visited Pororan with a couple of younger relatives from Malasang. She wanted to 'eat fish and rest a little' on the island, and at the same time wanted to refresh the Pororans' knowledge of the details of their relation. Recorded below is the '<u>rot blong tumbuna</u>', the ancestral migration route of the highest-ranking *ngorer* of Plisoh on Pororan, whose *tsunon* was Francis, as Rosa recounted it:

> That is all right, I will talk of our road. All of us come from Punein [a mountain in the Solos language area]. This is the first place of all Buka people. They used to live at Punein in caves ['holes'], already separated into the two birds, Naboen and Nakarip. When a <u>kros</u> [fight or argument] broke out, people left the mountain. They moved

around the area until they came to a place called Mau. At Mau, the *tsunon* filled a coconut shell with *gogoa*. They threw this coconut shell down onto the ground. It broke, and the *gogoa* scattered all over. In the same way, the people who had lived together at Punein were to disperse. From Mau, different groups followed different roads. Our ancestors walked along and eventually came to a place called Telatu [an inland village]. They built a *tsuhan* there. At Telatu, they split up again. One of their women moved to Malasang [an east coast village]. With her went the *tsuhan*. It stays there now. Our *tsunon* look after it and look after our people. Another woman went to Poka [a west coast village]. The third woman, Gitei, went to Pororan. A warrior brought them there. Because there was no one else at these places, each of these women 'married back' into her own *pinaposa*.

Rosa made a pause here. Kil moved her head from side to side thoughtfully. Tsireh nodded heavily. Francis smiled into the distance. Talmits and a few other women of her generation kept their eyes on the ground, looking a little uncomfortable. Rosa then finished her story by listing the names of the *pinaposa*'s *hahini* at Malasang, starting with the woman who had arrived there from Telatu and ending with her own mother. After that, Francis took over. Speaking quietly and modestly as usual—and as befits a person of his status, who 'has others who talk for him'—Francis indicated to Rosa the direction of the spot at which Gitei and the warrior had first landed on Pororan. He promised to show it to her later. Then, he listed the names of the Plisoh *hahini* on Pororan, though he cautioned us that he might not have remembered all of them. 'What if I lie to you', he said. Finally, he called over one of the small children playing at the other end of the hamlet. 'Here, this one, this is Gitei', he said. The Malasang women got excited. Rosa hugged the girl, who looked confused, and told her that she had a namesake at Malasang, a slightly older girl called Gitei, like her. The other women who had accompanied Rosa from Malasang, too, went to inspect and hug the little Gitei, and the round broke up.

For me, this story of the mountain, the separation of different groups and the migration of their *tsuhan* that were then re-emplaced in different locations bore immediate resemblance to other Melanesian and Southeast Asian origin stories talking of original unities being decomposed (McKinnon 1991; Mimica 1988), and with an aesthetics of centre and periphery, immobility and mobility, source and issue. Not all of Rosa's listeners on Pororan were equally convinced by her story—and given my argument about radically different assumptions about places among them, this may not be surprising. The Pororan Plisoh gathered at

Kil's house that night, after Rosa had gone to sleep, and discussed matters among themselves. The discussion began with Maru asking into the round: 'Malasang, what kind of place is that?' Kil shrugged. 'Who knows. I haven't gone yet.' Tsireh, however, told her the same as he had told me, many times, about places on the Buka mainland in general: 'A real place. A mountain, and *tsuhan* stand there.' The mountain may be a reference to the Buka east coast road rising as the coast becomes steeper when one approaches Malasang from Buka Town. But perhaps more immediately on his and Maru's mind at that time was the mountain of Punein. If so, one may detect another meaning in his reply: mainland places are the origins of mobile people, of human life as we know it today. They are full of capacity—which the Pororans of course locate on the reef in their own story of Sia and Hulu.

Maru continued: 'Did you go there?' 'I didn't go', said Tsireh. 'Did you see that road that Rosa was talking about?' asked Toapal, Kil's sister's son. 'No. I only know the road of our *ngorer*, not Francis's. Some of it', responded Tsireh. 'And you don't want to tell us what it was like, and if it was like that one Rosa talked about', suggested Toapal. Tsireh began:

> After the ancestors scattered at Mau, our people continued down the mountain [downward-outward arm movement]. They followed the [Gagan] river to the coast [downward-outward arm movement]. Some went to the coast and then to Pororan. Others went other places [downward-outward arm movements in different directions]. Others again are still staying somewhere there, in the bush, along the river. I returned there to meet them when I was young [inward-upward arm movement]. We went up the river by boat, and we took that branch river, deep inside the bush. Then we left the boat and walked inside, we almost went missing in there, and then we met them. They knew we wanted to return, so they had come to look out for us. They took us to their houses, and I stayed with them for a while to hear their talk. Then we had a feast, and then we went back down the river again [downward-outward arm movement]. Ehee. We went around in the deep bush there.

His account provoked lively story-telling. Unlike Rosa's story, his, underlined as it was by familiar arm movements, was something everyone in the round could relate to. 'Did you go by *sirok ta neh?*' [a spot along the river known to the Pororans from stories of headhunting (see chapter 3)] asked Talmits. 'Did you see crocodiles on the river?' Honik wanted to know. 'No, we didn't see any then', replied Tsireh. 'But I saw one another time, when. . . . ' 'No, <u>papa</u>', said Maru. 'Never mind the crocodiles now. That road of yours, it is clear, it is straight. But the road of that woman, Rosa? Do you think it is true?'

Other people then asked other questions about Rosa's account. Talmits asked: 'Is it true that our ancestors married back in the same *pinaposa*?' Kil's sister Rotia wanted to know: 'Rosa told me that Gitei is a name belonging to our *pinaposa*, and nobody else should use it. But Mateuk's [a Pororan Naboen woman's] daughter is called Gitei, too.' Tsireh said he was tired and would explain the next day. The next day, of course, was too busy, but a few days later, when he came across Talmits, Rotia and Maru at Kobkobul, Tsireh sat down, accepted a cup of tea and a freshly baked bun that Talmits offered him and began talking about Rosa, who had left by then. 'Those people are gardeners. Kil told me about their large gardens. She said they have large bananas, very well looked after.' He paused meaningfully. Then he told us what he had told me earlier, that women grew the same way as bananas on the mainland, by being cut, taken to a new garden, planted and watered. 'And that's it. Our *pinaposa*, too, grew like that, from Mau to Telatu to Malasang, Poka and Pororan.'

'Ah', said Maru, 'this warrior, Kuntali [she filled in immediately the name of the male ancestor she knew so well from her father's stories], he took this woman, Gitei, and he planted her here, on Pororan. And she grew on the island.' 'That's it', said Tsireh, 'and that is why we, her children, must return to the mainland, where our mother came from, every now and then. There, we can learn about her road.' Talmits, who had wanted to know if it was true that the first woman of her *pinaposa* on the island had married a man from her own group, could now answer her own question, too. 'Kuntali is the gardener, who made this garden for her. Had he been of another *pinaposa*, this woman Gitei would have returned to the mainland relatives later, and her children would have followed her back there. But Kuntali was our person, our ancestor. It was his own garden in which he put Gitei. So we can stay now. Nobody can send us back to where we came from.' 'That's it', said Tsireh. 'Sometimes, of course, the women who went to new places and opened up a rope of the *pinaposa* there did not marry back. For example, another Gitei of our *pinaposa* went from here to Tohatsi. She got married at Tohatsi. Her husband belonged to another *pinaposa* there. However, his people wanted her and her children to stay. So they gave them a place to live there and told them that this was their little place now. That Gitei at Tohatsi did not come back to Pororan. Her children, too, only come to visit from time to time. Still, they know they stay on their father's land. And their father's people can send them back to Pororan any time.' Talmits looked thoughtful. 'Will they do that?' she asked. 'No', said Tsireh.

'Gitei's children have been staying there for a long time. Few people know that this Gitei did not marry back into her own *pinaposa*.' Talmits concluded that these matters were difficult. Maru nodded: 'Their things, the mainlanders' things. Hard for us to know.' With that, the two of them set back to work on making buns.

Rotia repeated her questions about names, and why it was that on the island, children of different *pinaposa* could have the same name, while Rosa had said this should not be the case. I had asked myself this question before. At Tegese, I had come across disputes over people 'stealing names' familiar from the anthropological literature on Sepik River groups (Harrison 1990). On Pororan, by contrast, I noticed and people confirmed that 'names are free—who would want to own names?' Tsireh said that on the island, people did not care much since they knew who was who, but that really one should try not to confuse the mainlanders by 'letting names go around'. 'Mainlanders know the children, the fruit of their banana by their names. That's how Rosa knows that we came from her place: she saw Gitei, and she heard her name, and she knew that Gitei was a child of her *pinaposa*', he added. Rotia nodded.

From the perspective of Rosa's migration story and Tsireh's explanation, we may, first of all, review Kil's visit to Lasi, as Lasi may have thought of it. Kil described her own movements as highly indeterminate 'going around', and the result as getting for free things she had looked at. Lasi, however, might well have perceived of Kil's visit as a rather ordinary return of relatives, whom she gave bananas and other things to. Here, relations between saltwater and mainland relatives worked out without frictions arising because each could make sense of them from their own perspective, without getting into the other's way. This was not the case when Rosa came to Pororan and told her account of ancestral migration. The reactions of the Pororans to Rosa's story show that only some of them could grasp the generative pattern underpinning it. Rotia, Talmits, Toapal and Maru, among others, had difficulties. I have presented those in detail because they show what happens when Pororan Islanders, with their lack of interest in the dichotomy between immobile, powerful centres and mobile people on the periphery (see chapter 3), deal with accounts of themselves— their own *pinaposa*—that are underpinned by this dichotomy. Maru and Toapal especially looked in vain for the feature that is necessary for the islanders to judge the 'truth', as Maru put it, of their own accounts of relations: firsthand observations of the 'road' at issue. Rosa's story offered no such observations. Instead, it was an account of 'roads' made up of women linking up named places. It was, as Tsireh's references to bananas in the beginning of his explanation indicated, an account grounded in an aesthetic of source and shoot, place and road. This aesthetic is not familiar to the Pororans from their own narratives of places and groups on the island, which are objectified in movements of particular shapes that appear out of *roror*.

Nevertheless, Francis, Tsireh and Kil accepted Rosa's account, judging from their calm and appreciative reactions. Tsireh, moreover, was able to explain to the others the generative pattern that gave her story its cohesion, or 'truth'. Note that Francis, Tsireh and Kil are *tsunon* and *hahini*, while those who found Rosa's story difficult to understand are not. In the following section, I will show what experiences allowed Tsireh especially to speak so knowledgeably and confidently about mainland stories and understandings of relationships. The key, as I will show, lies in his experiences of the ceremonies that made him *tsunon* [*hatsunon*].

Hatsunon

The firstborn [*hamua*][7] daughter and son of a *hahini* (herself a firstborn daughter of a *hahini*) 'have a position', or 'have a number' that comes from the ancestors, through their mother. As is the case with ordinary children, their relation to their mother is not established once and for all at birth, but is a gradual and reversible process that others observe by watching the child's movements relative to their mother. However, the movements of a young *tsunon* and *hahini* are not only informally observed by others at the village. They must also be formally 'witnessed' by persons of respect, in ceremonies that the child's relatives host in his or her name. Two gradually expanding sets of persons must witness a *tsunon* or *hahini*'s position, beginning with the mother's pregnancy and ending after the person's death. One consists of the child's *pinaposa* relatives, most immediately the mother's brother but also more distant relatives at other locations in Buka. The other consists of the child's father and paternal relatives, other *tsunon* and ordinary villagers 'at his/her village' [*ipinapu tanou*].

This process of 'witnessing' begins when others recognize that the *hahini* is pregnant.[8] Her matrilineal relatives will then provide a pig, most likely obtained from relatives on the mainland, which will be eaten by the *tsunon* at the village and the ancestral spirits who are said to eat with the *tsunon*. By providing pork, matrilineal relatives beyond the island come to 'know' [*atei*] and show their concern for the child already before it is born. By eating the pork, the *tsunon* at the village similarly come to know and care about [lukluk long, *ngot (ne)*] the as yet unborn child. In the case of a woman of very high rank, the entire *hagung ni tsunon* [meeting of the *tsunon*][9] may attend the occasion. More common would be a delegation of two or three, who were selected so that their rank would match that of the pregnant *hahini*. Along with the *tsunon*, it is said that ancestral spirits eat the pork. They, too, thereby enter into a relation with the *hahini*'s unborn child. After that, it is important that the *hahini* no longer leave the island.

When the *hahini*'s child is born, the birth will be witnessed as her pregnancy was, again with pork. Further ceremonies of witnessing follow as the child of rank performs particular activities for the first time. Most important among these, according to the islanders, is the child's first journey beyond the island. For example, the future Plisoh *hahini* and *tsunon*, Solohi and Tukan, took their first longer journey beyond the island to Tohatsi, on the Buka east coast, when they were in their teens. Kil, Talmits and some other members of Plisoh accompanied them. At Tohatsi, the local *hahini* of their *pinaposa* took them to a spirit pool, for them to get to know the *pinaposa*'s localized spirit [masalai] there. At a feast, made from a pig supplied by the Pororan Plisoh, the *pinaposa*'s *tsunon* at Tohatsi formally acknowledged Solohi and Tukan's rank. Upon their return to Pororan, their paternal relatives 'washed their legs', that is, poured water over their legs to remove the salt of the journey. Afterwards the Pororan Plisoh hosted another feast (with another pig), for the paternal relatives, 'the people at the village' and the Pororan *tsunon*, at which these people, too, acknowledged the position of Solohi and Tukan as the future Plisoh *hahini* and *tsunon*.[10]

A *tsunon*'s position is openly stated and confirmed by a larger number of people, including both matrilineal relatives and those at his village, at a feast held about a year after his predecessor's (usually his MB's) death, for lifting the final mourning observances. On this occasion, his matrilineal relatives will travel to his village of residence for witnessing his assumption of the position, along with the people there. A *hahini*'s position is witnessed by large numbers of people at her *sinahan*, when her husband pays the bride price and her relatives bring her to his hamlet (see chapter 5). Unlike ordinary women, who walk at the centre of a tight cluster of female relatives with a pandanus leaf cape over their head, a *hahini* is 'carried above' in a seat on the shoulders of her relatives, widely visible to those who gather to see the event, as I was told. Finally, after death and during the wake for a *tsunon* or *hahini*, their rank is marked when a paternal relative paints their hair and face with stripes that are specific to each bird.

Ceremonies of witnessing are considered to be dangerous to the person of rank (except for those conducted after death). As already noted, the islanders are highly ambivalent about persons 'looking' at others [*ngot*], for instance when fishers return from the sea. The same holds for such ceremonies of witnessing. When *tsunon* and ancestral spirits—both very powerful others—'see' and come to 'know' the person of rank, they draw him or her into relations beyond anyone's control. These are potentially beneficial, but also potentially dangerous. For instance, the islanders frequently pointed out, with reference to numerous specific examples, that children of rank often fall ill after being introduced to ancestral spirits. Once known to the ancestors as persons of importance to their relatives, they are also more likely to be killed by the ancestors when their matrilineal relatives do not live in peace among themselves. Furthermore, other humans who see them, especially those who see the *hahini* at her marriage, may become envious from seeing a healthy person of rank, and may aim to kill her through sorcery. However, the witnesses of a person's rank are not entirely in control of the relation they thereby enter into, either. *Tsunon* are given pork, not only as a medium for witnessing, but at the same time also as a form of recognition or reward for their witnessing, which puts them in close contact with powerful spirits. At important occasions, they also receive money.

Because ceremonies of witnessing are dangerous, the islanders say that they aim to postpone them, either by postponing the activity that will require formal recognition (such as the first journey),[11] or by postponing only the ceremony. Secondly, they always include the younger siblings of *tsunon* and *hahini* in those procedures, so that they can take over if the *hahini* and *tsunon* die, without the necessity of further ceremonies. The Rimoldis have suggested, for Hahalis, that the acknowledgement of status is postponed so that rank can be shifted relatively easily to a younger brother/sister should the *tsunon* or *hahini* die or (in the case of a *hahini*) not have children to continue the line (Rimoldi and Rimoldi 1992: 175). On Pororan, the connection posited between moments of witnessing and a person's death is so close that a stronger argument may be made: The postponement of ceremonies is not an attempt to avoid wasting effort on a person who might die (for unspecified reason), but an attempt to increase the likelihood that the person of rank will live (see also Sagir 2003: 49). Nevertheless, to opt out of these ceremonies, or to opt out of the relations that a child of rank enters into through them, is not a possibility. Rank is imposed on the firstborn children of a *hahini*, beginning before birth, by matrilineal relatives who provide a pig and thereby 'push him/her up', expecting the child to 'go ahead' and engage in dangerous, geographically far-flung and temporally deep relations on their behalf. Their demand upon the child is recognized by the *tsunon* who eat the pig. Matrilineal relatives and *tsunon* may agree to 'remove the position' from a particular person. For example, when the highest-ranking *ngorer* of a *pinaposa* is seen to be in danger of dying out, their position can be temporarily moved to another *ngorer*, which then 'hides' the first. Nevertheless, where such shifts can be avoided, rank remains with those who have been constituted by these relations from the moment their presence became visible to others.

Pororan accounts of 'witnessing' seem to provide yet another ethnographic case of a specific Melanesian conception of agency, investigated by Marilyn Strathern (1988) through analyses of a range of ethnographic instances. In this conception, a person's agency is elicited by a witnessing other, or a 'cause'. Often, there is a visual 'bursting out' of the internal capacity of the agent into the open that is staged at performances. Something is drawn out of, or extracted from the emergent agent, who is thereby 'decomposed' to reveal particular capacities or intentions. Strathern foregrounds the assumption of partible persons, the imagery of bodies as containers—of children, of wealth–, the role of visual perception in turning them inside out and the importance of gender to the emergence of forms out of one another. Finally, she emphasizes temporality, and the reversal of the roles of cause and agent over time. This makes it necessary to stage a single act as a performance, to lift it above ordinary time by the suddenness of the appearance of a new form (see esp. M. Strathern 1988: 290ff.). While she herself has not applied this model of agency to the study of hereditary rank, Mark Mosko has. He has argued that hereditary rank among the Mekeo in PNG is better conceptualized as Strathernian 'decomposition' than, following Sahlins (1985), as '*super*composition', that is, the hierarchical internalization of social relations within a single person (Mosko 1992: 699). He adds that Mekeo hereditary leaders, unlike the cases described by Strathern, are decomposed twice, thus revealing a 'quadripartite' (Mosko 1985) internal structure of which they divest more than ordinary people.

With regard to Pororan *tsunon* and *hahini*, it seems clear that the process of 'witnessing', too, brings a capacity into the open. This capacity, however, is not an internal bodily structure or state, and it is not evinced in sudden outbursts, set apart from the processes of reciprocal constitution of agency by their staging as singular performances. Instead, the capacity made visible here is a capacity to make others move. First, the movements of pork and of the *tsunon* who gather to eat it show the capacity of the child to 'pull' high-ranking others, who thereby 'put *nitsunon* on the child', once before and once at birth. When they are in their teens, the children of rank 'return' those movements, and return the power 'put' on them, by visiting at least one group of matrilineal relatives beyond the island. This return of power once installed upon them is acknowledged in the washing of their legs, both at their destination and upon their return to Pororan. The gesture of washing legs (pouring water, from above, over the legs of a person), like the gesture of 'throwing pork away' is one of *tsomi*, of pity and condescending concern by the host, the 'cause' of the journey. Unlike at the *hahini's* pregnancy and after the birth, those who move (the child's relatives) bring the pig they eat themselves now, rather than receiving it as payment by the host. The cause of their movement—the hosts—thereby retains superiority.

So much can be said if one considers acts of witnessing from the outside, from the perspective of someone at the village watching and discussing the movements of the young person of rank. From the perspective of the moving person themselves, the experience is a different one. The night after Rosa gave her account of ancestral migration, Tsireh told us about his own 'return' to matrilineal relatives as a young person. Far from talking about a (coordinated, orderly, 'straight') 'return' all the way through, in his brief narrative he highlighted experimental movements of going 'deep into the bush', nearly going missing and then, almost by surprise, coming across relatives who had been waiting already. Nevertheless, what to him appeared as an oscillation between a purposeful 'return' and 'going around in the bush' was acceptable to his mainland relatives as a return along an ancestral road to their place. While there, he heard their talk. As he explained to me on a different occasion, this was talk, specifically, about ancestral roads, the mountain of Punein, their place and other places. Upon arrival to the island, he was formally recognized by the Pororan *tsunon*, too.

Such experiences of having one's movements recognized both by mainlanders and by islanders were unique to people of rank. In those people, the mainland *tsunon* recognized their own children, the children that they had 'put *nitsunon* on', which was now returned to them. Where the Pororans might perceive erratic movements 'deep into the bush', the mainlanders perceived the return of a power that came from their own place, along a 'road' they themselves had created. They formally recognized this return, and explained to the child what it had just done, where it had returned to (and come from), and other details of mainland relationality. Thus, Pororan persons of rank came to know the mainlanders' perspective, and came to be formally recognized as knowledgeable persons, made knowledgeable by mainland relatives themselves. Ordinary people 'without a number' were treated differently when they 'returned' to the mainland. They did not have their movements recognized and explained as a return along a road to a particular place. They were not likely to learn about the differences between their own and their mainland relatives' perceptions about their relation, since those questions fall into the responsibility of *tsunon* and *hahini* only.

Although particular relations differed, from my observations, Pororans 'without a number' were treated friendly but condescendingly, as '*tsomi*, the people from the sea; they have no sweet potatoes of their own, so they come'. Thus, ordinary people on Pororan had difficulties understanding the 'roads' that mainlanders valued so highly: they had not 'seen' or experienced them for themselves.

Conclusion

Beginning in chapter 2 and running up to this point, I have aimed to contribute, from a particular ethnographic and theoretical perspective, on a theme that has preoccupied all Buka ethnographers. This is the relation between the two institutions that people in the area themselves have consistently pointed out to be the two most important ones: matrilineal kinship and inherited rank. Let me re-trace my steps. I began with two hand movements, one running downward-outward and inward-upward, and the other running inward-upward and downward-outward. One was associated with the relation between mothers and their children, and the other was associated with the relation among fathers, their wives and their children. I then introduced the theoretical question of what relates and what defines people. One may perceive of the downward-outward and inward-upward movement as a claim to the capacity to relate—to extend help outward to people and receive help in return. This does not mean, however, that the capacity to relate is limited to the relation between women and their children. Although giving help is especially appropriate within one's *pinaposa*, it is also routinely extended beyond, especially to one's father's people but also more widely. In parallel, one may perceive of the inward-upward and downward-outward hand movement as a claim to the capacity to define: to elicit movements that make particular relations visible. Again, it would be a mistake to therefore reduce definition to relations between fathers and their children.

In chapter 3, I have attended to some of the processes of definition that are associated with the *tsunon*. *Tsunon* define themselves as being 'above' others as they create places in which power resides. In the first section of this chapter, then, I have moved on to show how they define groups, as well. They ask, entice or command people to move in a particular way, but for rank, a place or group to indeed appear 'defined', ordinary people must 'hear their talk' and move accordingly. Whether these movements define or relate the group is, of course, a matter of perspective. Let us take the example of the men whom Sakuan told to gather building materials for the houses in the colonial village, and then to catch fish for the feast to celebrate the completion of the houses. From his perspective, they bring materials inward-upward that are then deployed downward-outward. From their perspective, they more likely leave his place in the morning, go around a little and run into some fish, and then return in the afternoon—that is, they help him as they would matrilineal relatives, with no particular attention to his rank.

Finally, I have considered relations between Pororan Islanders and their matrilineal kin on the Buka mainland. For Kil, these were bound up with more general processes of asking for help and returning favours. Her movements were also, however, meant to help Francis 'define' his own rank and the *pinaposa* of Plisoh through a reconciliation ceremony. They can thus be framed in terms of definition or of relation, depending on whose perspective one takes, Francis's or Kil's. In the process, moreover, Kil and others on Pororan were exposed to Rosa's attempts of defining her own position 'above' them, as well as of defining their *pinaposa* by describing its 'road' of migration. Here, it turned out that Rosa was relying on different 'objects' altogether, namely on roads that began and ended in places and on a generative pattern modelled on banana growth, rather than on observable movements that began and ended in *roror*. I noted that the ability to perceive the difference requires rank, and that therefore rank makes a difference when Pororan Islanders engage in relations with *pinaposa* relatives on the mainland.

What can one say, having come thus far, about a question that many Buka ethnographers have addressed, the relation between rank, or *nitsunon* and *pinaposa*, or matrilineal kinship? It would not be correct to associate these two with my two starting points, the two hand movements of contrasting shapes, although this would be tempting. It is true that downward-outward and inward-upward hand movements objectify *pinaposa* relations, but *pinaposa* relations also require, for becoming apparent among all other relations of mutual help going on, the defining actions of a *tsunon*: inward-upward and downward-outward. It is true, secondly, that inward-upward and downward-outward hand movements objectify the capacity of a *tsunon* to define. However, *nitsunon* is first imposed upon one (downward-outward) by one's matrilineal kin on the mainland. It must be returned (inward-upward) before a *tsunon* can be known as such. The second analytic possibility, more correct than the first, is to speak of a dialectical relation between *pinaposa* and *nitsunon*, each constitutive of the other. This is not particularly original in Buka ethnography (see esp. Rimoldi and Rimoldi 1992). As the Rimoldis have noted in their insightful accounts of experiments with matrilineal kinship and the work of the *tsunon* in the Hahalis Welfare Society, however, the devil is in the details of Buka creativity. For Pororans, this means that the devil is in the movements. From my analysis, guided by Pororan movements, a few statements about the relation between *pinaposa* and *nitsunon* can be made, in relation to earlier Buka ethnography (see esp. Blackwood 1935; Rimoldi and Rimoldi 1992; Sagir 2003).

The first concerns the question of what 'inherited rank' is on Pororan. It is not a substance. When the Pororans say that rank is 'put on' a person, especially on the head, they are referring to a movement (not a thing or substance) coming from 'above', from someone who already has status. These are the movements of the *tsunon* at the village and of the child's own matrilineal group who 'witness' the child's status. What is the role of the mother, of which the Pororans say that they are the 'road the *tsunon* comes on'? Because she had her status witnessed in the previous generation, the *tsunon* now know which child to go to and witness in this generation. She thus guides the process of formal recognition that makes her child a person of rank. These observations lead me to emphasize again what the Rimoldis (1992) especially have noted: that rank in Buka both comes through one's mother and needs to be activated. I add, however, that on Pororan at least, these are not two separate processes, one of internal transmission of rank through the mother and one of external recognition by the *tsunon*, but only one. Rank is at the same time perceived, created and made visible for all to see in the *tsunon*'s acts of witnessing the child of a woman who was recognized the generation above.

The second point concerns the ranking of different *pinaposa* relative to each other. On the Buka mainland, two principles are crucial to arguments over rank: priority of settlement and genealogical proximity to the founding ancestor of a hamlet (Sagir 2003). Sagir has situated these principles within a comparative Austronesian framework. Rosa's migration story is consistent with his observations, and can usefully be analysed in the terms he lays out. Tsireh's detection of plant imagery in the account matches up, furthermore, with the Austronesian comparative material that Sagir has drawn on (see esp. Fox 1971; see also Fox and Sather 1996). Pororan claims to their own ancestors 'pulling' people', too, are bound up with claims to having 'come first', and may at first sight appear very similar. Note, however, that the generative pattern underpinning those claims is different from that underpinning Rosa's story. This becomes apparent if we focus on the conceptual connection between *tsunon*'s claims to rank and fathers' actions of pulling on Pororan, established by hand movements. Here, it becomes clearly apparent that Pororan acts of 'pulling' and 'putting' are not claims to cutting a sapling and implanting it in the ground, but of giving shape to movements. Transported to the claims of *tsunon* to have 'come first', 'pulled others' and given them places to settle on, there is no reason to think of those primarily as claims to first settlement, or indeed to control over land. They are claims to have elicited particular movements. The implications of this difference are potentially far-reaching, both for arguments over land and marine tenure and for further investigations into relational metaphors in Austronesian saltwater settings. Unfortunately, they cannot be pursued any further here.

Thirdly, it is important to differentiate between contrasting perceptions of rank and of matrilineal kinship on Pororan and on the mainland on the one hand, and a shared 'traditional leadership system' stretching all across the Buka area on the other. Within this system, Pororan persons of rank have the chance, in the course of their ceremonies of 'witnessing', to learn about mainland understandings of matrilineal kinship and traditional leadership. At the same time, they find themselves— their own status—formally recognized by mainlanders, despite the fact that, as they know, the mainlanders' understanding of what is being recognized differs from their own. Ordinary people on Pororan, meanwhile, are stuck with the rather vague observation that 'mainlanders are entirely different kinds of people', and feel less confident in dealing with them. Thus, the unified system of 'traditional leadership', as Buka people call it and as it is enshrined in the Bougainvillean constitution, provides a space within which local differences can be perceived—at least from a saltwater perspective—and needn't be resolved. This point will be taken up again in chapter 6.

NOTES

1. Why exactly will become clear when I describe a *sinahan* in chapter 5.
2. Some people dated Mulul's attempt at *tsuhan* building to 1999, others to 2002.
3. Yaming is the now uninhabited island just north of Petats. In colonial times, it was a coconut plantation. Some of Kitou's ancestors are said to have turned into stones that still stand there.
4. A masalai, a local spirit who takes the form of a shark and is said to have killed many people near the spirit's home passage between Petats and Pororan.
5. My informants across Buka as well as ethnographic sources are unambiguous on this point. From the other side, from northern Bougainville, Thomas Rabans (pers. comm.) offered some migration accounts that confirmed a different origin point for those people.
6. People with formal roles in the peace process played a role in facilitating initial meetings between former relatives, but colleagues and Town friends, too, sometimes brought former enemies together. Reconciliation was not always initiated in Town, of course. However, it could more easily be initiated there.

For instance, when a senior politician once drove into the hamlet of a political adversary in Crisis times by car in 2005, his emergence from his car sent the women of the hamlet running back into their houses. This was a case of political adversaries, not of ex-combatants. The strong reactions of the women, and the obvious tension that the arrival of one at the other's hamlet caused, may indicate why many people, especially those immediately involved in the violence, chose Town as a setting for re-establishing connections.

7. *Ha-mua* = make front.
8. No child of rank, to my knowledge, was born on the island during my stay. I therefore rely on the Pororans' detailed explanations here.
9. All men who gather for meetings at the *tsuhan*, that is, the *tsunon* of each *ngorer*. This chapter follows Pororan usage and refers to the *hagung* as 'the *tsunon*'.
10. They have not yet taken on the tasks of *hahini* and *tsunon*, since Kil and Tsireh are still alive and active.
11. In northern Bougainville in 1930, the occasions for formal 'witnessing' that were postponed were multiple (Blackwood 1935): *tsunon* child emerges from house ten days after birth, not five days as for commoner children (186–87); *tsunon* child is first carried on the mother's pack at about the age of four, later than commoner children (189–93).

CHAPTER 5

Marriage and Mortuary Rites

In the previous chapters, I have followed Pororan movements, especially the standardized hand movements of different shapes that the islanders use to comment on relations in the past and present. Two questions will be addressed now that have arisen in the course of this investigation of the Pororans' objectification of relations in movements. One has already been stated explicitly: What roles do other modes of making relations apparent play in this heavily movement-centred mode of objectification, especially human bodies? Secondly, how exactly can we understand the relation between the hand movements in which relations are depicted in a 'finished' (see, e.g. Wagner 1986b) form on the one hand, and the step-by-step unfolding of movements and relations on the other? How is the multiplicity of perceptions and contingent possibilities transformed into particular relational outcomes, and how are these opened up in their turn to novel possibilities?[1]

To recall a few situations mentioned in previous chapters of which we may ask this question, Tsireh said that he went around deep in the bush and nearly went missing when he 'returned' to have his status witnessed by his relatives. However, in the end, he did 'return', and not only to his mainland relatives but also, afterwards, to the island. There, he was recognized by the Pororan *tsunon* as having performed a movement of a definite shape. How did he make the transition from wandering to return, without thereby losing the sense of the contingency of his achievement? Secondly, how did Kil find her way back from 'going around' in Lasi's garden towards 'returning' a banana sapling to Maru, who had contributed marine produce to take to Lasi's? And how did she juggle the 'return' with her own strong sense of having gone around and received things for free? In the discussion of people's return from the sea (chapter 1), I have already indicated one element that seems important: the mechanisms of looking and having things attached to oneself, and the details of facial expression, gestures and the directionality of bodily movements that make relations appear one way or the

Notes for this section begin on page 162

other. Here, I pursue the issue further through an in-depth investigation of bodily movements, looks and their interconnection on very important occasions: marriage and mortuary rites. In those, the Pororans are most keenly interested in making relations appear in a single form—without, however, losing the sense of their contingency.

Both marriage and mortuary rites are explicitly labelled as occasions 'when you can see', as people told me excitedly every time a *sinahan* [bride price; the ceremony of paying bride price] or a mortuary feast was scheduled. Nobody ever spelled out for me what I would see, and of course there were lots of possibilities. The most anthropologically interesting one was the processes of objectification, more carefully and consciously managed by the *tsunon* and *hahini* on those occasions than in everyday life. At *sinahan*, the main aim was the 'tightening' of a relation between spouses and in-laws that was actualized on the background of all other possibilities—without making this relation appear less novel, contingent and therefore exciting to the participants in the ceremony. To this purpose, the Pororans not only managed movements during *sinahan* carefully, but they also deployed 'objects' neglected in everyday kin relations: decorated human bodies. Secondly, at death, the Pororans' stated aim is the opposite of 'tightening'. It is to 'throw out', that is, to finally release the spirit of the deceased, to forget and to open mourners up to novel relations (see also Battaglia 1990). Through a discussion of the transformation of movements at death, I shall address some older anthropological questions about personhood, forgetting and Melanesian expressive forms from a saltwater perspective.

Sinahan

I report here on a *sinahan* that was held on Hitou Island in early 2005, which I attended as a member of the husband's group. Both partners were from Hitou, but many Pororan Islanders were involved as relatives on one or the other side. The couple had already been living together for two or three years, but it had taken the husband and his relatives some time to gather sufficient money for the bride price. In late 2004, they had signalled that they were ready, and negotiations over the sum and the details of the ceremony had begun. It had been decided that the bride price would be assembled at Kil's house, since Kil's father had been a prominent *tsunon* of the husband's *pinaposa*. Because of that and because she had a lot of experience, Kil was appointed to lead the husband's side in their singing and dancing, as well, together with Tsireh. In early February 2005, Kil told me of the date of the ceremony and urged me to attend. 'Then you will see', she said. So I went, along with about fifteen other adults from Pororan, who joined about 25 relatives of the husband on Hitou. An approximately equal number of people took part on the side of the wife.

Salu and I set off from Lulutsi and walked over to Kobkobul at about 10 A.M. in the morning of the *sinahan*, carrying a basket of sweet potatoes each to take along to Hitou. The paths leading into Kobkobul were busy. Relatives of the husband, men and women, were carrying their contributions to the event into the hamlet. Under Kil's watchful eyes, some younger women of her *pinaposa* counted and moved all the baskets that people had dropped here and there onto one big pile, and put the rice bags and other store-bought food and bananas onto another pile. Kil, who had kept an eye on the people coming and going, recalled who had brought what, identified whose contribution was still missing, and sent a younger relative to go and chase them up. When Kil was satisfied that the piles of baskets and other things were complete, male and female members of her matrilineal group moved them over to Mulul, the hamlet at which Albert would land with his boat that would take us to Hitou (the reef off Kobkobul was inconveniently shallow). Albert had not arrived yet when we reached Mulul. Tsireh, too, was missing. Kil sent Honik to look for him.

While some women re-counted the baskets and commented on the size of particular relatives' contributions, and while others wandered off to chew betel nuts with the women at Mulul, a woman pulled me over to a young man who was watching the cardboard box in which the *sinahan* was kept. The woman asked Kil to open up the box up for me. Women, men and children from our group and from Mulul approached and formed a circle to see the *sinahan*. There were five laplap in the box, and five envelops containing a string of shell money and 500 Kina (about $190) each. Kil held the open envelops with dignity. 'Write that down', she said to me. 'This is kastom'. Then, she put the laplap and envelops back into the box and tied it shut with a rope. The spectators dispersed.

At this point, Albert arrived with the boat, and Kil's younger relatives loaded it with our cargo. Tsireh finally arrived, too. Kil pushed him towards the boat, climbed on herself and ordered the other women into the spaces in between and around the cargo in the centre of the boat. Then she chased off Honik, who had taken centre position, with the words 'And who are you, a *hahini*, that you sit on top of all the food, right in the middle of all of us?' Honik giggled, slid off the boat and splashed through the water to its very front, where she climbed back on. Kil told the other children to join Honik there, while the men squeezed around

Albert in the back. Off we went, under the shouts and cheers of the people at Mulul. 'Never mind Hitou', Tsireh shouted back to them. 'We will take to the open sea! We will leave Kessa (on the northern tip of Buka) aside and go straight to Nissan, to Kavieng (the capital of the neighbouring province), and when we run out of petrol, the sea will carry us all the way to the Philippines!' The children in the front cheered. 'Paah', said Kil, 'keep quiet over there!' Her smile, however, said otherwise, and she leaned over to my side of the boat, tucked on my shirt and shouted across the noise of the engine: 'If we drift off now, at least we will have plenty of food!' Salu joined in by pointing out that she would love to see her firstborn in Kavieng again, and drifting there would be cheaper than going by ship. Meanwhile, Tsireh had begun singing the song that we would sing when dancing into the village on Hitou: 'Oh in-law, you must bring our woman!' The women joined him, for practice.

We landed on the Hitou beach at some distance from the village. Albert and some young men took the cargo by boat into the village, to the wife's hamlet. Kil instructed the women to unload two baskets of mixed garden produce (taro, cassava, bananas and coconuts, two of each kind on top of a large heap of sweet potatoes) that we would carry with us for the ceremony, and the women got off the boat with the baskets. We gathered at the edge of the coconut plantations to put on decorations of fragrant leaves that we had brought along. We also splashed each other generously with baby powder, for beauty and for the fun of it. The husband's relatives from Hitou joined our preparations and took the occasion to explain to the Pororans how exactly they were related to the husband. Some of the young men met up with a group of Hitou and wandered off into the coconut plantations to drink, taking Tsireh along.

Albert came back after a while to inform us that the wife's side was almost ready, and what about us? Kil sent one of the women to round up the men drinking in the coconut plantations, especially Tsireh who would have to take the lead. The women formed tight rows for the dance formation, with Kil in the front and two women by her side carrying the mixed-root baskets on their backs. Salu pulled me towards the centre of the cluster of women. Tsireh finally re-joined our group and was handed a bow and an arrow by one of the Hitou men. He pointed the bow at us and into the distance and said: 'Ha! We will go and get our woman now!' A Hitou *tsunon* joined him in the front with a conch shell. Other men took their position along the sides and in the back of the cluster of women. The children were all around and in everybody's way. Trying not to kick them or each other, we started shuffle-dancing in slow tap-steps into the village, singing: 'Oh, in-law, you must bring our woman now!'

In between our own singing, blowing of conch-shells and Tsireh's loud war shouts, we heard noise coming closer from inside the village. 'What's that', Salu said excitedly, tap-stepping impatiently on the spot as Kil and Tsireh held us back. 'Slow down', said Kil, 'that thing is still far away'. She kept us back at one short side of the Hitou soccer field, which we had reached by then, until we could see the 'thing' on the other side. The thing was a group of people. 'Ii!' called the women in our group, surprised. From my position in the centre of the women, I could see a man threatening to throw a spear our way. 'Watch out, their arrows!' one of the men on our sides called, though none came flying. Now we could hear their singing, too: 'Oh, in-law, you must give us our bride price now!' Tsireh challenged us to go ahead: 'What's that now? That's our woman! Let's go and get her!' Shouting fiercely, he pointed his arrows at the other group and ran up and down along our line to motion us forward. 'Slowly', Kil called back to us from the front of the cluster and refused to give way. With other women pushing forward from the back, we tap-stepped almost on the spot. The singing, conch-shells and war shouts had turned into a deafening noise. Stuck in the centre of the cluster of women, Salu and I could not see properly what was happening ahead. Salu's decoration had slid off her head and was hanging over her eyes, and as she struggled to put it back in place, her elbows hit a couple of women around her in the face, who started yelling at her. Several of the smaller children wiggled and pushed their way through the tight cluster to their mothers, crying with confusion.

Finally, Kil led us forward towards the other group. Salu stretched her neck to see better, and eventually elbowed her way towards the front of the cluster, pulling me behind her. 'Look at them', Salu cried out with amazement when she had gained a clear view. 'They are beautiful!' 'Look, they are wearing leaves, too, and powder! Don't they look smart?' added another woman. 'They look just like us!' The tension was giving way to sheer admiration of that other group, complete with women on the inside and men on the outside, looking bright and war-like. 'That's it', said Kil, apparently satisfied.

Loudly and unexpectedly, Salu shouted out the name of a neighbour and friend of hers on Pororan: 'Siatun!' She waved frantically towards the other side, 'Siatun, come out, I want to see you dance!' Siatun, a *hahini* of Naboen and an older woman with some standing in the village, stepped outside the cluster of woman and performed a little solo, waving her leaf decorations at Salu. The women on both sides cheered. Salu broke out of our cluster, and the two ladies stood in the space between the two groups and chatted away. Other women did likewise, including the younger ones, who had to elbow their way out of the centre of the cluster.

Suddenly and with a collective 'ii', however, the people in our fragmenting group stood still for a moment, then moved all towards the same spot in the middle of the wife's group, were held up by the older women and the men with bows and arrows and moved backward a little only to approach again. Finally, they formed a circle around 'something, you see!' as they whispered excitedly. This 'something' turned out to be the wife that we had come to 'get', lavishly decorated. She had been hidden until then under a pandanus cape. Now, she was visible for all who were near enough to her in the crowd. Her skin was glistening with coconut oil. Her hair had been rubbed with oil mixed with charcoal. It was pitch-black. Yellow flowers were placed above her ears. Painted in red across her head and in various colours on her face were the decorations of her matrilineal group. A string of *beroan*, shell money, was crossed over her chest and back. Around each of her arms, a band of banana fibres held a clay pipe in place. She was wearing a grass skirt, and around her ankles hung the same leafy decoration that everybody else was wearing. She kept her eyes down and looked embarrassed.

Tsireh called me to the front, so that I would see what would happen next. He explained, not just to me but everyone, that Kil would now 'circle' the wife and husband with taro, so that they could eat together in the future. The wife and the husband, who had played no special role so far among the men in our group, were led by relatives to sit down on two plastic chairs that a woman from the wife's side had put up next to each other in the middle of the circle formed by the crowd. Kil took a taro root out of one of the baskets on the table, passed it above, around and under the outstretched arms of the husband, and in front of, around and behind his legs. Then she held it to his mouth, and he pretended to take a bite. Afterwards, Kil did the same with the wife. Meanwhile, on the side and with hardly anyone turning their way, Tsireh motioned the young man carrying the *sinahan* to hand it over to a *tsunon* on the wife's side. This being done, Tsireh returned to stand next to Kil. 'Now you can eat together', he said to the couple, and turning towards the spectators: 'Let's all eat now!'

Some women from the husband's group had already gone ahead, and others followed them now to a stretch of beach where a large canvas of the kind normally used for fastening cargo on a boat or truck had been spread out for the women to sit on. The women aimed for that canvas, while the *tsunon* sat down at a table further up on the beach, where they would be served food first. I sat down on the canvas close to Kil, with the younger women from Kil's matrilineal group. Several women from the wife's side brought us food. They began with betel nuts and sticks of lime for chewing, as is usual at feasts. Everyone was handed two nuts and one stick of lime, in an order that, as I had learned on a previous occasion, depended on the particular relations of kinship and rank among the recipients. Knowing this, I learned a lot from watching the distribution, especially once Kil ordered the women around me to 'explain who is who, and why they get their betel nuts when, so that she can write it down'. On the betel nuts followed leaf-wraps of boiled rice topped with meat. While the husband's people were eating, the wife's people who were not busy with the distribution came around to shake hands with every single one of them: 'We are in-laws now', they said to each other. After the wraps and after the hand shaking had subsided, tea and scones were served, and then the party broke off. I went with Salu to sit under the house of her sister Soaka for a while, and then the boat took us back to Pororan.

Tightening a Relation

It should be clear from the above that *sinahan* has a conventional structure prescribing what is to be revealed at what point in the proceedings. Kil knew this structure well. She physically imposed it on everyone else and carefully manipulated who could see what, and when. Her method of manipulating perception was by 'bossing (our) movements' [bos-sim wokabaut], as the Pororans pointed out to me later. As mentioned previously, the islanders hate having their movements bossed around ordinarily, but *sinahan* is an exception. Here, people cooperate to make something appear, step by step and in a highly specific sequence, for everyone to see and admire. What appears, ostensibly, is the wife. Her appearance is followed by the circling of husband and wife so that they can eat together in the future. However, as people pointed out to me later, this is not the most important part of the ceremony. Much more important is the transformation of a movement of open-ended destination—we could have drifted to the Philippines instead of going to Hitou—into a tiny, closely controlled, hardly noticeable movement—that of the bride price between two men at the edge of the circle of people standing around the newly married couple. This movement 'tightens' their relations as in-laws—and the fact that nobody is looking, I shall argue, is central to the achievement of this 'tightening' against the usual Pororan interests in keeping relations open-ended. In the following paragraphs, I re-trace the achievement of this transformation of movements.

From a far distance, as the two groups shuffle-dance towards each other, neither the direction of their movements nor the numbers or particular shapes of bodies involved are apparent yet to the members of the respective other group. The participants' excited shouts draw attention to this and to the uncertainty of what will happen next. 'Something is walking about over there!' as Salu, shuffle-dancing next to me, pointed out when making out the other group in the distance. 'Huh, what are those people doing? See, over there, can you tell? What is going around there?' Kil kept us back at that point, so that we would meet the other group in the middle of the soccer field, where there would be enough space for the ceremony.

As the groups draw closer to one another, gestures of enmity, or more importantly gestures of mutual recognition become apparent. Participants see the men in front of the other group, their weapons pointing at them. They also hear the singing that makes explicit an interest complementary to their own. 'Give us our woman' sounds up against 'give us the bride price'. At about the same time, the women of the other group become visible behind the men. Furthermore, as participants gradually come to appreciate the form of the other group in its entirety, they recognize in the other a mirror image of themselves. This is made explicit in the comments of the women as they shuffle-dance along: 'See, their women are so smartly dressed, too!' Shouts of admiration punctuate the singing. A connection between the two groups appears highly desirable now.

As the groups draw yet closer to each other, connections are shown to be already there, in the persons that now come into view. Participants recognize persons whom they are related to in particular ways 'on the other side', and will call out to them by name. Salu at this particular *sinahan* recognized her neighbour Siatun who was leading the women on the other side, and shouted across the noise of the singing and the instruments: 'Siatun, that is it, we will be in-laws now!' There is a more abstract aspect, too, to the emergence of a possibility of connections between the two groups. This can be found in their decorations, as they become visible to people 'on the other side'. Each participant is decorated with things taken from land and sea. Green fragrant leafs are hung around people's bodies, and white baby powder (a substitute for lime powder made of corals) decorates their faces. These appear side-by-side on the body of a single person. We may take this as an indicator, visible on the body, of the person's capacity to move far and wide, to the different spots where lime and vines can be found, or where baby powder can be bought. This makes him or her an attractive person, full of relational potential.

At this point, when the two groups meet, the wife emerges between them. With her various decorations from diverse origins, she radiates mobility and the potential for connections to others. Everyone's eyes are on her. The Pororans point out that this is a dangerous moment for a woman, for with the looks come wants [*ngil*], here as when fishing people return from the sea. The islanders make veiled reference to envy and sorcery, as well as to admiration and love magic when talking about this moment. However, while the woman is holding all the looks and focusing all attention on herself, something else happens: the *sinahan* changes hands. The movement is so small, and everyone is so busy looking at the bride and the ceremony after which the couple can eat together, that this movement is not affected by 'looking', 'wanting' and interference from those around. This tiny, easily missed movement, said Tsireh, was 'the tightening of their relation—they are in-laws now'. Young people sometimes downplayed the *sinahan* when talking to me as 'just a present'. Kil, however, told me repeatedly, lowering her voice conspiratorially, that this, really, was the whole point of the ceremony: the handing over of the *sinahan*.

Her and Tsireh's commentaries on the movement of the *sinahan* indicate that, from the perspective of the woman's relatives, the movement of money that the husband's people hand over to them objectifies their own capacity to grow and produce a person, or relations, of value to others. The bride price is money that 'they pay for our woman'. The wife's relatives also understand the movement of the bride price to foreshadow the return of their daughter with her children later in life. From the husband and his relatives' people's point of view, by contrast, the movement of 'throwing away' [*hamok*] the money finishes off the movement of gathering it together from various categories of relatives. It thus objectifies their capacity to create movements of a particular shape, as fathers do, and stakes their claim of likewise 'making [the woman and her relatives] grow' in the future.

The movement of the bride price, then, might be understood to reaffirm the contrasting interests that the two groups already held in this marriage before the event. However, the two contrasting interests now appear as two sides of one mutually beneficial relation. This transformation has partly come about through the earlier revelation of already related persons 'on the other side'. I further note, however, a contrast between the noisy earlier revelation, aided by marine and bush decoration, and the calm, quiet and short-distance movement of handing over the bride price. The latter requires no further props or decorations, and no further movements of persons, which the Pororans always suspect may go off in an unexpected direction. In fact, it requires that other people be distracted from it, so that they will not look at and meddle with it. If the handing over of the bride price is a show of contrasting interests, then it is also a show of the ideally formal, highly constrained, and (hoped to be) predictable behaviour between in-laws. The Pororans, of course, are not ordinarily interested in predictable behaviour, but in 'going around'. That is why the movement is performed just when participants are distracted by an extraordinary, because human bodily object of open-ended relationality and excitement: the decorated body of the bride.

Having seen them through to their completion, the movements of the two groups of in-laws, one with the wife and the other with the bride price, could now be summed up as a hand movement that takes a downward-outward and inward-upward shape from the perspective of the wife's people, and an inward-upward and downward-outward shape from the perspective of the husband's. Doing so would be a description of *sinahan* as an 'image' that impresses its viewers by binding up and into itself opposed elements of social life or an 'ethos' (Wagner 1986b). However, if we did so, we would miss something: the Pororans' interests in the temporality of the revelation, and the contingency of its outcomes. In analytic terms, we would miss the question that movements as a particular mode of objectification pose so strongly, not only but especially when they are carefully orchestrated in ceremonies: how do open-ended revelatory sequences acquire a single form?

Mortuary Rites

I pursue this question further through a description of Pororan mortuary rites. In those, a more complex revelatory sequence unfolds than that at *sinahan*. In the course of my discussion of this sequence of rites and revelations after a death, I shall offer saltwater views on three questions discussed in the context of mortuary rites by other ethnographers. Firstly, what imaginations of the person become apparent in them (see esp. Battaglia 1990; Munn 1986)? Secondly, how is forgetting achieved (see esp. Battaglia 1990; Küchler 2002)? Thirdly, what are the expressive forms in which people present themselves to themselves in the context of mortuary rites, the occasions that provide a focus for people's aesthetic, economic and political activity, and 'engage pervasive cultural concerns' (Foster 1995: 96)?

Table 3 • Schedule of Pororan Mortuary Rites

Name of event	Activities observed on Pororan
Death	Wailing sets in, the body is washed and laid out for mourning.
Showing grief, crying over the body	Women assemble to cry over the body inside the deceased's house. Men stand around, make the coffin, and dig the grave.
Burial	The body is placed into the coffin and carried out of the house. Often, a service is held at the church, or the coffin is opened for mourners to bid farewell to the deceased at the *tsuhan*. Burial takes place at the village cemetery, established by missionaries in order to end the practice of sea burial.
Mourning period (9 to 29 days)	No sweeping or other cleaning in the village. Large gatherings, large fires and noise are avoided. Close relatives of the deceased wear black, do not comb or cut their hair and do not wash.
	Garden food and pigs are assembled, mostly from mainland relatives, in preparation for *bung malot*. The timing of the feast depends on estimates of how long preparations will take.
	Various smaller rituals may be performed, including 'tracing the footsteps' and one or more *hahats* [fire sacrifice] to communicate with the spirit.
	If the deceased is a person of rank, female matrilineal and paternal relatives may choose to remain confined in the deceased's house. They eat only banana and cassava, do not wash, and leave the house only briefly. *Hahur* [mourning songs] may be sung in one or more nights between death and *bung malot*.
Bung malot [ten-day feast] (days 10 to 30 after death)	In the morning of the feast, on the tenth day after the death, the mourners wash in the sea. Matrilineal and paternal relatives gather their food contributions at the deceased's house. Baskets of garden food, topped up with pork, are handed out, ideally to everyone who came to cry over the body. The *tsunon* eat first. With them eats the deceased's spirit, who is then expected to depart.

Persons at Death

The wailing after a death appears to physically draw Pororan Islanders to the hamlet where the death has occurred. Children interrupt their games and run towards the wailing, either out of curiosity or because an adult relative had called out to them: 'What is that? You run and check!' Gradually, the adults present at the village follow. Those who suspect the death of a close relative, perhaps because he or she had been ill, or those informed by children that the dead is 'your person!' drop whatever they were doing. They sometimes pick up a face towel at their house but usually just move very quickly, sometimes running, towards the hamlet from which the wailing originates. The persons who will come running include (so not present at the moment of death) the deceased's mother and sister, the spouse and children, matrilineal relatives, paternal relatives and in-laws who co-operated closely with the deceased, and finally nearby neighbours, schoolmates, colleagues and age-mates with whom the deceased maintained close relations. Other villagers follow at a later point in time, which they decide upon on the basis of the degree of co-operation they had had with the deceased and his or her immediate relatives.

Relatives living or currently staying further away, for example work-ing in Town, are usually informed of the death through a messenger. They react in similar ways as those who hear the crying at the village. Men silently quit their work and leave for the place where the death has occurred. Women more commonly collapse to cry, usually on the spot and on the shoulder of a close relative or a friend [poro], and then make arrangements to travel to the location of the death. Employers in Buka Town never, to my knowledge, question the absence of an employee who has 'gone to cry'.

When they arrive, closer relatives first and others later, at the ham-let of death the women push into the door of the house where the body lies. They make their way through the increasingly dense crowd of women in the room and collapse straight onto the body or onto other women hanging over it. The room becomes increasingly hot, smelly and noisy with growing numbers of crying women inside. A *tsunon* of the deceased's *pinaposa* usually presides at the deceased's head. Other men come inside to view the body only briefly. Afterwards, they sit or stand around outside, in the hamlet, talking quietly and chewing betel nuts. The deceased's male matrilineal and sometimes paternal relatives make a coffin somewhere at the edges of the hamlet. Members of the deceased's *pinaposa* eventually hand out betel nuts to the mourners and serve them food, brought by mourners only distantly related to the deceased. The usual etiquette of serving the *tsunon* first is not strictly followed on such occasions. In addition, mourners do not—or pretend not to—care what precisely they eat (nuts gathered together if the hosts are less affluent, bread spread generously with peanut butter for the most wealthy). Women continue to cry over the body, taking turns for some women to eat and relax their voices while others keep the wailing up, from death until burial. Ordinary villagers are usually buried in the afternoon of the day of death. Pororan Islanders are reluctant to keep a dead body and the spirit that is assumed to be hovering around in the village in the dark. *Tsunon*, however, must be mourned over for one night before they are buried.

'Death . . . objectifies the person' (Wagner 1986b: 177). In other words, it makes personhood, and particular persons, an object of regard. Other ethnographers have noted two aspects to the point: At death, mourners construct themselves as persons in the eyes of others, by showing their compassion, their relation to the mourners, and their capacity to behave appropriately in what is often a highly conventionalized set of activities. They do so, secondly, through the objectification of a particular person, the deceased. In most places, this objectification focuses on the body of the deceased. For instance, on Sabarl, when a body is prepared for burial it is washed, dressed in finery, the skin is oiled and the face painted, and ornaments are hung around it. Food is placed next to the head, a con-cave potsherd put over the mouth, and the body becomes the centre of a display of garden food, sago, small luxuries and wealth items such as shell necklaces and ceremonial axes around it. The deceased is made into an 'effigy of the social person' (Battaglia 1990: 163). On Pororan, by contrast, attention to the body itself is minor. Women wash and dress it at the onset of mourning, but besides that, little effort is made to pre-serve the physical appearance of the deceased; instead people press for a quick burial. Furthermore, wealth items, be they food, shell wealth or other things, are conspicuously absent.

The Pororans objectify the deceased and the mourners as compas-sionate persons and relatives in the mourners' movements. The island-ers' commentaries on the felt need to rush to the hamlet of mourning, and their deliberations of when would be the right point in time to go indicate both aspects and their close interconnection. For instance, when word spread at mass of the death of Jimmy, a sixteen-year-old who died while fishing on a Sunday morning, Jennifer wanted to go to his hamlet straight after church. She knew him as a distant paternal relative, a friendly and helpful boy and stated her distress at his death. Salu kept her back by saying: 'Hey! Are you his immediate sister, or why would you run there straight? You stay. We will show our grief later.' When the women collapsed on the body, ideally in rough order of their felt 'closeness' to him, they objectified their grief, and thus themselves as human beings with emotions, their relation to him as they knew it, and their knowledge [*atei*] of proper behaviour among relatives, who must support one another especially after a death. They also objectified his relational constitution. I suggest that their gathering made apparent all the relations that, in his lifetime, the deceased's movements used to keep apart. Now, they all came tumbling down onto the body, and made the place heavy, as Pororan Islanders say (see also Munn 1986).

In addition to their relation with the deceased—and thus, collectively, his relational constitution and their own personal attributes of compassion and understanding—the movements of mourners to the hamlet and straight onto the body objectify the cause of death that Pororan Islanders most commonly identify: a failure to attend properly to particular social relations, for which ancestral spirits eventually killed a person. For instance, after Jimmy's death, people most immediately suggested that of course, the spirits were angry because he had not kept the Sunday rest. He had therefore acted disrespectfully against the *tsunon* of the village who had encouraged people to rest on Sundays, and against the spirits of his ancestors who had done so in the past.[2] Who those spirits were was not specified. Gradually, however, general opinion shifted, and many villagers suggested that Jimmy's relatives' failure to kill a pig at his deceased grandmother's final mortuary feast had caused her spirit to linger on and eventually kill Jimmy. In both suggestions, relations—matrilineal or relations of respect—had failed [pundaun, fallen down]. When Jimmy died, people commented that either his own or his relatives' behaviour had failed him [pundaunim em, made him fall down]. It was this 'collapse', I suggest, that the women objectified when they collapsed crying over his body. At this time, women come in extraordinary close physical contact with various others, including those with whom they stand in a relation of respect and with whom they avoid physical contact in everyday life. For example, in-laws who usually keep a distance from one another may cry on one another's shoulders over a dead body. Moreover, women who do not usually get along, or women from different locations who may not know one another at all, cry together in this room. Relative rank, too, is not attended to at this moment.

By physically collapsing over the body, Pororan Islanders turn the collapse of social relations, which first became apparent in the form of spiritual intervention (which, as the islanders state, is very difficult to either predict or control), into a form that human beings can understand or feel their way into, and that they can collectively assume control over. Various prohibitions that the entire village keeps may be understood in the same terms. When children are admonished to play quietly, soccer tournaments, village assemblies, *tsunon's* meetings, dances or other celebrations are cancelled, and no rubbish is removed from hamlets, the village as a whole takes the death onto itself and into its inhabitants' physical actions. Those are then, gradually, altered to remove the 'burden'. One might say that, in their movements at death and during the mourning period, Pororan Islanders personify death, as death personifies them. In its personified form, death can be acted upon.

The argument that human beings personify death and then act upon it is not new. However, this personification has commonly been described in terms of bodily 'icons', persons who take death upon themselves by tying mourning bands around their wrists, blackening their bodies and wearing heavy skirts, for instance. These are gradually removed, and human life thereby reconstituted (see Munn 1986: 167–78). Battaglia (1990: 194–95) argues that *segaiya* on Sabarl constitutes a gradual opening of bodily orifices (ears, mouth, sexual organs, eyes) that open mourners to new relations after a death. She draws an analogy to a Sabarl story of the first human being, who was blocked inside the creator before the creator cut a vagina through which it could appear. On Pororan Island, by contrast, I suggest that personification at death—of the deceased's relational constitution, of mourners and of death—is achieved in the mourners' movements. How death is then transformed, and the deceased forgotten, will be the focus of the following sections.

Objects of Forgetting

A person is not only objectified, but also forgotten through the mourners' movements. What I render here as forgetting is referred to, by Pororan Islanders, as 'sending the spirit off', which is stated to be a key aim of mortuary rites. The process of forgetting begins when the body is placed into the coffin and carried out of the house. Wailing grows strong at this moment. I was told that the women show their grief 'because their child is leaving now'. When young men then carried the coffin out of the house and through the village to the church, where a service was to be held, they did so at the highest possible speed, forcing others to jump aside. It was explained that they did so in order to prevent the spirit from lingering on. At Lontis, I observed how the *tsunon* who hosted the mourning walked ahead of the coffin, holding a bundle of croton [*limoto*, Haku] in his hand into whose leaves lime had been placed. He invited the spirit to sit down on the lime. Then he walked a small circle [*hasoma*] in front of the house, which would prevent the spirit from returning inside. On Pororan, however, it is the high-speed movement of the coffin itself that is supposed to separate the spirit from his or her former home.

It is said, however, that the spirit will only be satisfied and leave the living for good when the relations that constituted the person of the deceased have been 'straightened', implying both a clarification and the removal of arguments among his relatives. The process of straightening relations begins before burial. For instance, at Jimmy's death, a service was held at the church before his burial. After the service, people rose from their church benches to pass by the coffin at the altar roughly in the order of 'closeness' of their relation to Jimmy.[3] First went his mother, father, siblings and aunts, uncles and cousins who had known him well, matrilineal and patrilateral. More distant matrilineal, and then patrilateral relatives followed. His friends and other school children came next, who had come in their classes 'so that they can see this'.[4] Finally, the longest time at the coffin was given to the (unrelated) men who had found his body, 'because they are carrying a heavy burden'.

The quiet negotiations between close relatives in their church benches about when to get up and approach the coffin indicated that the relations that were being made apparent here were not considered self-evident, but had to be worked out as people went along. Clusters of relatives rather than a neat row of people approached the coffin and arranged themselves in space only gradually when they reached it. After the funeral and during the following days, the order that emerged on this occasion was commented and acted upon. At their hamlets, people asked immediate relatives explicit questions, such as 'Who is he/she to Jimmy?' that were answered by kin terms. In that way, what used to be a highly patchy, and not necessarily mutually compatible understanding of his relational constitution before his death was 'tidied up' and made explicit afterwards. 'The community'—as Pororan Islanders sometimes call themselves collectively, often in the context of mourning—came to a shared understanding of who Jimmy was.

However, this understanding was adjusted so as to exclude him almost the moment it was made explicit. From the islanders' calculations of 'who is he/she to Jimmy?' others emerged such as 'if X is Jimmy's paternal relative, he must be my mother's paternal relative, too. Then I am his *pian hatuhan* [the child of a male member of a *pinaposa*].' The result of their objectification of his relations, then, was his eclipse from them, and their transformation. One might say that, as they 'walked out' his relations, they also walked out of them, in ways that were facilitated but not constrained by the relations whose objectification was the purpose of the event.

The same doubling of making relations apparent in movements and turning movements and relations to novel ends becomes especially obvious at an event called 'tracing the footsteps'. I observed such an event at Lontis on the Buka mainland after the death of Magata, a Haku *tsunon*, and Pororan Islanders confirmed that they, too, conduct it sometimes, in similar ways. Magata's mourners 'traced the footsteps' all the way from the hamlet of Tegese, where people had cried over the body, to Buka Town, where Magata had worked. They drove along the Buka east coast road by truck, all the way singing mourning songs. They stopped at Magata's matrilineal and paternal relatives' houses, many in the Haku area, some at Hanahan where his *pinaposa* is said to have their main location, and some at other places along the road. They also visited the shops where he used to stop and the houses of his friends. At each stop, the *tsunon* in charge of the event and Magata's sister led the mourners in a procession from the road to the doorstep and back again. The sister, dressed in black mourning attire and her head covered with a pandanus leaf cape, cut small pieces off a taro root and let them fall to the ground.[5] In Town, the mourners visited in this way at all the bars and shops Magata used to visit, the market, the bank, and finally the company where he had worked. That is, they physically enacted and thereby made visible the most important movements and relations of Magata's during life. Upon reaching Town, however, the group of mourners gradually decreased in numbers. Participants departed, individually or in small groups, for going shopping and, more generally, 'going around to rest' before returning by truck to their hamlets.

The mourners' dispersal in Town made the dissolution of the deceased's footsteps into his mourners' indeterminate 'going around' especially apparent. But in addition, the entire event was shot through with mourners' small digressions from Magata's footsteps. For instance, on the truck along the Buka main road the mourners not only sang mourning songs and cut taro, but also 'took a rest' from singing to tentatively chat with others on the truck, some of whom they had never met before. They also, occasionally, walked off on their own to buy a bottle of coke at a roadside store, rather than joining the procession to a particular house. Here, it became apparent that the event was not entirely determined by Magata's relations that were being straightened; people were turning these to novel directions. From this perspective, one might understand some aspects of Jimmy's church service, too, as *roror*, going around, although of a less obvious kind. For instance, mourners looked around to see who was standing where around the coffin, or they made tentative attempts at conversation while standing around after church, which eventually turned into a working out of relations among mourners. Pororan Islanders perform in movements, then, what other Melanesians achieve through attention to bodies (e.g. Battaglia 1990), material objects (e.g. Küchler 2002) or the exchange of wealth items (e.g. Foster 1995): a dialectical process of closing and opening up relations, or of gathering up the deceased's life force and dispersing it, as New Irelanders do when they make and then leave to rot the wooden carvings called *malanggan*. Where they differ from all those whose mortuary rites have been mentioned above with the exception of Sabarl Islanders, however, is in their insistence on the 'incompletion' of this process, as we shall see.

Bung Malot: The End of Mourning

Bung malot, the ten-day feast, is ideally held on day ten after the death. It is the end of mourning, when the spirit of the deceased joins the living for the last time for a formal meal. In the case of a person of rank, when the feast must be larger, it can be postponed until day thirty. During this time, the close matrilineal and paternal relatives of the deceased elicit contributions of food—sweet potatoes, rice, fish and pork—that is finally handed out to those who came to cry over the body of the deceased, in order to 'finish their sorrow'. On the morning of the feast, the relatives bring their contribution—the matrilineal relatives usually to the house of the *tsunon* of their *pinaposa*, the paternal relatives to the *tsunon* of theirs. From there, each side brings its contributions to the house of the deceased, where ideally, the feast is held. The *tsunon*, seated on chairs and benches around a table, receive betel nuts and their food baskets first. These contain, on top of the usual layer of four boiled sweet potatoes and a leaf-wrap of rice, the largest portion of pork, two laplap, a packet of sugar or another store-bought item, and an envelope with money, for 'witnessing' the event. With them eats the spirit of the deceased. In many cases, a basket is put aside for the spirit, and the spirit is invited to eat by a short speech given by one of the *pinaposa*'s *tsunon*, or by a whispered prayer. The women in attendance—ideally, all those who came to cry over the body—meanwhile settle down on a canvas spread out at the feast site, usually on the beach. Men usually just stand around the edges of the hamlet. When the *tsunon* have started eating, the women receive betel nuts 'to warm the belly' and then their baskets, smaller ones, filled with sweet potatoes, smaller leaf-wraps of rice, and smaller portions of pork. Ideally, these are distributed in the order of 'closeness' of the recipients to the deceased. Kil always explained, or made sure that someone else was around to explain to me why a particular person would receive his or her baskets at one or the other time.

However, her careful explanations on those occasions clearly fell short of what was happening around, as she admitted. Once, at a *bung malot* held for a Plisoh man, the women handing out baskets at the deceased's house to those who would take them to the guests on the beach were pushing and shoving each other. Some said we should start the distribution, while others said we should wait till the *tsunon* had finished chewing their betel nuts, and others again complained that things weren't in order, and could we not count the baskets again so as to make sure there were enough? The arguments didn't go unnoticed, and eventually, Tsireh got up from his place at the table of the *tsunon* and came over to inquire if the women could not for once get their act together. Eventually, a disorderly line of women carried a first round of baskets to the beach. There, however, they found that some of the closest relatives of the deceased and most active supporters of the *pinaposa* during the mourning period were not there to receive their baskets, and after some noisy deliberation, their baskets were taken back to the deceased's kitchen house and put aside for them there. Of those guests present, some refused to accept their food baskets. They tried to hand it back with emphatic statements of 'paah, I am tired of this' [*tsii*, mi les] or immediately passed it on to a child that happened to be nearby. Others looked inside their baskets and complained that their piece of pork was smaller than that of other people. Others again loudly declared that they weren't hungry. Salu had a brief look at the basket that she had been handed, then left it on the canvas, walked over to a relative's house and took a meal there instead. When I asked why, she said that she didn't want to eat 'in people's full vision' [long ai blong olo man stret]. Others expressed similar sentiments: 'I don't want to eat with everybody looking', 'I don't want people to look at me', 'I feel shy eating in front of other people'.

Everyone attending a *bung malot* seemed to share this nervousness about looks [*ngot*]. The *tsunon* told me they felt exposed to the looks, envy and sorcery that they attract by 'standing up in the eye of the people' [sitting at a table] in order to 'witness' the event. The hosts, too, felt vulnerable, although their concern was mostly with the 'looks' of the spirit of the deceased.[6] The spirit, they feared, might be dissatisfied with the way mourning had been conducted, and might kill another person. In addition, the hosts felt their reputation, although not their physical well-being to be at risk from sharp comments from the women in attendance about the quantity and quality of the food served. These women, in turn, felt vulnerable to looks from others whom they met at the feast, and sometimes more explicitly stated fears of sorcery and love magic transmitted in food. Women of childbearing age tended to avoid eating anything at all at feasts, according to my observations, although they were likely to give in to the temptation posed by freshly boiled or grilled pork upon their return to their hamlet. Only old women stated without ambivalence that they enjoyed the excitement of *bung malot*, which they said they enjoyed 'watching'.

The problem with looks at *bung malot* appeared to hinge on the subtle difference between 'looking to' [a direction or cause, *ngot ne*] and 'looking' or 'looking strongly' [*ngot*] already noted in the context of fishing. Ideally, *bung malot* is an occasion for 'looking to' relations. The hosts of ten-day feasts say that at this occasion, they 'return' food to those who 'looked to' them when they were grieving a death. What is indeed perceived to happen, however, is 'staring' among and between hosts and guests. 'Staring' is said to trigger unexpected and unpredictable action by one or the other, and the emergence of valued, but highly uncertain and potentially dangerous relations. Staring is what happens when people hand fish over upon their return from the sea. It creates a radical open-endedness of relations where, in fact, *bung malot* should achieve closure: a straightening of relations among the relatives of the deceased that exclude the spirit, who has to leave for good after the feast.

There is a contrast to *sinahan* here. During *sinahan*, the 'tightening' of relations is achieved by replacing the multiple, difficult to control movements of a crowd of mobile people with the small gesture of handing over of a card box containing money and other things between two people. This happened precisely as everyone's 'looks' were firmly attached to the decorated body of the wife, who had just emerged from under her pandanus cape. As nobody was looking at this moment of closure, nobody was likely to 'want' anything, that is, nobody was likely to interfere with it. At *bung malot*, by contrast, everyone is looking at the movements of the baskets, at those who distribute them, those who receive them, and at each other while eating. People are observed to interfere, or are suspected of interfering with those movements and with each other. Without the kind of distraction provided at *sinahan*, the looks of people create interferences that prevent the closure of relations.

One effect is that the spirits do not reliably leave Pororan. The presence of spirits of the dead [<u>tevil</u>, *nomnomi*] around the island, and at night even inside the village is a taken-for-granted aspect of Pororan life, although older people educated by white missionaries are somewhat embarrassed by it. People take a torch when walking around at night in order to avoid bumping into spirits, and especially when a person is already sick or otherwise weakened, it is important to watch her back, the side from which spirits come and make her ill. In addition, people maintain relations with spirits of particular relatives who 'look after us here', as explained by people whose houses I stayed at and whose spirits I therefore had to be introduced to. Kil occasionally received visits from her deceased husband at night (like other spirits he had no difficulties with locked doors). She then went to fetch a plate of rice for him, sat down with him while he ate and informed him of the latest news concerning their children. Then she asked him politely to leave, so that we could go back to sleep. The room in which I was staying at Salu's had been empty for many years because her son, who died young, had been laid out there for mourning and was known to still frequent it. Others felt uncomfortable in his presence. A more benign presence around the house was Salu's mother Stella, who kept an eye on things when nobody was home. Some spirits are more dangerous than others, though. The house of a deceased *tsunon* is torn down and the spot left empty for this reason.

Another effect of *bung malot* being carried out the way it is on Pororan, besides the continuing presence of the spirits, are sorcery accusations, which are illegal, but nevertheless used to run high on Pororan after *bung malot*. People falling sick in the weeks after a *bung malot* suspected that someone had 'looked' at them then, or had perhaps 'put something on my food'. Instead of giving the deceased's relations a pleasant finish, then, *bung malot* tended to bring out old arguments, old disagreements about relations among persons, and the sense of insecurity about others' intentions that is so pervasive on Pororan.

This lack of closure is immediately connected, I suggest, to the lack of an expressive form prominent elsewhere in the region: an image. Where other people present images to themselves, the Pororans, it seems, look at each other. Let us take, for comparison, Usen Barok mortuary rites, in which a striking image provides closure to the relation with the deceased, in a 'closed' expressive form at the end of mourning. Wagner (1986b; see also 1987, 2001) argues that in two kinds of mortuary feasts and in their temporal sequence, Usen Barok enact their 'ethos', an ideal of comportment and of relationships to which the self-containment and mutual nurture of the two moieties is central. Nurture and containment are enacted in mortuary feasting at the *taun* [men's house]. In 'closed feasts', which take place immediately after a death, food is provided by the moiety opposite to that of the deceased, and no food must be taken out of the *taun* enclosure. In 'open feasts', the flow of food is reversed. After these two feasts, the Barok hold the *kaba*, at which the dead are 'finished' and a new leader [*orong*] is installed. The *kaba* takes place outside the enclosure altogether, and 'works' by a series of systematic inversions of Usen Barok ethos. For instance, when host and guest moiety openly compete in decorating the *kaba*, the *kaba* reverses the usual distinction between containment and nurture. The containing image of the *taun* and 'ordinary' feasts is itself contained at this event by the incipient power, explained in a later analysis to be a power *over* rather than *of* society (Wagner 2001: 46), of the neophyte *orong*. Out of his will alone, unconstrained by reasons, concerns and symbols, the *kaba* is performed (42). From the vantage point of the *kaba*, which Wagner suggests offers a synchronic, explanatory image to the Usen Barok of their culture, a new definition of ethos is possible, namely 'a style of improvisatory action in response to demonstrated contingencies' (Wagner 1986b: 216).

There are ethnographic resonances in Buka to the three-tier analysis that Wagner extracts from the Barok sequence of feasts. These lie not in feasts as such, certainly not on Pororan, where usually only a single feast, the *bung malot*, is held.[7] They lie, instead, in the directionality of people and food, from the moment of death through activities such as 'following the footsteps' to *bung malot*. Is *bung malot*, then, an image of Pororan social life, as the *kaba* is of Usen Barok 'ethos'?

Bung malot certainly 'elicits' and 'contains' movements and relations, and thus does conform to Wagner's definition of an image. However, this image does not 'work as an image'. It does not make for a moment of revelation on Pororan. The islanders do not use *bung malot* to explain anything to themselves or one another. Why would that be? My suggestion is the following. 'Images' in Wagner's sense are stoppages of movements. At the moment of their stoppage, movements lose their distinctive quality of gradually revealing multiple forms, and posing questions about the single one that will terminate the sequence. Images thus keep relations on hold, and thus render their future highly uncertain. Those moments are the opposite of revelatory to the Pororans. They may nevertheless be valued, as moments that 'hold' the open-endedness of relations, in non-revelatory form, as 'looks'. An example of such valued non-revelatory moments are returns from the sea. In the context of *bung malot*, however, where 'looks' involve the entire community and the spirit of the deceased, they are deeply disturbing.

If 'images' in Wagner's definition do not make moments of revelation on Pororan, as the example of *bung malot* shows, then we need to broaden our theoretical scope and methodological attention to expressive forms beyond 'images'. In the following section, I describe one such form.

Hahur: 'A Mark of Being Human'

The death of a *tsunon* or *hahini* requires specific ritual activities. The body must be placed, not on an ordinary bed, but 'above' on a high bed for the wailing. Furthermore, a wake is held, nowadays usually lasting one night but longer in the past, either at the deceased's *pinaposa's tsuhan* or at his or her house. Although *tsunon*, too, have no longer been buried at sea since colonial times, their hair is still thrown into a particular hole on the reef, and their possessions are scattered nearby. After burial, close female matrilineal relatives, paternal relatives and in-laws of the deceased may choose to remain in confinement inside his or her house. This is called *gum* [sindaun sori, sit down in mourning]. They leave the house only briefly and with their heads covered under pandanus leaf capes, do not wash, dress in black, and eat only cassava and especially bananas [the 'food of the place'] for the mourning period, which usually lasts for twenty-nine days after the death of a person of rank. The moments that I think give the strongest impression of island life, and that the islanders value deeply, are sessions of singing mourning songs held during one or more nights during the mourning period for a person of rank, often from nightfall to sunrise. Their number, duration or omission is, however, entirely contingent upon the decisions of the closest relatives.[8] These sessions are called *hahur*.

Ideally, 'everyone', including the entire village and any visitors who were drawn to the place by the death, gathers at the deceased's *tsuhan* in the evening before *hahur*. Women sit down on the benches that run along the sides of the open-walled *tsuhan*. They sing wordless mourn-ing songs accompanied by the beats of a large slit-gong. They hold twigs or bundles of leaves in their hands. Facing the centre of the *tsuhan*, they swing the twigs out into the *tsuhan* and back towards themselves with small movements of their wrists to the rhythm of the slit-gong, in a movement that resembles the ways in which they throw out fish-ing rods, as they say. At intervals in the course of the night, the singing grows stronger. The deceased's sister and another close female relative, who have left the deceased's house for the night, sit down on a bench placed in the open space of the *tsuhan* for them. In their black mourn-ing clothes and with pandanus leaf capes covering their heads and upper bodies, they sit and wail. One or two women at a time get up from the benches to dance around them. Tap-stepping forwards and backwards, they move their arms and upper bodies as if they were paddling a canoe. Emotions run high, and women switch from sobbing to cheering for the dancers to excited whispering when they point out to each other vari-ous signs indicating the presence of the spirit of the deceased, such as a firefly that appears in the roof of the *tsuhan*. Most memorable about the event, however, are the movements that the women perform in and around the open space of the *tsuhan*. They energetically paddle their imaginary canoes, with whole-body movements much more pronounced than those they usually perform at sea. They may perform sweeping movements, imitating the sweeping of the village. The women along the benches, too, never sit still. Small as it is, the movement of throwing out the twig keeps their entire bodies continuously in motion.

The movements of *hahur* are described as <u>mak blong man</u>, a sign of being human. This, then, is the expressive form in which Pororan Islanders most comprehensively present themselves to themselves, on what they say are the most highly valued occasions of island life. A <u>mak</u>, in common Pororan usage, can be something that holds something else as a potential. Alternatively, it is what remains after that which it marks has disappeared. To my mind, the notion of <u>mak</u> expresses a process of transformation. Is it an image, comparable to the kaba?

Hahur, like the *kaba*, can be understood as an image that closely juxtaposes many of the movements and relations introduced in previous chapters. It is a condensation or gathering into a single event of persons and spirits, wailing and laughing, and of distinctions of gender, rank and kinship. This begins with the presence of women in the *tsuhan*, which is normally reserved for men.[9] It continues with close physical proximity, among others, of in-laws who usually keep a distance from one another, and with sexual license unthinkable at other occasions. Furthermore, laughing and loud wailing, dancing and hitting with twigs—'because they are in grief'—the women participating in *gum* who have emerged from the house of the deceased for the occasion all intertwine. Moreover, spirits, the separation of which from the living is the purpose of mortuary events, are also included in *hahur*. For example, women hear the dim beats of another slit gong alongside their own, and note the sweet smell of a particular flower, associated with graves, sweeping across the *tsuhan* from time to time. Both indicate the overlapping of their own gathering with a dance held by spirits 'in the bush' nearby. Fireflies in the roof of the *tsuhan* indicate spiritual presences at the *tsuhan*, too, which people are usually keen to avoid, but which they welcome on nights of *hahur*: 'You come! You come now and dance, enjoy with us! And then you will leave us forever', the women call out to the deceased.

Furthermore, during *hahur*, the women who sit along the sides of the *tsuhan* and sing hold twigs in their hands that they swing in and out, in and out for hours and hours. These movements of swinging twigs or leaf bundles in and out are likened to movements performed when fishing with a rod. One might suggest, then, that in the nights of mourning after the death of a person of rank, activities are displayed in which Pororan Islanders locate the beginnings of the human world. They perform the <u>mak</u> of this world as it is described in the story of Sia and Hulu. In these inward-outward and upward-downward movements, with their indeterminate beginning and end points, one might perceive both the downward-outward and inward-upward movements by which the islanders objectify matrilineal kinship, and the inward-upward and downward-outward movements by which they objectify a *tsunon*'s achievement of 'pulling' others and settling them down at a particular place. Pororan Islanders witness the past and potential of human relationality when watching and performing the movements of *hahur*.

Wagner's notion of 'figure-ground reversal' appears suitable, then, insofar as *hahur* draws into a ceremonial setting and foregrounds what usually remains at the background—the movements of fishing and, as the story of Sia and Hulu suggests, the beginnings of the human world. Through the foregrounding of their processes of emergence, human relations—more specifically, the relations of matrilineal kinship, rank and power that constituted the person of rank in whose name the event is held—are delegated to the (past or future) background.

However, 'figure-ground reversal' seems too tight a term for giving proper weight to the particularities of the processes that *hahur* brings into view. These are the processes of dissolving movements and social relations into movements of *roror*, and re-perceiving them in tense moments of 'looking', 'eating' and 'wanting' in which *roror* culminates (see chapter 1). These processes of transformation are highly open-ended. All sorts of movements and relations dissolve into *roror*; from *roror*, they re-emerge in a form that is beyond the control of any particular person involved. The islanders' acute sense of the indeterminacy of the transformation of movements and relations, too, is 'marked' in the movements of *hahur*. These movements are highly variable. For instance, the swinging in and out of twigs, which the women told me mimics the swinging in and out of a fishing rod or line and which is dominant throughout the night, occasionally turns into tap-stepping backward and forward, movements of paddling a canoe, or of sweeping the floor when a woman gets up to dance in the centre of the *tsuhan*. The women's movements increase and decrease in vigour, expand and contract in space, and change shape without losing their distinctiveness. That is, the movements of *hahur* gather into themselves and mark various movements and activities of human life as irreducible to one another. They transform them into and out of one another in an open-ended sequence. Furthermore, Pororan women performed, for me and for their own entertainment, any and all of these movements when I mentioned *hahur* to them. I also observed, more than once, older Pororan women move into the forward-backward tap-steps of *hahur* while sweeping the space in front of their house or when testing the elasticity of a fishing rod for an outing the next day, and I also heard them hum mourning songs. Kil's little performance on the reef was another instance (see chapter 1). Ad-hoc audiences sometimes formed on such occasions and cheered, and children happily lined up behind the woman and followed her movements. On such occasions, *hahur* gathered up into itself and temporarily kept on hold everyday life far beyond its obvious time and setting.

Following up on a point that Wagner (2001) makes in a later discussion of Barok mortuary rites, I suggest that *kaba* and *hahur* correspond to two different ways of appreciating a figure-ground relation in Euro-America. One is to focus on the 'closed', self-referential image of a dialectical relation (Wagner 2001: 43). Such 'closed' images are, for example, Gestalt Psychology's images that make a spectator's eye oscillate between an encompassed and an encompassing object (a vase, or two faces), which are perceived alternately as figure and ground. The *kaba* is such a closed image. But secondly, one might also focus on the open-endedness of processes of figure-ground transformation.[10] This is how *hahur* is apprehended on Pororan. Although the movements of fishing provide a 'closed' or containing image of Pororan understandings of the processes by which social relations appear and disappear, the open-ended transformation of these movements during the night of singing and dancing indicates people's strong interest in indeterminate transformations, or revelations.

Finishing Mourning on the Mainland

Hahur is held on the mainland, too. However, on the mainland, it is labelled as 'fun' or 'play' of no consequence to ordinary life, comparable to that of the Baining 'play' (Fajans 1997). On the mainland, *hahur* is 'finished' along with the entire mourning period at *bung malot*. 'Now you need to watch', Ngasi alerted me once as we attended a *bung malot* together, just as Kil had on Pororan. 'Now you will see who is who here.' Here, unlike on Pororan, I did. So did everyone else. The *tsunon* among the guests sat around the benches of the *tsuhan*, and the women stayed outside on canvases. First, the *tsunon* were handed their baskets, not jointly as on Pororan, but one by one. The *tsunon* of the host group stood next to a helper calling out the name of each recipient, in a particular order of rank that Ngasi explained to me, and everyone watched on as another helped brought him his basket. The distribution of baskets to the women outside proceeded in batches. A stack of baskets was given to the senior woman of a *ngorer*, and she distributed them to her relatives, who were sitting close together. The women of the host group co-operated silently and efficiently. No complaints about stares occurred. 'That's it. Everything is straight now. It is over now', Ngasi said, obviously relieved, as we left the event. 'It is over', she repeated a couple of times along the road, increasingly brightly. 'All this heaviness is gone.

The heaviness of preparing for the feast. The heaviness of the smell. This time of craziness at night is over.' (I understand the 'craziness at night' as a reference to *hahur*, as well as to the disturbances caused by spirits that had woken people up again and again in the mourning period.)

On Pororan, of course, nothing was over after *bung malot*. *Hahur* spilled over into everyday life, and the spirit remained among the living. The lack of closure that Pororan *bung malot* afford, especially by comparison with those held on the mainland, offers an ethnographic version of the paradox noted by Jane Fajans for the Baining of New Britain: 'the maintenance of a coherent cultural identity by an incoherent culture, and the continued stability, resilience, and successful self-reproduction of a structureless society' (1997: 4–5). Unfortunately, the Pororans' ways of establishing continuity with the past, and of maintaining a distinct identity without making an 'image' of it were not recognized in the context of formal Bougainvillean politics in 2004–05. They were not recognizable as <u>kastom</u>. <u>Kastom</u> and the Pororans' reservations against reviving it will be discussed in the following chapter.

NOTES
· · · · · · ·

1. My theoretical interest is related to that of Knut Rio (2007) in writing about 'Thirds' on Ambrym, Vanuatu as a Melanesian conceptualization of what keeps re-appearing in Western science as the problem between structure and process. I do not engage further with Rio's work here, however, because unravelling the ethnographic contrasts between Ambrym and Pororan Islanders' interests in separating and tracing the connections between process and structure, respectively, would take up too much space here.

2. The Sunday rest was only introduced to Pororan by missionaries in the early twentieth century. Nevertheless, in 2004–05, it was said to be an integral part of 'good ancestral ways' [<u>gutpela pasin blong tumbuna</u>] at all places where I stayed in Buka. The Pororans often told me that their ancestors, especially those who had been catechists at the mission school at Burunotoui, had been better Christians than their descendants are nowadays. Through them, the Sunday rest had become a part of 'good settled life at the village' [<u>gutpela stap long ples</u>].

3. <u>Ol lain blong en stret</u> [his immediate relatives] went first, as my neighbour at church pointed out, followed by those who were <u>klostu</u> [close] to him and then those who were <u>longwe liklik</u> [a little further away].

4. Explanations of what they were meant to see included: a very young dead person, so that they themselves will keep the Sunday rest; a young dead person killed by matrilineal spirits, to teach them that it is bad to quarrel within one's *pinaposa*; who is who at the village, because at this time, it will be clear; and the procedures that should be taken after a death.

5. Neither the *tsunon* in charge and his relatives nor the Pororans, who said that they too cut taro along the road, could explain the significance of this.

6. Spirits are sometimes encountered on Pororan in human form, but with glaringly bright eyes.

7. At other locations, feasts are also held on the first and fifth day after death, but the islanders excuse themselves on the grounds of a shortage of pigs—or of 'human beings' and 'proper thinking' as some add half-jokingly.

8. At each of them, mourners have to be feasted with pork, which is why, according to the islanders, they are often called off on Pororan. The description of *hahur* below is therefore based on my observations at the hamlet of Gogonuna, Lontis Village, on the Buka north coast. Although I have never observed *hahur* on Pororan, the islanders' descriptions suggest that it is performed in a very similar way.

9. I was also told that after the death of one of the eminent Pororan *tsunon* of the past, the Pororan *hahini* were asked to play soccer in men's trousers and shoes. This would be an extreme example of condensing, and thereby making apparent the contingency but significance of gender differences.

10. As exemplified, for example, by a quotation attributed to Max Ernst, and printed on a wall at the Max Ernst Haus in Brühl: 'I suddenly felt my "visual faculties" enhanced such that I saw the newly created objects appear on a new ground.' I note, but make no point of it here, that Max Ernst has drawn extensively on what was then called 'primitive' or 'tribal' art.

CHAPTER 6

Movements and Kastom

Pororan interests in keeping relations open-ended will be held up here against the Bougainvillean government's suggestions of 'reviving <u>kastom</u>' in 2004–05. My purpose in doing so is three-fold. Firstly, I aim to draw together my argument about Pororan Islanders' mode of objectifying human relations in movements up to this point. Secondly, the political implications of this mode of objectification for Pororan Islanders will be highlighted. Finally, the contrast between Buka mainlanders' mostly positive responses to the government's suggestions and the Pororans' reservations offers a perspective from which to explore what precisely it is about the objectification of social relations in movements that sets their saltwater sociality apart from that of people 'in the bush'.

<u>Kastom</u> has been a subject of interest to anthropologists working in the Pacific since the early 1980s, when researchers across various disciplines attended to processes of post-colonial nation-making (e.g. Anderson 1983) and the 'invention of tradition' (Hobsbawm and Ranger 1983). Since then, a lively literature, some of it with an echo far beyond Pacific anthropology (esp. Hanson 1991), has emerged on Pacific 'inventions' of tradition, called <u>kastom</u> or <u>kastam</u> in many areas of Melanesia (Bolton 2003; Foster 1992; Jolly and Thomas 1992; Keesing 1992; Keesing and Tonkinson 1982; Leach 2003b, 2004; Linnekin and Poyer 1990; Otto 1992). One point emerges very clearly from this literature. This is that <u>kastom</u> has developed in highly particular ways, and with very particular outcomes of inclusion and exclusion among various constellations of persons, institutions and interests.

For instance, Lissant Bolton's (2003) analysis of the history of the Vanuatu Cultural Centre and, within it, the Women's Culture Project demonstrates the historical specificity of the interrelation of notions of <u>kastom</u>, place, and gender in Vanuatu. Bolton shows how the understanding and work of particular persons and institutions, among them radio producers and the staff and director of the Cultural Centre, have

Notes for this section begin on page 185

contributed to the emergence of, and changes to the salience and specific connotations of <u>kastom</u>. Intended as a means of promoting national integration, no attention was paid at first to the inclusion of women in <u>kastom</u> activities. This has since changed, and Bolton has analysed the role of the Women's Culture Project, in particular, in this change. Her work shows how hard it was for women to gain recognition for their activities, knowledge and skills as <u>kastom</u>, without surrendering to a Western feminist agenda that does not fit Melanesian women's ambitions. My aim here is to similarly outline, although more briefly, historically specific notions of <u>kastom</u> that were employed in Bougainville in 2004–05, and to argue in ethnographically specific terms why Pororan Islanders, in contrast to many ni-Vanuatu women and in contrast to Buka mainlanders, were not excited to participate in Bougainvillean activities of 'reviving <u>kastom</u>'.

In Buka, the term <u>kastom</u> was employed in 2004–05 in two different ways. The first is broadly inclusive. Buka people say: 'Our <u>kastom</u> here in Buka is all the same.' 'The clans', 'the chiefs' and '*tsuhan*', or 'matriliny' and the 'traditional leadership system', along with mortuary and marriage rites, were the most commonly stated or implied components of 'Buka <u>kastom</u>'. For instance, Buka people in Town and in the villages pointed out to me and to one another their *pinaposa* connections across the area, and the ease with which people found distant relatives at various locations who supported them on travels. They also remarked that all places had *tsunon* and *hahini*, and that *tsunon* of different locations closely interacted, for example, when *tsunon* of one local branch of a *pinaposa* witnessed the 'first achievements' of a future *tsunon* of another local branch. Buka people also noted shared or overlapping stories of migration, and the participation of people from across the area in one another's marriage and mortuary rites. Especially among people active in formal politics in Buka Town, attempts were made to integrate 'Buka <u>kastom</u>' with the <u>kastom</u> of other ethnographic areas in Bougainville. It was pointed out, for instance, that all of Bougainville was matrilineal (although the exceptions of Buin in the south and, arguably, Nissan Island in the north were noted) and had 'traditional leaders', although not all inherited their status. In addition, Buka *tsuhan* were compared, for instance, to Nasioi men's houses through the common Tok Pisin term <u>haus boi</u>. Pororan Islanders, too, lay a claim to <u>kastom</u>, and to participation in wider Buka sociality in these terms. People's use of the term <u>kastom</u> in this broadly inclusive sense was not delimited by the colonial or postcolonial political setting (see Leach 2003b; Keesing 1992). It was used, instead, for drawing attention to particular valued relations that are traced further back than the term <u>kastom</u> itself existed in Buka.

More prominent in Pororan Islanders' usage of the term kastom, however, was another sense, namely that of kastom as a particular process of documenting, establishing agreement upon and reviving knowledge of the past, as promoted by politicians in Buka Town. The islanders told me that some time before my arrival, the *tsunon* brought the news of the government's interest in kastom from their meetings with other *tsunon* in Buka Town. They reported that all Bougainvillean communities were asked to straighten and write down their kastom. Where exactly the request originated, was of no concern to the islanders. What mattered to them was that the government had asked people to document genealogies and migration histories, that is, to 'write down the clans', and to clarify and put down in writing traditional leadership and land ownership. In addition, cultural shows and the teaching of ancestral craft skills (such as mat making) at schools had also been suggested. Some islanders speculated that documents of genealogies, migration stories and land claims were to provide evidence in case of land disputes, so that those would not, as in the mining area in 1988, develop again into long-term fighting. In addition, cultural shows should instill pride in young people that was independent of fighting experiences. While not everyone made such strong connections, a vague idea that the revival of kastom was aimed at promoting peace after the Bougainville Crisis appeared to be shared.

It is in this second sense that Pororan Islanders claimed very firmly and somewhat sadly that they did not know about kastom, that they were confused [faul] about it, and that they tended to screw it up [bagarapim].

Their sense of exclusion should give pause to think. The Pororans have a very keen sense of the indeterminate fate and mutability of all human relations. It is on the basis of the assumption of the indeterminacy of human relationality, I suggest, that they participate gladly in wider Buka sociality. Furthermore, the islanders perceive the talk and power of their own *tsunon* to be contingent upon their own performances of those movements that the *tsunon* elicit. Why, then, would the islanders accept the suggestions of the government regarding kastom as immutable ones, to which one could either live up to or with regard to which one could fail?

From my own perspective, gained from travelling back and forth between the island and Town and having access there to white people as well as Bougainvillean politicians, the government's suggestions of documenting kastom appear historically specific, contingent upon the interests of particular people, and therefore challengeable and mutable. I suspect—although I am lacking firsthand knowledge of the region prior to 2004–05 for evidence—that the genesis of the project of 'reviving kastom' could be traced in formal workshops and negotiations during the peace process, as well as in informal conversations between Bougainvilleans and others in the region. Such conversations were taking place in 2004–05 between politicians and politically interested people with access to Buka Town or Arawa, local staff of NGOs, foreign advisors to the government, staff of donor agencies, and members of the Truce Monitoring and later the Peace Monitoring Group. In 2004–05 and on a visit in 2006, I had some occasion to observe such discussions and witness the excitement, to Bougainvillean and foreign participants, of linking Bougainvillean experiences and political imaginations to those of other Pacific Islanders through the terms of kastom, tradition and, sometimes, culture.

However, few Pororan Islanders had any share in, or even knowledge of this excitement in 2004–05. Serious efforts were made by Bougainvillean politicians and foreigners to consult ordinary villagers about autonomy and their needs as Bougainvillean communities. However, despite the availability of radio and interpersonal communication through the workmen who went back and forth between the island and Town, information that reached the islanders was often incomplete and outdated. The excitement of face-to-face conversations with people from various countries and regions that characterized discussions in Town did not come across. For most islanders, 'the government' was 'above' at its buildings, which were frighteningly neat and frequented by white people. Their comments suggest that, while particular people 'at the government' could be tapped, the suggestions made about 'reviving kastom' were beyond their reach in 2004–05. Correspondingly, the Pororans told me of the project of reviving kastom as a demand that was simply to be accepted and implemented. When they found this difficult, they perceived of these difficulties as an insufficiency on their part, not on the government's.

My own research was perceived of, initially, as guided by essentially the same interests in kastom as those of the government, as utilizing similar methods for collecting knowledge, and therefore as not at all suitably located on Pororan, where people did not know about kastom. When I first arrived, the islanders knew already what I had come for. Given that I was an anthropologist, it had to be kastom. Some suggested quite strongly that I find a better place for research, because they, as they pointed out with some embarrassment, knew very little about kastom. However, sensing that they had no objections against my presence on the island other than that they feared my research would not turn out well with them, I suggested that I might nevertheless stay, and that we might work out a way of how my research could, perhaps, come along to my and their satisfaction. With the support of particular people on the island, my presence was soon acceptable, as far as I know, to all islanders. Many greatly enjoyed the stories of snow I had to tell. Reservations about my research remained strong, however. Although I downplayed those aspects of my research that were most immediately related to government projects—the documentation of clans, of rank and of resource management—from the beginning, the islanders noticed my reliance on the same basic methods that the government had suggested for reviving kastom: writing things down, drawing maps, and drawing genealogies or otherwise mapping relations. They also pointed out to me that I thought they were stupid whenever I reacted, as sometimes happened, with impatience to their firm statement that 'we cannot know this now', or 'who knows', which were their most common answers to my questions. However, gradually some of the islanders began to respond to my insistence that it had to be my and not their stupidity that was causing the problem. They began to tell me what else I should ask, or how to find out for myself what they told me firmly they could not tell me. Most importantly, they told me to watch people's movements. In response to my efforts to make a point of my availability to questions, challenges, criticisms and random conversations, the islanders gradually formulated such challenges and told me how to write them down.

From these challenges and criticisms, it is possible to specify the particular divergences in understandings and interests that prevented Pororan Islanders not only from fulfilling some of my default expectations of how I would learn about island relations, but also from fulfilling the government's requests at reviving kastom. The following sections will pursue these divergences. My focus will be on the three governmental suggestions most widely discussed and most forcefully dismissed on the island in 2004–05. These were the documentation of 'clans' or 'matriliny'; the 'straightening' of 'traditional leadership', that is, of the relative rank of all Pororan tsunon and their respective ngorer; and 'straightening the ground', that is, working out land tenure. Through this discussion, I take up again the topics of mothers and relations of pinaposa, of fathers and tsunon, of places and groups, and I aim to state the significance of the Pororans' objectification of these in movements in terms of wider Bougainvillean interests.

As will be shown, the Pororans' reservations about 'writing down kastom' allow for specifying three points of difference between objectifying relations on paper or in movements, and three qualities of relations to which the Pororans' mode of objectification draws attention. First, the single form in which relations appear when written down on paper cuts off what Pororan Islanders are keenly interested in when watching movements. This is the gradual and indeterminate process by which relations come to appear in a sequence of forms, and the question of the form that they will take in the end. Second, because they appear in a single form, these relations are exposed to the interference, and perhaps appropriation of others, who may turn them to their own ends. The Pororans like to avoid this. Third, writing down relations on paper in a single form would cut off, including physically, Pororan possibilities for extending them into the future through movements.

Apparently, the objectification of social relations in roads that link places is more compatible with the objectification of social relations on paper. Buka mainlanders, who privilege roads over movements in their apprehension of relations, were happy to respond to the government's requests of writing down the clans and straightening traditional leadership. While the mainlanders were closely involved in Bougainvillean cultural politics, the Pororans opted out. This had tangible consequences, as will be shown below.

'Writing Down the Clans'

In discussions about <u>kastom</u> that I overheard and took part in at Buka Town, it was often stated that a good knowledge and strong sense of matrilineal kinship among Bougainvilleans were crucial to a lasting peace in the region. Matrilineal relations had provided support in times of hardship during the Bougainville Crisis, and had provided the framework in which people could grow up safely, with respect for others and with knowledge of <u>kastom</u>. As Moses Havini, a prominent Bougainvillean politician living in Sydney at the time wrote:

> The concept of peace in Bougainville society was and is in its own intrinsic values. Found within its matrilineal family system and the very fabric of its society. The matrilineal system established values since time immemorial that [were and still are] synonymous with stability . . . every individual is significant in the family; each family is a valued member of a clan, each clan is an asset to one of the four tribes constituting North Bougainville society. Every person is therefore an asset to Bougainville society in the same way as a citizen is an asset to a nation. . . . (2000)

According to the Pororan *tsunon*, the intention of the government was that by writing down genealogies, meeting more frequently and formally, and, very importantly, running Australian-introduced microfinance societies with matrilineal relatives, people would re-gain a sense of the importance of mutual support in their clans, which in many areas had been disrupted by the Crisis. Clans or matriliny, then, would re-gain the integrative function that the above quote suggests they had in the past, and that would provide a foundation for Bougainvillean autonomous political structures. Written genealogies in particular should make an object of these relations.

However, as the Pororan *tsunon* who tried compiling such genealogies noted, no one on the island appeared to take any interest in them, and people seemed much more interested in watching and performing movements and everyday tasks instead. With regard to my own genealogies, which I drew during conversations with the islanders and with their help, the Pororans often pointed out their deficiency. Put briefly, the potentially open-ended expansion of connections traced through women that Pororan Islanders value so highly did not become apparent in them. The islanders used to stipulate connections, in a breath, that ran in various directions and far beyond the circumscribed space that paper appeared to offer. When trying to capture these connections in my notebooks, I was faced with the choice between two evils. One was to cut the connections to the size of the paper, and thereby dismiss one of their key qualities, their expansiveness and open-endedness. I did so once, to the anger of the islanders who told me to get a bigger notebook. The other option was to fill many pages with genealogies and accounts of relations of co-operation as they became apparent at particular moments in time, and to accept their incompleteness. The latter was, it seemed to me, the approach of one of the local priests, who had spent many years collecting such knowledge and observed that there was always more to it. It was also, I think, what those *tsunon* were trying to communicate who refused to show me the genealogies they had begun to draw on the grounds that they were 'not finished'.

More specifically, writing down genealogies seemed insufficient to the task of documenting connections traced through women without omitting the highly valued potential for novel relations to emerge at any time. On various occasions, the shape and genealogical levels of my drawings of genealogies seemed to animate the Pororans to stipulate further and further connections. They enjoyed criss-crossing my genealogies with their fingers, drawing lines that linked people in many different ways. They also used to triumphantly point out multiple ways of connecting blocks of genealogies that I had laid out separately. These reactions to my attempts at writing down genealogies were entirely congruent with Pororan women's more general tendency to respond to my questions that were phrased in terms of *pinaposa* by expanding connections further and further. For example, when I asked three women who were sitting on the beach chewing betel nuts about their respective *pinaposa*, they said that they were all of Mulul, and wasn't it obvious that they were all of 'one mother' since they were sharing their betel nuts? When a fourth woman joined them and was handed a betel nut immediately, I stipulated that this woman, too, must be of Mulul. The women laughed and said well, no, but yes, for the purpose of chewing betel, 'I think we are all of one mother'. They immediately and quite seriously set about the task of reckoning connections to this woman that had their history in the exchange of ripe bananas, in help with making copra and other small gestures. From this and other occasions I learned what Pororan women valued: the possibilities of expanding connections, and relations of mutual help that appeared sometimes burdensome but also necessary and highly valuable. But I learned of nothing that could have been very easily 'put on paper' in genealogical drawings.

This is not to suggest that the values that Pororan Islanders locate in 'following one's mother' cannot be rendered on paper. Susan McKinnon's account of the tracing of female bloodlines and asymmetrical relations of alliance between wife-givers and wife-takers in the Tanimbar Archipelago, Eastern Indonesia is worth mentioning here. It contains diagrams of relations traced through women that I suspect Pororan Islanders would immediately recognize as images of the value of 'following one's mother' (McKinnon 1991: 113). The fact that Tanimbar has not, to my knowledge, been described as matrilineal should not distract one from these parallels that may be drawn between Tanimbarese careful tracing of their lines of blood through women and the value that Pororan Islanders locate in 'following one's mother'. With respect to the islanders' interest in open-ended processes and the indeterminacy of relations, anthropologists have drawn attention to the value, to some people, of surprise (e.g. Astuti 1995; Rutherford 2003). In addition, various ethnographies exist that describe kinship as process and attend to its imaginations in ethnographically specific ways. An example from a matrilineal group close to Pororan is Susanne Küchler's processual analysis of matriliny among the Tikana in northern New Ireland (Küchler 2002). Küchler's analysis grounds in the Tikana image of a skin as both a passage and a container. Matrilineal kinship, she argues, is best understood as a process of expanding and contracting relations in analogy to the operation of a skin. My analysis in previous chapters aimed to build on such approaches, remaining very close to the ways in which Pororan Islanders speak about following one's mother. The Bougainvillean government's expectations about matrilineal kinship offer an external perspective on these, from which the islanders' particular interests can usefully be reviewed. At the same time, the comparison shows that in Bougainville, objectifying relations in movements makes it hard to conform to government standards. The question is thus one of regional political, as well as theoretical interest.

Straightening Traditional Leadership

Forerunners to the government's suggestion of reviving traditional leadership as a tool for promoting peace, law and order, and stability may be traced far into Bougainvillean history (see Regan 2000; for the Haku language area, see Sagir 2003, 2005). Arguably, an origin may be located in the system of indirect leadership by the German colonial administration. From German colonial times, attempts were made to include traditional leaders, sometimes called chiefs, in formal government, usually at its lowest, local tier. The aim was to thereby draw on traditional authority as, presumably, the cheapest and most effective way of governing dispersed villages. This basic proposition has continued to hold conviction across Papua New Guinean independence and Bougainvillean separatism. Local Government Councils and Councils of Chiefs have drawn on traditional authority for purposes of governance in various ways. As early as the late 1960s, Bougainvilleans noted the importance of tradition, including that of leadership, for avoiding novel problems that would now be described in terms of 'law and order' (Hannett 1969a, 1969b). When young Bougainvillean intellectuals returned from their studies on the Papua New Guinea mainland with ideas of Bougainvillean independence, they acted mindfully of traditional leadership and carefully included traditional leaders in their lobby work for independence from Papua New Guinea. The Rimoldis' ethnography of the Hahalis Welfare society gives a close-up view on the role that traditional leaders have played, and on shifting perceptions of what their role ought to be, in a particular political movement of the late colonial period, the Hahalis Welfare Society (Rimoldi and Rimoldi 1992). Questions of traditional authority again became virulent before the outbreak of the Bougainville Crisis, when increasing economic inequality was seen to undermine it (see Ghai and Regan 2000).

During the Bougainville Crisis, various innovations were made to include traditional leaders in formal political structures. Traditional leaders played an important role in various areas as advisors to younger leaders of armed factions. At the same time, many remained sufficiently uninvolved in acts of physical violence for serving as important mediators in the peace process (although their influence varied, depending on the particularities of Crisis history in their areas and villages). The success of traditional leaders as mediators and their resulting position of authority in post-Crisis Bougainville provide the immediate backdrop to discussions about the importance of <u>kastom</u>, and especially traditional leadership, for enduring peace. Oral accounts that I collected suggest a variety of relations of association, support, competition and strong opposition between traditional leaders and the fighters and leaders of various factions. Nevertheless, in 2004–05 Bougainvilleans and foreign advisors generally portrayed traditional leaders as a hopeful alternative to the rule of young men who terrorized villagers with guns or who burnt down houses. Pororan Islanders' statements on these matters were clear: the *tsunon*, who discouraged the 'young people' from joining the fighting on one or the other side, are to be credited for the fact that no fighters of either faction ever made an appearance on Pororan, and that the island remained a peaceful place during the Crisis.

However, the government's suggestion to clarify who these leaders were, and to discuss, identify and document their relations of relative rank, met with no enthusiasm on Pororan. In contrast to *tsunon* at other locations in Buka, the Pororan *tsunon* made no attempts to address this issue explicitly. Instead, they took great care to keep their divergent versions of the island's history to themselves, and to tell them only to members of their own *pinaposa*. (And to me, once they assumed that I had a sufficiently clear understanding of island life so that I would not confront other *tsunon* with them directly.) The simplest and most commonly stated reason against 'straightening' migration stories was that it might trigger bitter arguments and divisions, and perhaps even fighting between the followers of different *tsunon*. That is, what the government had intended as a measure to promote peace would not work in this way on the island.

Why should the government's strategy not work on Pororan? I draw here on another ethnographic case, that of the Arosi of Makira, who similarly avoid confronting one another over questions of settlement history and the relative status of matrilineages (M. Scott 2000, 2007). Privately, knowledgeable people from different matrilineages tell stories by which they claim for their lineage the status of *auhenua*, of autochthonous lineage, in their own settlement area. However, they do not confront members of other matrilineages with these stories, and may not even disclose them to younger members of their own matrilineage, out of fear that those might do so and thereby spoil village peace. The fragile consensus among the Arosi is that in the coastal area where they have been living since the colonial period, none of the matrilineages with living members in the present has the status of *auhenua*, of autochthonous lineage in the land. Scott reports and analyses several stated reasons for the Arosi preference of such a consensus over confrontation, and for claiming ignorance rather than knowledge of their lineage history in front of others. He explains that the arguments that knowledgeable people aim to avoid are highly undesirable because Arosi lineage histories are not, as reported from elsewhere in Melanesia, strategic knowledge to be kept secret until a moment when they can profitably be revealed, for instance in land disputes. Instead, a lineage history 'describes the very ontological nature of a matrilineage as an entity inseparably fused with its ancestral land . . . ' (60). In challenging the history of other matrilineages, Arosi challenge 'the fundamental nature and possibility of the other lineage's existence' (61). Conversely, in exposing their own knowledge, they expose themselves to such fundamental challenges. Another twist to the problem is that, in claiming for their own matrilineage the status of *auhenua*, knowledgeable people would effectively undercut their own credibility in doing so. Claims to status run counter to the behaviour appropriate to the members of the *auhenua* lineage. These people must be peaceable, generous and welcoming to others at their village. Making claims to *auhenua* status explicit, then, is the surest way of diminishing respect among the villagers for one's own knowledge, and one's lineage's status.

Pororan Islanders state similar reasons for not talking openly, and for not confronting one another over questions of relative rank. The *tsunon* only gradually began to tell me migration stories in which their own claims to having 'pulled' and 'settled down' other groups were made explicit. In similar terms as the Arosi, the Pororan *tsunon* noted, most generally speaking, the potential for anger and fighting among their followers, should they begin to argue over their histories. Also like the Arosi, they considered 'talk about power' to discredit the knowledge of those who claim it for themselves. As for the Arosi, saving their knowledge for land disputes did not appear to be their main concern. No such disputes had occurred for some time in the past, and none were anticipated in the near future.

While the stated reasons of Pororan *tsunon* for not talking about power resonate with those that Arosi state for not disclosing lineage histories, their most basic underlying assumptions differ. Scott (2000) argues that Arosi claims to ignorance and their fear of the occasional outbursts of challenges to one another's claims to *auhenua* status is a post-colonial and Christian transformation of a wider Solomon Islands social polarity of continuity and destruction. The particularities of Arosi claims to ignorance about lineage histories must be located, furthermore, in the context of the Arosi poly-ontology. Arosi think of the original state of the world as one of already differentiated matrilineages that gradually became 'entangled' through co-residence, mutual help and exogamous marriage. Where differentiation is the original state of the world, Scott suggests, the main concern of human action is creating cohesion, or the continuity of social life at a multi-lineage village. Knowledge of lineage histories however, once made explicit, would achieve the opposite. The articulation of exclusive claims to *auhenua* status would pose a threat to the integrity of the village. For this reason, although at times such exclusive claims are necessary to assert the difference of the *auhenua*, Arosi more commonly tend to avoid them.

On Pororan, I suggest that claims to relative power go to the heart, most specifically, of the power [*nitsunon*] of the *tsunon* who makes them. They are perceived to diminish it immediately. The reasons for this perception must be located in the context of some basic Pororan assumptions about and appreciation of certain qualities of relations, which movements, as objectifications of relations, draw special attention to. One may hear such basic assumptions and concerns speak through the islanders', especially the *tsunon*'s, more specific stated reasons for not confronting one another with mutually incompatible migration histories. A *tsunon*'s talk about his own power is said to 'shoot his own leg' for two reasons. Firstly, a *tsunon* who perceives a need to talk about his own power, surely, is no *tsunon* at all, since no one else is 'witnessing' his status, and no one is making his power apparent by moving in relation to him in particular ways, which resembles the movements known to the islanders from stories of the past. If he was powerful, it would be obvious from his 'pulling' of people to his settlement, and his 'throwing away' especially of food, and of generosity more generally, at feasts and when hosting guests. This makes the most general assumption of Pororan Islanders about relations apparent: If they cannot be perceived in people's movements, they cannot be known to exist.

While it is crucial that relations are perceptible (in movements), it is equally crucial that they are not fully exposed, all at once and in a single form and moment. If they are, they will 'finish'. The islanders often state gloomily: 'Husat itoktok long paua, bai dai hariap.' [Whoever speaks of power will soon die.] The logic is the same as when the *tsunon* or the wife at a *sinahan* 'stand up' in everyone's vision. Talk, just as visibility, can attract the envy of competitors, as well as the anger of the ancestors. This is why the islanders reacted with anger and refused to answer when I asked them, early on in my fieldwork, who was *tsunon*. They said they would not tell me. When I asked, then, how else I could learn who was *tsunon*, so that I might behave respectfully towards them, they told me to watch people's movements. The *tsunon*, they pointed out, are those whose heads people take care not to be above. Here, then, movements achieve what 'straightening relations', as suggested by the government, will not: a revelation that draws people's attention to a person's power, but avoids making it apparent in a definite form that would 'finish' it.

It follows that the islanders' reservations about reviving <u>kastom</u> must be understood through a fundamental incompatibility between the islanders' basic assumptions about relations and the government's basic assumptions about 'traditional leadership'. The government expected clarification, and therefore peace and stability, to result from discussing ('straightening') and eventually agreeing on and documenting ('writing down') a single and binding version of relations of rank. To the Pororans, however, such a process of discussion would immediately put into question the very 'traditional authority' of the entire meeting of the *tsunon* that the government was intending to strengthen.

But while this may explain why the islanders avoided 'straightening' and 'writing down' relations of rank, it cannot do away with the problematic political and practical implications for Pororan Islanders. The islanders' reservations about agreeing on a single hierarchical order of representatives meant that Pororan *tsunon* remained relatively unknown and invisible to the government during my stay on the island. It was notable how little was known about them beyond the island, in contrast to the *tsunon* of other locations. This posed serious problems to Pororan Islanders' dealings with outsiders. None of the *tsunon* provided a clearly apparent point of contact for the government, NGOs or foreign donors, for instance. While several *tsunon* entertained relations with such outsiders, none of them could speak for, or was seen to represent, the community as a whole. As a consequence, Pororan Islanders were somewhat marginal to regional affairs, including projects such as the distribution of water tanks to communities. Although the Pororans, like others in the region, had a Council of Chiefs, with chairs who should have provided such points of contact, they were not visible enough to be effective in this regard.

However, not only relations with outsiders but also relations to people at other locations in the Buka area were channelled through Buka Town and the meeting of the *tsunon* there, and were thus affected by the Pororans' relative invisibility. In 2004–05, relations between *tsunon* of the same matrilineal group in different locations were most commonly re-established at formal political meetings (for practical and financial reasons). It can thus be expected that, in the longer term, relations between those *tsunon*, too, might be coloured by the Pororans' relative lack of prominence at those meetings. If so, the implications for saltwater-mainland relations would be profound. I have shown in chapter 4 how those hinged, in 2004–05, on the formal recognition of island *tsunon* by their mainland counterparts, which allowed them to be complacent about the differences between mainlanders' account of their shared relations and their own sense of it. Should those processes of formal recognition be affected by the relative invisibility of Pororan *tsunon* at those meetings, the capacity of Pororan Islanders to maintain their saltwater mode of apprehending relations, despite the contrasts to the mainlanders', would most likely be reduced.

Straightening the Ground

According to the Pororans and to my own observations in Buka Town, the suggestion that people sort out their claims to land at the village were made much more tentatively, and had a much more ambiguous status on the government's agenda than the documentation of matrilineal kinship and the straightening of traditional leadership. Some people argued that land tenure should, in fact, not be discussed at all yet, because of its association with the Bougainville Crisis. As they explained, the Bougainville Crisis had come about, in the end, because a group of Nasioi traditional landowners who were unhappy with the mining agreement wanted to re-gain control over their land. They broadened their base of support by linking their claims to their particular piece of land to broader demands that Bougainvilleans control Bougainville. The connection appealed to people, and the conflict spread. However, the Bougainville Crisis ended not with Bougainvilleans' full control over land, but with a temporary status of limited autonomy until a referendum over independence would be held. In 2004–05, the compromise formula of autonomy was officially supported by all but those leaders who had shut themselves off in the 'No Go Zone' around the mine. However, under the official consensus lay muted disagreements, disappointment over the outcome of the peace process in some, and disappointment over having become involved in the Crisis in the first place in other cases. Many of those disappointments, and many of the practical difficulties that politicians in Buka Town were struggling with, had to do with claims to particular pieces of land.

One such problem, for instance, concerned recent settlers in particular districts of Arawa Town, formerly inhabited by employees of the mining company. Some of those districts were being re-claimed by 'traditional owners', who argued that they should 'boss' their own land, now that Bougainville was autonomous. The recent settlers, meanwhile, demanded the government's protection as people displaced by the Crisis.

The problem was confounded by the fact that small arms were still in circulation, and reportedly quite a number of them in the districts at issue. Another, less immediately explosive but nevertheless serious set of difficulties concerned Buka Town itself. Here, the government owned too little land for housing the growing administration. Some traditional landowners were claiming exorbitant amounts in rent for government offices and employees' homes, as people working within the administration complained. This was seen to threaten the development of an adequate administrative infrastructure for the Autonomous Region. Thus, administration staff and politicians in Town were treading around questions of land ownership carefully. They avoided any statement that could further raise the emotional stakes and monetary demands made in the context of arguments over land and its traditional ownership.

At the same time, land ownership was too closely bound up with issues of traditional leadership and matrilineal kinship, as well as with sentiments of autonomy for not being included in the revival of <u>kastom</u>. Privately, even those members of the administration fully aware of the problems that strong claims to land were causing 'spoke strongly', as Buka people say, about the land they themselves owned in their village. In the introduction, I mentioned the profound sense of security and strength that living and working on their land gave Buka mainlanders. It should be obvious from my discussion of roads linking places on the mainland, and of banana metaphors for the growth of women and of matrilineages in the previous chapter that rights to particular pieces of land, to staying there, growing things there and making connections from there were crucial to Buka practices of kinship, and to the *tsunon*'s work of 'looking after the place'.

The problem on the Buka mainland, then, was how to turn land ownership from a problem—a source of the Crisis, and a source of difficulties in the context of formal peace-making and setting up the administration—into part of the solution. Land tenure had to be made part of the revival of co-operative relations within the *pinaposa*, and the capacity of *tsunon* to settle conflicts over land had to be strengthened. Some people on the mainland addressed the issue head-on, by making maps or describing the boundaries of their own land to their relatives. Some even began negotiations over disputed boundaries, with remarks such as: 'See what happened when the Nasioi didn't straighten their ground? They drew everyone into it, and we had the Crisis. We will straighten this thing here before something bad happens.' Other people took the opposite approach and kept quiet about disputed areas, waiting for 'things to settle down first, and then we will straighten this'.

I assumed that the Pororans merely belonged to the latter group when several *tsunon* asked me very seriously in the beginning of my fieldwork to stay away from researching land tenure. Gradually, however, it became clear that they had a different reason from that which mainlanders worried about, which were arguments over disputed boundaries. Tsireh told me to leave land issues alone because, as he put it, 'This island is too small to fight over ground. Some young people are starting that way. But why cut it up, this little thing, and mess things up. You leave it, or you might confuse those young people and things will turn out badly.' In other words, there should be no boundaries at all, and I should not try to research them so as to not give further motivation to some young people who were arguing that there should be: that one should 'straighten the ground'.

One of those young people with an intense interest in land boundaries was Hanun. He wanted to know which piece of land particularly was his *pinaposa*'s, assuming that he could then lay claim to it. 'Then I will know which land I hold. And nobody can boss me around there', he said. Hanun was not the only one investigating the matter. In 2005, I heard rumours that Kil's son Chris was making plans of building a hotel on Manuan, the small, uninhabited island that the Pororans used for fishing. Some people told me that he had worked out that Manuan belonged to three Pororan *pinaposa* jointly. One was Plisoh. He planned to buy out the other two and then build the hotel and make lots of money. Kil had heard the same rumours, assured me they weren't true but looked worried and said 'what is my child doing again, cutting up the ground, causing nothing but trouble, thinking only of money?' Musong—according to her source, the hotel was to be built within the year—came to inquire with Kil, angry and concerned: 'And where we will go fish?' Tsireh, who was around and listening, flew into a rage at this point. 'It is all the government's talk of straightening the ground that is giving everyone here bad ideas. No good thinking!'

The government's requests that people 'straighten the ground' put the *tsunon* on the island in a quandary. On the one hand, they were proud of their own knowledge, and they wanted the young people to learn about their ancestors, including the places of the past. On the other hand, all agreed with Francis, who put matters clearly: 'sapos ol isave, bai ol isalim'. If they know, they will sell them (the places they can claim 'through their mothers'). The *hagung ni tsunon* therefore agreed among each other that, if their young people asked them about land, they would say: 'Who knows now where our ancestors stayed?' Tsireh, for instance, would talk about Kuntali and Sakuan, but he would only point his head in the direction of the spots he was talking about. Only when talking to Kil or other close, reliable relatives, would he be more specific. Salu left her grandchildren, who would have loved to come, at home when we went to Keketin. Before she showed me the site of her *tsuhan*, she had discussed the matter with the *hagung ni tsunon*, who had agreed for her and Rokayo to take me to Keketin, but who reminded me of my promise to make sure the labels in my maps of the island did not correspond exactly to the locations of the places they named. In light of those arguments, Salu and Rokayo's calm assertion that Keketin was a place of the past that they remembered but did not want to re-open becomes a political statement against 'straightening the land'.

The strategy that the *tsunon* had suggested in the beginning of my fieldwork already for my maps mirrored their strategy for placing the houses of *tsunon* and *hahini*. Several *hahini* and *tsunon* on the island had their houses, as they pointed out to me carefully, 'somewhere near' the site of the colonial *tsuhan*, but not at that site exactly. Siatun giggled when she told me that her house, the house of a high-ranking *hahini*, stood up 'not straight at all', a little bit outside the area that her *pinaposa* had occupied in the colonial village. Then she became serious. 'Some people say I should re-locate. Re-locate where? Someone else is staying at the old spot. Should that person re-locate, too? Should we all break down our houses now and line them up as they were in the past? The island is full of people now. Many more than there were back then. Where do those others go, eh? Crazy thinking.' In front of young people, all *tsunon* and *hahini* vigorously argued that 'we are all islanders': 'Our island is small', they would say. 'We are many now, and we must make space for each other. Do not worry about the places of the past—leave them. Do not try to cut the island up. The pieces would be too small— maybe just enough to put a chair on it. You could no longer go around. What would you do then, sit on this land of yours?'

Secretly, however, the *tsunon* suspected each other of leaking impor- tant knowledge to young people that would allow them to claim land, for settlement or for 'selling', on the grounds of their membership to a particular *pinaposa*. As a precautionary measure, Tsireh was therefore re-positioning his *pinaposa* members so as to 'hold' places that were indisputably theirs. He did so without telling his young people the rea- sons for why he was putting a particular person where, and what the history of this spot was. All he told them was to 'hold this little spot, so that our people can come here if some "landowner" throws them out of where they are staying now'. His pattern of moving people was intricate and systematic. Without going into details, all I can say is that Tsireh had literally inverted the 'traditional' pattern of virilocal marriage and bihainim mama that he taught his young people. His greatest concern was who would do this—who would remember the places of the past without giving their exact location away so that they could be 'sold'—after his death. His predecessor, he said, might not understand that his *pinaposa*'s well-being and island life itself depended on the success of this undertaking.

The practice was not entirely new on the island. Salu's uncle, the *tsunon* of her *pinaposa* in the past, had placed Salu at Lulutsi without telling her why exactly, for instance. However, according to the Pororan *tsunon*, the government's request to 'straighten the ground' had made young people more persistent in their attempts to find out which piece of land they could possibly claim 'traditional ownership' to. Others, in turn, had become more nervous about being expelled from their current location by people who claimed traditional ownership to the spot. Tsireh described this as a generational conflict, with young people trying to claim their own land and older ones aiming to preserve the habit of sharing the island's limited land base. However, factions were more mixed if one looked at the statements of particular people, and even more tangled if one looked at their actions. Tsireh was not the only one walking a tightrope in trying to afford his *pinaposa* protection against landowners without allowing them to become landowners themselves.

Why exactly did the government's suggestions of straightening land ownership have these unexpected and unwanted effects on Pororan? I shall suggest one answer by looking briefly into the connections between matrilineal kinship, leadership and land on the mainland and on Pororan, respectively, and how the government's suggestion affected those connections. On the mainland, it is assumed that the *tsunon* of any particular *pinaposa* holds a particular piece of land that belongs to his group. What this 'holding' involves has only been touched upon briefly in what has been a saltwater ethnography. However, the basics should be clear: the *tsunon* assigns land for garden plots and houses, holds feasts and co-ordinates the activities of his people in gardening, feasting and other ventures. All of those activities take place immediately on and with the land and around the *tsuhan*, the physical centre of his power there. Given this 'landedness' of relations of matrilineal kinship and of power, 'straightening the ground' was perceived to be a necessary part of straightening kastom after the Crisis.[1]

On Pororan, as I have shown in previous chapters, traditional leadership was not vested in land, and land was not 'held' by the *tsunon* on behalf of their *pinaposa*. The *tsunon* co-ordinated the activities of people, but not on or around a particular piece of land or a physical centre of power, such as a *tsunon*. As an effect, land was not immediately bound into relations of *pinaposa* and of rank. Thus, a slippage became possible between 'straightening the ground' and 'cutting up the island', that is, dividing up among its members land associated with a *pinaposa* through particular people and events in the past. However, while land is not crucial to relations of kinship and power on Pororan, space as a capacity for moving and creating relations in movements is. And, as Tsireh's seamless move from 'straightening the ground' to 'cutting up the island' indicates, cutting up the land would have cut this capacity to move into pieces, too. Neither the slippage from traditional ownership to individual property nor that from land to space was likely intended by the government. But as it was, the call to 'straightening the ground' was making Pororan Islanders more rather than less vulnerable to conflicts over land, and potentially also to exploitation to foreign investors, though none had arrived yet in 2004–05. The Pororans perceived of it, moreover, as a threat to island life with its emphasis on freedom and 'going around' wherever one wanted to.

A Pororan <u>Kastom</u> Event

Despite their reservations against reviving <u>kastom</u>, the Pororans did, from time to time, pitch a claim to <u>kastom</u> themselves, and on one occasion, they did so exceptionally successfully. In 2005, Kil's son Lawrence was running for a seat on the Autonomous Bougainville Government. Central to his election campaign—and, as many people suggested, the single most important cause of its success—was a performance that the Pororans put on jointly to show their support for his candidacy. In this performance, Pororan Islanders made the values of island life visible to themselves and recognizable to others as <u>kastom</u>. They let others know, in an apparently convincing way, what they as 'saltwater people' or 'crazy islanders' (their term) had to offer to Bougainvillean autonomy. Below, I briefly describe the event and comment on its significance.

When Lawrence registered his candidacy for the elections, Pororan women paddled him with brightly painted mock paddles in a mock version of a *mon* from Kuri Village Resort along the Buka main road to the administration office. More than ten women, as well as many of the *tsunon*, had come from Pororan the night before the event. They practised their song at the workers' quarters, Kuri's 'backside', while the Pororan workmen put together the *mon*. The *mon* consisted in a wooden stern and bow painted in black and white and connected with ropes that the women would hold in one hand. In the morning, the women dressed up smartly and decorated themselves and the *mon* with fragrant leaves and lime powder. Lawrence's face was painted by a paternal relative with half the pattern of the *tsunon*. *Gogoa*, red soil from the Bougainville mainland that was used as a dye on ceremonial occasions and which Kil had brought from her storage on Pororan, was rubbed into his hair. Then the island's *tsunon* took Lawrence in the middle and pushed him towards the centre of the *mon*. The women lined up along the ropes that formed the *mon*'s sidewalls.

Shakily, the *mon* set off from Kuri's backside towards the main road, paddled by the women with their mock paddles. Some of the workmen jumped on in front and shouted *peki, peki* [reef] backward to warn the women of potholes in the road. As the *mon* progressed along the main road, the women sang loudly: 'We bring our child to the meeting of the *tsunon* [here, the government].' One of the *tsunon* beat a small slit-gong. Onlookers gathered along the road, and some of them, who knew Lawrence and the Pororans, slipped under the ropes of the *mon* to join them. Tightly packed with people and much more slowly than it had set off from Kuri, the *mon* finally pulled into the court of the administration office. Here, the women descended, Lawrence went inside to register, and the workmen folded the *mon* up to take it back to Kuri. Spectators clapped and followed the Pororans to Kuri to chat with them and celebrate what was generally judged to be a brilliant performance. The Pororan women looked deeply satisfied. The *tsunon*, who received most of the congratulations and wishes of luck to Lawrence for the elections ahead responded calmly and with dignity: 'He has already won.'

The image of the *mon*, paddled along a road in a way that drew attention to the danger and uncertainties of a sea journey, was not new to Bougainvillean spectators. Similar performances had been staged throughout the peace process when former enemy groups met for reconciliation ceremonies. The performance was also classified, at least by some spectators, as a 'cultural performance', or kastom (while the Pororans only ever spoke of it as 'paddling the *mon* in Town'). In addition, the *mon* itself was stated to be an item of shared Bougainvillean kastom.[2] This performance, then, was the only occasion at which I saw Pororan Islanders enact most enthusiastically what others recognized as kastom, in a way that these others admired greatly and that made the Pororans name 'go above everyone else's' for the following days in Town.

But at the same time, spectators from other locations pointed out to one another that the details of the performance were typically Pororan. Who else would have staged, with so much laughter, exaggeration and funny dancing, a dangerous sea-journey along an all too familiar stretch of the Buka main road? Who else would have given Town an air of adventure, and the office workers along the road a welcome occasion

for a break, they asked. Furthermore, and more significantly, the somewhat haphazard movements of the *mon* could only be understood,
from a Pororan perspective, as a display of *roror*, not unlike that given
by women who paddled an imaginary canoe across the *tsuhan* during
hahur. The comments of the workmen and their warning shouts of *peki*
made this explicit, as did the conversations among the women on the
mon. Along the road, one woman asked another: 'Will we make it, or
will we get stuck on the reef? Oh, this *mon* is becoming very heavy with
people, and very slow! What if we capsize!' As she put this question,
she shook the rope of the *mon* violently, triggering excited shouts of
'wind now, a strong wind!' The other woman shouted back to her: 'We
will make it! This is a good *mon*, and we are strong mothers! We will
paddle our child all the way up! And once we have dropped him off up
at the government [the administration office], we will go all the way to
Pororan . . . no, we will go all the way to Buin!'³ This was one of the rare
moments when Pororan Islanders were able to present to themselves
and others, and to receive wide recognition for the value and potential
of indeterminate movements. Arguably, paddling the *mon* through Town
they re-enacted, this time in full vision of other people who might or
might not have known this story, the origin of human relationality as
recounted in the story of Sia and Hulu.

In his campaign speeches across the constituency, Lawrence drew
heavily on shared memories of the *mon*, and on demonstrations that
those present had given to those who had not seen the performance in
Town. With reference to the *mon*, he impressed upon his audience the
potential of the moment of Bougainvillean autonomy. All possibilities of
good government, good leadership, peace and a settled life at the village
would be open to Bougainvilleans. He asked his audience to pause and
think: What would they want Bougainville to be like? Unlike some other
candidates, Lawrence was explicit about the dangers ahead, and about
the possibilities that the peace process or autonomy might not turn out
as expected. To this purpose, he drew on the image of Bougainville as a
mon on high sea, which required the travellers' close co-operation and
full support and would nevertheless always remain in danger of capsiz-
ing. Memories of the performance lent these figures of speech a specificity that made members of audiences on Pororan push one another in the
ribs and laugh. The mainland inhabitants of the constituency, too, were
apparently convinced, or at least gave Lawrence a majority of votes.

The idea of a Pororan Islander winning a seat on a government that
was placing such high value on the project of 'reviving kastom' appears
counterintuitive, given the islanders' reputation across the area for
consistently 'screwing up kastom'. One might suggest however, that it

only demonstrates what Pororan Islanders observe on a daily basis, and what I have pursued across various aspects of 'island life'. This is that novel and valuable relations emerge out of indeterminate movements of *roror*. Sometimes people are attracted and get stuck in them in unexpected ways.

With the *mon* and with Pororan Islanders' frustration about their apparent inferiority in matters of <u>kastom</u> in mind, I have aimed to focus in my ethnography on what Pororan Islanders openly state they excel in. They excel in alerting one another to the possibilities that things may turn out differently, and that human relations always retain an edge of indeterminacy. Knowledge of relations, where these are apprehended through the observation of movements that are always just emerging from, and always about to dissolve back into *roror*, is by necessity incomplete. 'Finished' knowledge can only be had of the dead—and even then, the Pororans avoid the closing in order to keep their spirits with them. In stating that they 'know very little about <u>kastom</u>', Pororan Islanders thus claim the vitality of island life. And in 'going around at sea' in Buka Town in preparation for the elections, they have staked a claim to the indeterminacy of the future, and thus the vitality of the Autonomous Region of Bougainville, as they perceive it.

NOTES

1. How realistic the expectations were that this 'straightening' would indeed increase clarity, rather than merely increase occasions for disputes, is not for me to judge. Given my limited knowledge of the complex histories of *pinaposa* relations in mainland villages and the mutually incompatible claims to land resulting from them, I have reservations.
2. When I visited Buka in 2006, a wooden mock *mon* decorated the entrance of the new parliament building.
3. A reference to headhunting raids, which were often noted to have taken the ancestors 'all the way to Buin'.

Conclusion

The purpose of this conclusion is, firstly, to sum up my argument from previous chapters. It may be read as one of the hand movements that Pororan Islanders use to describe particular movements and relations: a summary after the fact, and of a particular form that has been achieved at a certain moment. Needless to say, this form will change as movements go on. Secondly, I will point out some connections between my findings on Pororan and different sets of anthropological literature that may offer starting points for future research.

The Argument

The ethnographic stimulus for and throughout my research with Pororan Islanders has been the Pororans' enormous interest in movements. I first became aware of it because it stood in striking contrast to Buka mainlanders' interests in 'following roads'. The Pororans pay greatest attention to the physical movements of persons around them. Other movements they take note of are those of the tides, driftwood, fish, and baskets of sweet potatoes that could stand in, for instance, for absent grandchildren. When not on the move themselves as part of their everyday subsistence activities on the island and at sea, the islanders were busy observing, sharing and discussing among one another the movements of persons in particular. Specific observations of the movements that were unfolding around them were turned, step by step, into an understanding of the current state of relations of mutual help and competition, of gender, parenthood, rank and clanship. These understandings were deepened among those in particular positions as well as among a handful of interested others, through accounts of the pasts. Accounts of the past, like accounts of relations in the present, were elaborations upon the movements of particular people and their effects. They included movements of migration and island settlement, and of the dealings of

Notes for this section begin on page 198

powerful people with outsiders, including those whom they encountered on headhunting raids, as well as white people in colonial times. Finally, movements were central to ritual occasions on the island, including both marriage ceremonies and mortuary rites. Attention to bodies and their appearance was rare, and where it did occur, it had the effect of distracting people's potentially disruptive attention from a crucial transformative process carried out in the form of a movement.

Movements do not stop on Pororan. People continue moving until they become very old and die. After that, their spirits continue to move among their relatives. Thus, the crucial opposition of Pororan social life is not one of mobility versus stillness, which has been so prominent in the regional literature (e.g. Bonnemaison 1984, 1994; McKinnon 1991; Weiner 1991). Instead, the Pororans' accounts of themselves, their gestures, their dwelling on particular verbs of movement such as 'going around', 'returning' and 'pulling' indicate their interest in oppositions internal to human mobility. My account of Pororan sociality has been structured along those oppositions. The most fundamental of them is the opposition between *roror*, indeterminate going around, and movements of a definite shape that can be summed up in the movement of a hand or arm. The latter are *maror*, roads that create, and make visible for all to see, particular relations between the moving person and the one at whom the movement is directed. The former, however, is the most important feature of life 'at sea', according to the islanders.

Roror gives persons a 'rest' from ordinary social relations. It becomes most obvious and is described most explicitly in fishing activities. Fishing, the Pororans' main subsistence activity and an important source of cash, is not work but 'going around at sea' [*roror itasi*]. This going around, although it involves a multitude of particular movements of human bodies, canoes and other tools, is stylized as an unpredictable, random way of moving. *Roror* is unconstrained in space or by ordinary conventions of time and is mindless of ordinary social relations. The haphazardness of movements at sea is attributed to the 'will' of the person that moves outside his or her ordinary relations, to unexpected encounters with fish and to the will of ancestral spirits that interfere with the movements of fish, wind and rain, tides and thus also with those of the fishing person. *Roror* ends when the fishing person feels a fish on the line, which brings to mind those who will want to eat it. The fish will be taken off the hook and fishing may be resumed many times, with each fish prefiguring the re-emergence of social relations that will be established with the fishing person's return from the sea.

Returns from the sea with fish are one of the most ordinary events of everyday life on Pororan, but are also among the most tense and the most highly valued moments of 'our being here at sea'. Their special quality derives from the 'looks' [*ngot*] that those who want [*ngil*] the fish give the person who brings it. The looks elicit movements of particular shapes. Fish is either condescendingly 'thrown away', or is respectfully handed 'up' to the person who wants it. Which one it will be is highly contingent in each instance. It depends not the least on the facility with which each person involved in the encounter employs verbal statements accompanying the movement of fish, as well as body language, gestures and facial expressions. The particular form of relations that appears through them is confirmed and 'conventionalized' with a return for the fish a day or more later, handed in the appropriate direction, up or down. I have linked this process of making relations disappear and re-appear, of leaving them behind and re-creating them upon one's return to the story of Sia and Hulu that locates the origins of human life with two siblings 'going around on the reef'. In everyday fishing as in the story, people have something 'stuck' to themselves, first a marine creature and then the 'looks' or attention of others that transforms random 'going around' into relations of a particular form. In their claims that anyone can fish anywhere and at any time they like on Pororan, the islanders claim for themselves the 'freedom' to create relations anew any time. This 'freedom', they say, sets life at sea apart from life 'in the bush'.

The two possible movements of fish when persons return from the sea, and the return that is later made for the fish are the beginnings of the two conventionalized 'roads', one running downward-outward and returning inward-upward, the other running inward-upward and then downward-outward. These appear over and over in accounts of the past, in formal explanations of relations that some *tsunon* gave me of island relations, and in people's comments and discussions of movements they observed in everyday life. They are drawn with hands and arms into the air, and they are marked by distinctive verbs of movements with meanings particular to those kinds of relations. The downward-outward and inward-upward road is invoked verbally or through gestures to describe relations of mutual help, which are especially appropriate but not limited to matrilineal kin. In movements of this shape, people and most commonly women extend relations to others. The movement is expansive. The inward-upward and downward-outward road, by contrast, 'defines' (Wagner 1967) persons. It is an act of 'pulling' and releasing that objectifies the capacity to cause others to move, and thus to make relations of particular kinds apparent. Depending on who pulls and releases whom, the relations that appear are relations of kinship, of rank or of clanship. Most importantly, 'pulling' is a capacity defining fathers who thereby make children grow, and *tsunon* who 'look after the place' and look after people who inhabit it.

It is important to my argument that 'pulling' is not the extraction of persons out of immobile places or from groups that are defined in this very process of having someone extracted from oneself and responding to it (see esp. Leach 2003; see also McKinnon 1991). It does not 'decompose' an original unproductive unity into a productive relational world (see also Mosko 1985). Instead, by attracting persons who were previously 'going around' randomly—as everyone does occasionally, although some more often than others—the Pororans make movements of a particular shape stand out temporarily on an original background of indeterminate mobility. This background, as it appears in the Pororans' accounts of themselves, their love for fishing and their saltwater environment, is the sea and the reef around them, in which everything is constantly in motion, and things temporarily get 'stuck' on other things and then move off again, in highly indeterminate ways. Furthermore, and again in correspondence with their observations of movements in their saltwater environment rather than with the Melanesian and broader Austronesian literature, the Pororans do not contain what they attract, or lodge the power of attraction in stable places. Instead, the power is demonstrated in movements of a particular shape, and the places that do emerge in the process are disposable. They move and change shape along with those who perform the action of 'pulling', and along with their particular activities: headhunting, colonial village building or hosting foreigners in Town. The same holds for the island as a whole, which acquires sand on one end and loses it on the other. Thus, their mode of objectifying relations by making movements appear out of and then letting them disappear into *roror* is a distinctive, saltwater version of a familiar Melanesian aesthetic of creating distinctions.

This saltwater mode contrasts sharply with that of Buka mainlanders. Mainlanders emphasize the importance of 'following roads' [*kura maror*] that do not disappear into and re-appear out of *roror*, but that connect named, powerful places 'held' by particular *tsunon* on behalf of their matrilineal groups. Here, roads are not summary accounts of movements of particular shape, but footpaths and paved roads physically imprinted on the soft but firm soil of Leitana, the 'high land'. They are said to date back to ancestral times. In 'following' these roads in their everyday lives, people show their awareness of, and continue into the present divisions of matrilineal kinship mapped firmly onto the land, in the form of roads and places. The conditions of making relations apparent in this form—directly on the land—is an environment of relative endurance and immobility. The 'high land', Leitana, affords those conditions. Beyond this physical grounding of relations in land, the aesthetic pattern underpinning the objectification of relations in roads that connect places is 'landed'. It is modelled on the growth of bananas. Growing bananas involves 'cutting' [extracting, separating] a sapling, moving it to a different garden and planting and watering it there. Main-landers make an explicit connection between banana growth and the growth of women, who are cut off from their relatives and moved to their husband's place, where they grow. From there, they return every now and then with their children. Similarly, entire *pinaposa* grow by the separation of a particular woman and her planting in a new place. From this place, her children return to visit their 'source' [the Tok Pisin term as ples is sometimes used for emphasis] among their mother's relatives, at their place.

Long-term research on the mainland carried out with attention to roads and places, bananas and the everyday practices of 'emplacing' (Rumsey and Weiner 2001) relations would certainly yield greater complexity than my own investigations. Those were carried out strictly within the frame provided by saltwater concerns, and were pursued only as deeply as necessary for exploring saltwater-mainland relations in Buka. A key to those relations lies in the system of 'traditional leader-ship' that stretches across the Buka area. In the context of ceremonies in which their rank is 'witnessed', Pororan *tsunon* and *hahini* are instructed by both island and mainland *tsunon* in the history of their *pinaposa*, and thus in mainland modes of making relations apparent more generally. This allows them to act as mediators in island-mainland interactions, and it frees their island relatives of the need to engage in any depth with mainland understandings of relations.

In 2004–05, Pororan *tsunon* were grappling with the challenge of mediating not only between islanders and mainlanders, but also between island modes of making relations apparent and the expectations of the government that they revive their kastom. This idea of reviving kastom had emerged primarily from Buka experiences of the endurance of 'tra-ditional' relations of mutual support and respect during the Bougainville Crisis. Those experiences generated the wish of strengthening those rela-tions, so as to utilize best the potential for peace that they afforded. This wish matched the ideals of a 'locally owned' peace process agreed upon by Bougainvillean political leaders and foreign advisors. Energized by this convergence of interests, kastom became central to peace-building in Buka. Specifically, the Pororans were faced with demands of recording relations of matrilineal kinship at the village, of sorting out the relative rank of their *tsunon*, and of addressing issues of land ownership.

The demand to document clanship, rank and land ownership in a definite form on paper ran up against the Pororans' perceptions of those relations and their value, in particular ways with regard to each of these aspects of <u>kastom</u>. Recording matrilineal kinship on paper could never do justice, as the islanders pointed out, to the expansive quality of relations of mutual help created by women. 'Writing them down' cut those relations short, instead of making their expansiveness, their most valued quality, apparent. 'Straightening' relations of traditional leadership was seen to undermine the power of the *tsunon* from two directions. Firstly, 'talk about power' would imply that the *tsunon*'s rank was not visible already in people's movements relative to them. In other words, it would imply that Pororan *tsunon* had no power at all. Secondly, the Pororans feared that in the process of documenting a single form—a single set of relations of rank—conflicts would arise, and once agreed upon, those who 'stood up on top' would be vulnerable to envy and sorcery. Finally, 'straightening the ground' was feared to result in the island being 'cut up' into individual pieces too small to do anything with. The government's intention in asking people to 'straighten the ground' was, of course, rather the opposite. Clarifying traditional boundaries of blocks of land held by traditional leaders on behalf of clans was meant to strengthen the capacity of the group and their leader to defend their land against encroachment. On Pororan, however, there is no corresponding assumption to that of the government about a one-to-one relation between leadership, clanship and land. As a result, a slippage became possible from 'straightening the ground' to establishing individual claims to land for business or other use. This, as some islanders warned, put at serious risk a saltwater sociality grounded in its members' capacity to go anywhere at any time they wanted, and to make relations appear anew upon their return.

In all these particular concerns, a general aversion of Pororan Islanders against the 'revival of <u>kastom</u>' can be discerned. This is an aversion against 'pinning down' relations once and for all, in a single, definite form. The same aversion re-appears, independently of government suggestions of 'reviving <u>kastom</u>', in Pororan rituals. Those resist closure. At marriage, a 'tightening' of the relations between in-laws does indeed occur. However, it occurs precisely at the moment when everybody's attention is directed away from it. This is the moment when a most unusual 'object' in Pororan ritual appears: a fully decorated human body. It evokes strong associations of multiple relationality and mobility and 'covers up' the tiny movement of the bride price taking place nearby, unobserved. In mortuary rites, perhaps surprisingly, no comparable moment of closure is achieved. No body is displayed, and no condensed, explanatory image of sociality appears that 'finishes' the deceased and mourning elsewhere (Wagner 1986b). Something formally matching Wagner's definition of an image does indeed appear at that point in time, but it is not revelatory. I argue that this is because 'images', in which movements are put on hold, cannot make relations apparent to people who are used to apprehending them step by step, as movements unfold. This requires that we look beyond images for a 'sufficient' expression of Pororan sociality. I look to the 'mark of what it means to be human' displayed in *hahur*, the singing of mourning songs after the death of a person of rank. This mark turns out to be an open-ended sequence of movements that are transformed into and out of each other.

In theoretical terms, I have responded to *hahur* and the observation of the non-revelatory role of images on Pororan by relying on the term 'objectification'. This term seemed most suitable for investigating the interplay between single forms and multiple possibilities that the Pororans are interested in. It has allowed me, further, to point to both the creative and the perceptive side of the processes, which go together although their weighting differs in different situations. With regard to ethnographic methods, the limited role of images in Pororan modes of making relations apparent implies that watching Pororan movements from the outside, as if they were images, would give a very limited understanding of Pororan social life. Much of what I have described in the previous account has been observed while I was moving myself, and through conscious attention to the difference that movements make to what one sees at any moment in time.

Pororan, Melanesia

The reason that I can state the impossibility of pinning down a single form of Pororan sociality with contentedness is because for me, *hahur* evoked something else, besides and more immediately than the multiple everyday movements of paddling canoes, sweeping hamlets and throwing out fishing rods. It evoked a Melanesian anthropological literature that had, again and again, come across 'a fluidity of structure' (Fortes 1984: ix), 'structurelessness' (Fajans 1997: 5), and phenomena such as *na tadak* in New Ireland, whose form and location are impossible to pin down (Wagner 1986b). Early ethnographers did not know what to do with the apparent shapelessness of some—not all—Melanesian societies. Gregory Bateson despaired over the 'unstudiable' Baining and moved on (Fajans 1997). The Mount Ok region on the Papua New Guinea mainland deterred various anthropologists, too, because kinship seemed to be lacking, social groups seemed to be lacking, and everything seemed to be in flux (see esp. Crook 2007). Peter Lawrence did not publish his material on Garia kinship at first, not because it was 'wrong' but because it did not fit currently dominant models of society, as became apparent with hindsight (Fortes 1984; Leach 2003).

In all three cases—Mount Ok, Baining and the Rai Coast—anthropologists have more recently made inroads through analyses focusing on processes. Tony Crook (2007) has studied in detail the knowledge-making processes, the making of 'skin', in Bolivip. By comparing those processes to anthropological knowledge making and the assumptions underpinning it, he has been able to throw light on the difficulties of earlier ethnographers in the area. James Leach (2003) has picked up a thread left by Lawrence, a focus on land and land use. Where Lawrence attempted to identify land-holding groups, however, Leach directed attention to the processes of creating persons and places through co-operation in gardening, and through the exchange of garden produce. Jane Fajans (1997) has become involved in the very aspect of Baining life that previous ethnographers had found dull. This is their everyday work, in which she argues they transform nature into society on a daily basis, in a process structured by particular values and assumptions that must be discovered within it, rather than outside. Similarly, I have located particular values and 'forms' associated with particular kinds of relations inside an analysis of the processes in which Pororan Islanders bring them out for others to see and comment on.

Several of the abovementioned ethnographers have noted, specifically, the necessity of exploring people's particular understandings of talk and its limitations, in relation to other modes of making relations apparent. Talk of the propositional type obviously does not sit well with any of those people's modes of perceiving, creating and revealing relations gradually, and with their sense of the uncertainties involved in those processes. Talk is cheap, say the Usen Barok, says Wagner and turns to an investigation of power through *tadak* and through images (1986b). The Baining are rarely willing to offer exegeses on their activities, according to Fajans, and thus she discovers them inside their productive activities, including their attention to food and human bodies. In the Mountain Ok region, young people despair over the talk of their elders that confuses them, offering multiple possibilities where they are looking for straightforward answers, as Crook reports. Crook turns this into an exploration of the tree-like shape of Bolivip processes of knowledge making, which branch out into multiple tips before returning to a single base, and of other imagery through which people in

Bolivip describe their movements along this shape. The Pororans' routine reply to my questions was 'what if I lie to you', and like the Baining, they often told me plainly that they did not know. I have followed the Pororans' advice and joined them in watching movements unfold. In the process, I discovered a richness of expressions, some supported linguistically and others silent that is hard to do justice to in words. At the same time, I have aimed to elucidate the particular—evocative, eliciting action, partially descriptive—roles that talk does play in relation to movements. I note a potential for further comparative research into talk and its relation to spatial practices in particular (see also Rumsey and Weiner 2001; Scott 2000, 2007; Weiner 2001; for a stimulus from another region, see Basso 1996).

Beyond these particular cases, the Pororans' interest in making relations apparent in movements resonates with a wide array of literature from the region, but in a particular way. By analysing movements as a mode of objectification, I have aimed to draw attention to this particularity. It lies in the Pororans apparently extreme insistence on the uncertainty of the outcomes of people's creative and perceptive processes, and thus of the relations that will appear in the end. In a milder form, this uncertainty appears in numerous ethnographies. Movements, however, make an object of it, while Hagen pigs lined up for exchange, for instance, rather conceal this uncertainty, at least at that particular moment and specifically from the recipient's point of view. The pigs, lined up for inspection, eclipse the possibility that they might have gone elsewhere. By contrast, the movements of baskets in a Pororan *bung malot*—arguably the event that comes nearest to a Hagen pig exchange—make a point of just this possibility of baskets going elsewhere. The aesthetic quality of movements that allows them to do so, while pigs cannot, should be obvious. A tethered movement is not a movement. Movements cannot 'be there' or not be there. They are always either just coming or just leaving—and if they are just coming, then one may reasonably expect that they will soon be leaving. Temporality, of course, is crucial to the gift (Mauss 1990) and has played a prominent role in analyses of Melanesian sociality since. Pororan interests in movements offer a local commentary on the issue.

Their acute sense of uncertainty, the problem of temporality, the unreliability of talk and the lack of structure that make Pororan sociality distinctly Melanesian from an anthropological perspective make it distinctly saltwater from Buka mainlanders' perspective. Buka mainlanders comment on the impossibility of knowing what the islanders are up to; about them 'going around' unpredictably and 'messing things up'; about 'things' (the clans, relations of rank) not being straight on the island, and about the islanders not apparently knowing (or talking about) Buka <u>kastom</u>. I switch perspective here from considering Pororan as a Melanesian, towards considering it as a saltwater location, in comparison to others.

Pororan, at Sea

In a different context but most usefully for my purposes, Alberto Corsín Jiménez (2003: 137) has asked: 'What happens when people's identity is not land-related?' I focus here in particular on what happens to people's senses of place and what happens to tenure under such circumstances. At the risk of simplifying their position somewhat, both Edvard Hviding and Nonie Sharp have argued that nothing happens, in fact. Melanesians' and indigenous Australians' ways of relating to the sea are parallel to their ways of relating to land. The problem is merely that Euro-American researchers coming from a different tradition of perceiving the sea fail to see in it what indigenous people see: distinct bodies of waters of different qualities, paths and boundaries. Edvard Hviding's argument concerning marine tenure in Marovo Lagoon, New Georgia is two-fold. Firstly, he explicitly extends Tim Ingold's (1986) argument of hunter-gatherer tenure as an integrative movement along paths to particular sites or locations to Marovo fishing movements. When fishing, Marovo people follow paths (*huana*) leading to particular fishing spots. In tracing these paths, they are transmitting knowledge of their lagoon, of fishing spots, seasons and the movements of fish dating back to ancestral times. The paths are marked by physical markers under water, such as distinctive features of the reef. These, argues Hviding, are clearly visible to the Marovo, and detectable if one goes fishing with them. The main problem with marine tenure in the anthropological literature is that too few people have studied it in-depth, that is, by going out to and looking into the sea. In addition to his argument about paths, Hviding also shows the salience of 'territoriality' (in Ingold's terms) at sea. He documents the immediate conceptual link in Marovo between territorial divisions (*puava*) and kin groups (*butubutu*) that are their 'guardians'. Some *puava* in Marovo lagoon are landed, extending upward into the forest and belonging to the people who used to live in the interior in pre-colonial times. Others extend outwards into the lagoon and across the barrier reef. Others again are mixed. *Puava* have boundary markers. Marine *puava* are marked by passages in the barrier reef and extend between those from the beach out into the open sea. Unlike landed *puava*, however, they are not further sub-divided. His findings sit well with those of other Melanesian ethnographers on the ownership of certain sections of the marine environment by kin groups (e.g. Carrier 1981).

Nonie Sharp (2002) has collected ethnographic evidence for territoriality and the importance of paths among Australian saltwater people, drawing together findings of other researchers as well as her own. Meriam Islanders' clan territory, for instance, extends outward onto the reef. They drew its boundaries into the sand for her, and she recorded songs speaking of the particular sounds that the sea makes in particular locations, owned by particular groups. As in Marovo, paths in Australia create 'associations between places and relationships between people through the points they connect in their journey' (Sharp 2002: 141). These paths are Dreaming tracks, continued into the present by people who trace them. As in Marovo, sea markers are crucial to tracks and territoriality in Australia, and Sharp documents a fascinating range of them, ranging from on-land markers such as rocks, through reef features such as pools, sandbars and passages, to tidal currents and the smell of particular reef areas at low tide. In documenting these paths and territories and the ways in which people create and perceive them in their movements at sea, Sharp and Hviding pursue the same explicit goal. This is to overcome the unthinking application of a Euro-American, historically specific association of the sea with unbounded movements and open access. They hope to strengthen the capacity of indigenous people to re-claim their territories under customary tenure regimes and to thereby protect themselves from encroachment and resource exploitation at sea.

In the final instance, I share this aim. However, my findings on Pororan suggest strongly that transferring to the sea what we know about land tenure, be it about territoriality or about paths that hunter-gatherers use, will not work in Buka, and perhaps in other areas where people highlight a contrast rather than a parallel between land than sea. The patterns of paths linking up places that Hviding and Sharp describe so vividly among Marovo and Australian saltwater people is much closer to Buka mainland interests in connecting places by following roads than it is to the Pororans'. Pororan 'roads', as I have argued, do not end up in places, but dissolve in and reappear from *roror*. Furthermore, the Pororans explicitly contrast mainland territoriality to their own, unbounded 'going around at sea'. This 'going around', as should be clear by now, is not the same as the freedom of the seas that Euro-Americans have historically depended on for the spread of capitalism. To the contrary, it is a highly localized form of movement, integral to the Pororans' very own saltwater sociality. *Roror* cannot be accounted for in the terms employed by Hviding and by Sharp for demonstrating the validity of indigenous people's claims to customary marine tenure. Worse, if applied without caution, assumptions derived from tenure in 'landed' settings threaten the islanders' capacity to 'go around'.

What, then, does happen when identity is not land-related? How else can we approach issues of place and tenure at sea? Fiona Magowan (2001) has argued that among the Yolngu, at sea and on land alike, persons are connected to places and to the ancestors through 'kinesis as a transformative agency where each transformation has its own dynamic and interactive agency arising from particular movement forms in the landscape and seascape' (23).[1] These movement forms are highlighted in ritual songs, through rhythm and onomatopoeia, along with other things that foreground subject-object transformations through movements. Magowan's is most explicitly an argument about transformative connections through movements, not about differences created from people performing and attending to different movement forms. However, it is only a small step from here towards an argument that perhaps in Melanesia, different movement forms, or interests in mobility create the much-discussed, highly salient distinction between land and sea, mainlanders and saltwater people. This, of course, is the argument that I have been putting forward throughout this book. Specifically, the contrast in movements at issue is that between the Pororans' interests in the oscillation between roads and *roror* on the one hand, and that of mainlanders' in following roads that connect immobile places on the other.

What appears in Buka as a contrast between two 'entirely different people', saltwater people and mainlanders, appears in various other forms across the Melanesian literature. On Tanna, the contrast is imagined as a temporal one, between an origin time of incessant mobility and a present time of immobile stones, territories and orderly movements between them (Bonnemaison 1984, 1994). In the beginning, a horde of stones was roving around the island. Talking and fighting, they circled the island on five different circular roads, each with a different diameter. Over time, however, the stones stopped moving, each for its own reason, such as attending to a sore leg. These stones—after an eventful intermittent mythical period—became the places animating the territories of different groups, conceptualized as canoes. Within them, people are rooted; the canoe itself, however, is mobile, and it pursues connections along 'roads' to allied groups on the island and beyond. Thus, in the present unlike in the mythical past, 'Melanesian identity is determined by both rootedness around the central place and controlled mobility along roads traversing the country of alliance' (Bonnemaison 1984: 133). Note the parallel to the saltwater-mainland contrast in Buka: incessant mobility that created roads on the one hand, and roads linking places on the other.

Finally, research from the Massim indicates a gendered division internal to both a single group of people and the human present. On Gawa, sociality and value are created through the transformation of particular kinds of mobility into and out of each other. Munn specifies a contrast between the 'heaviness' and immobility of the gardens of Gawa, and the lightweight buoyancy of movements at sea, especially in the Kula trade, with highly specific transformations turning one into the other. The dualism between these two domains is intertwined with a contrast between two different social groups, dala and kumila. Dala are exogamous, landholding matrilineal groups. Stones associated with the dala and its ancestors physically represent it in the land. They mustn't be moved, for they 'embody the heaviness of the soil as an enduring potential productivity immobilised inside the matrilineal dala land across the transient tillage and planting of the gardens' (Munn 1986: 81). The dala are grouped into four exogamous *kumila*, associated with the four winds that are evoked in sailing. Through the *kumila*, trade connections are made on expeditions to other islands.

Pororan Islanders are firmly on the side of Tannese roving stones and Gawan sailors. Their ancestors were sent to a tiny barrier reef island in order to catch fish for those who themselves remained on high land. In the ways specified in previous chapters, as fishing people they keep re-creating relations 'island-style', as they call it, despite the difficulties that governmental assumptions about the landedness of Bougainvillean traditions are causing. The Pororans' interests in movements, and specifically in the transformative relation between indeterminate 'going around' and roads offers a perspective from which the movements of Tannese stones, Gawan sailors and others on the 'mobile' pole of the familiar dichotomy may be subjected to further scrutiny, as a whole containing various parts as well as a part within a whole. (Melanesian sociality is known for its fractal qualities.) Among other things, a thorough investigation of these 'mobile' movements seems necessary for exploring marine tenure, certainly in areas like Buka where people themselves insist on the contrast rather than the parallel between land and sea. One never knows, of course, what else may come up, or where one will drift ashore if one follows movements that dip into and come out of *roror* in a highly unpredictable fashion.

NOTES

1. I thank the anonymous reviewer of an earlier version of this text who brought the Australian literature, and specifically Magowan's work, to my attention.

Hapororan and Tok Pisin Terms

Beroan	Shell money, made of white or red shell disks, measured in arm lengths, used as bride wealth and for other ceremonial payments.
Binits	New, anew.
Bung malot	Ten-day [feast]. Main mortuary feast, held ten days (but sometimes up to a month) after a death.
Gogoa	Red clay soil from the Bougainville mainland. Used as red hair dye for *tsunon* and *hahini* on important occasions, as well as for storing *paiou*.
Gum	'Sit down'. Voluntary confinement of female relatives of a deceased of rank in the house of death, from day of burial up to ten-day feast.
Hahats	Fire sacrifice.
Hahini	'Queen'. Firstborn daughter of the firstborn woman of a *pinaposa*, mother of the next *hahini* and *tsunon*. She 'continues the line', and is the 'road along which the *tsunon* comes'. Halia: *teitahol*. Haku: *tuhikau*.
Hahur	<u>Singsing sori</u>, sessions of singing mourning songs, held at the *tsuhan* in one or more nights after the death of a person of rank. Women sing wordless mourning songs, accompanied by the slit-gong [*tui*]. Some *tsunon* present initiate the songs.
Halat	Season in which the tide is low at night. October—March.
Hamois	Hide.

Hamok	Throw away (e.g. money, a fishing line). A downward-outward movement.
Hamua	Firstborn.
Hatsitsi	Respect.
Hatuhan	Make grow, cause to grow.
Heol	Ceremonial basket, used at mortuary and marriage ceremonies.
Hiningal	Time of the <u>galip</u> nuts [*ngal*]. Season when the tide is low during daytime. April—September.
Hitaku	Tree species of the genus carophyllum, according to Blackwood (n.d.).
Ias	Up, above.
Ka	1. Thing, something. Sometimes used to refer to persons. 2. Stay.
Kal atoh	Sago leaf (for thatching a roof). Opening gift for building a *tsuhan*.
Kakatun	Just stay.
Katun	Person. Also used, as an expression of respect, for ancestral spirits and <u>masalai</u>.
<u>Klostu</u>	Close, related.
Kohel	Basket.
Kopu	Down, below.
<u>Laplap</u>	Sarong.
Latu	<u>Bus</u>. 'Bush', referring to land, garden land, coconut plantations, and the Buka mainland.
Longon	Hear, listen.
<u>Longwe</u>	Far, not immediately related.
Malei	<u>Pisin</u>, 'bird'. Refers to Naboen and Nakarip.
Mamaluh	Rest, relax.
Maror	Road.

<u>Masalai</u>	Localized spirit that takes animal appearance. Sometimes but not necessarily associated with a particular *pinaposa*.
Mon	Large, outriggerless canoe of the past, used for fishing, trade and headhunting.
Mumua	Front.
Mur	Back.
Naboen	<u>Bikpela pidgin</u> [big bird], <u>pidgin bilong antap</u> [bird above]. One of the birds, also called *manu* [eagle]. Said to be superior to Nakarip.
Nakarip	<u>Liklik pidgin</u> [small bird], <u>pidgin bilong tambolo</u> [bird below]. One of the birds, also called *kekeleou* [fowl]. Said to be inferior, but in possession of stronger magic than Naboen.
Nakas	'Dog'. Warrior group, now occasionally claiming to be a separate bird. Relation to the birds is debated in Buka and among ethnographers.
Natasi	'Saltwater', 'sea'. Warrior group, now occasionally claiming to be a separate bird. Relation to the birds is debated in Buka and among ethnographers.
Ngil, mangil	Like, want.
Ngorer	<u>Wanpela rope</u>, <u>wanpela belly button</u>. Matrilineal group, dispersed or localized, whose members trace particular, known connections to a single known ancestress.
Ngot	Look.
Nin	Eat.
Nomnomi	<u>Tevil</u>. Ancestral spirit, spirit of the dead.
Paiou	Teeth money, made of dolphin or the flying fox teeth, used as bride wealth and for other ceremonial payments.
<u>Pasis</u>	Passage (between parts of the reef).
Peits	<u>Mausman</u>. The functionary of the highest-ranking *tsunon*, usually the *tsunon* of the second highest-ranking *ngorer* of a *pinaposa*. Also: *tson pipit*, *runner*.

Pian	Child. Fruit or sapling of a plant.
Pian hatuhan	<u>Mipela kamapim em</u>. Reference to the children of the male members of the speaker's *pinaposa*.
Pinaposa	<u>Wanpela mama tasol, ol pikinini bilong ol ipas wantaim. Clan.</u> Matrilineal group, dispersed or localized. Made up of two or more *ngorer*.
Pinapu	<u>Ples</u>, village, home.
<u>Poisin</u>	Lethal sorcery. A spell placed on food or a betel nut or on food; substance added to food; 'just thoughts' that can cause illness or death.
<u>Poro</u>	Friend.
Pos	Banana.
Rang	Talk.
Reban	People. Plural of *katun*.
Roror	'Go around'. Aimless, random, haphazard movement.
<u>Singsing sori</u>	*Hahur*, singing mourning songs.
<u>Ston</u>	*Remits* elevated reef part. Stone. Very old man.
Taun	Town. Usually Buka Town.
Tasi	Sea.
Tokui	To work, work.
Tsinih	Canoe.
Tsuhan	Meeting house for the *tsunon* and male members of a *pinaposa*, where feasts are held. Halia and Haku: *tsuhana*.
Tsunon	<u>Chief</u>, 'traditional leader'. The firstborn son of the firstborn woman of a *ngorer*. Halia and Haku: *tsuhono*.
Tui	Slit-gong, <u>garamut</u>. Comes in three sizes in Buka. An important aspect of Buka everyday life in the past. Nowadays used only on ceremonial occasions.
Wasim leg	The custome of pouring water over the legs of a person of rank after a journey, in order to 'wash off the salt' and acknowledge the person's status.

Pororan Travel Routes, 2004–05

Listed below are some of the routes Pororan Islanders used to travel to Buka Town in 2004–05. The relative advantages and disadvantages of each route were a common topic of Pororan conversations, which is why I record these details here. Costs are given in Papua New Guinea Kina. In 2004–05, K1 was equivalent to 0.17–0.19 of a British pound.

1. *Kura maror itasi* / <u>bihainim highway solwara</u>: taking a boat to town

Usually chosen only by boat owners (there were five at Pororan Village in 2004–05) and their close relatives, who travel free (but might contribute to the costs of fuel). Also used by people who can afford the passenger fare and who want to reach Town quickly.

Costs, one-way: K20 passenger fare. Free if close relations to boat owner. Cost of fuel: K100.

Duration: 45 mins—4h, depending on load, number of stops (Petats and Matsungan, for refuelling or chewing betel), and fishing excursions.

Perceived disadvantages: High costs; having to negotiate a boat ride (shameful even with distant relatives, and people are very ashamed to ask 'other people' for transport); having to submit to the boat owner's schedule; the shame and anger if a boat owner leaves early in the morning without informing the passengers he agreed to take, which is blamed on greed (fuel costs rise with load) and the desire to show superiority; fuel shortages on the island; wind may make Buka passage difficult to navigate.

Perceived advantages: Fast, pleasant.

2. *Kura maror [ilatu]* / following the [bush] road: going by road

a) Taking a passenger boat to the market at Karoola, then taking the Karoola-Town truck:

Often done by women travelling to Town for shopping or visiting relatives.

Costs, one-way: K2.5 boat, K7 truck.

Duration: Approximately 4–6 h.

Perceived disadvantages: having to be at the beach before sunrise to secure a seat on one of the market boats; the Karoola truck has a reputation for breaking down frequently; the Karoola feeder road gets muddy and bumpy after rain, requiring passengers to get off and push the truck; difficulties of finding transport back to the island once in Town (mentioned by women with small children).

Perceived advantages: Low costs.

b) Hiring a boat and truck for the journey:

Most commonly done by a group of Pororan workmen for travelling to Town on Mondays and returning on Fridays of Saturdays.

Costs, one-way: K 2.5 boat, K7 truck (passenger fare).

Duration: 4–16 h.

Perceived disadvantages: To Town: the frequent break-downs of the truck; to the island: having to travel through the bush at night (fear of spirits); break-downs of the truck make the islanders arrive late on the beach—their hired boat might have returned to the island. They then signal to the island by torch, send one person by canoe (borrowed from Karoola residents), or sleep on the beach. Women usually avoid this truck because of the men's heavy drinking. Women with children fear the cold at Karoola at night.

Perceived advantages: Arranged by a particular workman on a regular basis, therefore no organizational difficulties or shame of asking for transport.

c) Going through Kessa:

Usually for visiting Haku villages, most commonly after the Saturday market in 2004.

Sometimes used for transporting copra to Town on a truck belonging to a Haku relative. Not used much in 2005, after the Kessa market was discontinued because of arguments between the Pororans and the Haku. The Hitou, however, are said to have closer connection to Haku, and might have travelled through Kessa more frequently in 2005 than the Pororans.

Costs, one-way: K3 boat (passenger fare), truck depending on distance (max. K10 to Town) and passenger's relations to owner (no charge for relatives).

Duration: Depending on destination, from 2 h (waiting for boat's departure on Pororan, market, short truck ride) to 5 h (continuing by truck all the way to town).

Perceived disadvantages: Higher costs and longer duration than the Karoola route if the destination is Town.

Perceived advantages: Haku trucks are said to be better maintained, as is the road (except for the stretch between Kessa market and Lontis Village). Contact with Haku relatives.

3. *Kura ramun* / [following the river]: going up the Gagan River:

In 2005, a market between island (mostly Yaparu Village) women and women from Kohiso and Gagan, discontinued during the Crisis, was re-established. Some women used the occasion to visit Solos relatives. Others, with close connections to a prominent Solos leader and politician, visited his house at Gagan after the market, and took a ride on his jeep to Town.

Costs, one-way: K5 (boat).

Duration: Depends on duration of visit.

Perceived disadvantages: The majority of Pororan villagers, whose relations to this particular Solos leader were cool, never considered this option.

Perceived advantages: Yaparu women welcomed the establishment of a market that they say was bigger than the Kessa or Karoola market, and the connections to Solos relatives it helped to facilitate. The option of another transport route to the mainland appeared to be valued as a side effect, but no more.

Some Fishing Terms

Table B.1 • Fishing Methods and Species Caught

Method	Location	Species caught
Gathering shellfish	Reef	*Mamop* [clam shell], *Kessa* [shell-fish]: *telepoits, hit, teran, kabelu, kun, binivan, kevan, talas, kati Pisu* [seaweed] *Matats* [sponge—broken off reef with iron pole]
Fishing on the reef (with iron pole, or string and hook) and off the reef's edge	Reef, reef's edge	*Ku, noku, kinon, gereger, kot, mul, pail, kueina, nihon, buruh, kamou, kalipou* [eel], *lout* [octopus]
Fishing in the lagoon	Lagoon	*Kuia, monosing, mul, pail, rahalein, malat, kinon, togi*
Fishing in the open sea	Open sea	*Pinipun, sioh, kahik, tosabau, kalas, atun* [bonito], *kekek, tangili, pilpili, wak, baki* [shark]
Net fishing	Lagoon	*Sioh, luas, mul*
Spear fishing	Passages on the reef, open sea	*Baki* [shark], *numeh* [turtle], *toatoh* [turtle], *reki, noku, epah* [stingray], *bal, mamin, toben*
Going to the mangroves at night	Mangroves	*Kuk* [mud crab]

Source: Collation of questionnaire filled in by students of Year 3, Pororan Primary School, July 2006

Fishing Locations:

Lis: edge of reef, open sea (speaker on the island)
Loul: open sea (speaker at sea)
Balat: lagoon
Peki: reef
Manguru: mangrove

Equipment, Line-fishing:

Ahon: fishing string

Guap: vine for making fishing string

Hoat: bamboo rod, with or without string

Tsikul: bamboo (for making *hoat*)

Botol: Bottle (for tying the string around)

Huk: small, store-bought iron hook

Bona: fishing basket, for women to tie around hips when standing on the reef

Kohel: basket (generic)

Tsinih: canoe with outrigger [*hatal*], one or two seats

Hos: paddle

Hatiam: anchor

Equipment, Net Fishing:

Bian: net (generic)

Bianatsian: the largest kind of net

Kabir: a net of medium size (about 5 m long), used by young people to practice

Kesul: smaller net (about 3 m long)

Sasop: the smallest kind of net, used mostly for catching bait and very small fish

Equipment, Trolling for Bonito:

Palangon: troll

Ngats: hook

Nah: hook of turtle shell, attached to the hook base with string

Gol: base of the hook

Mon: canoe without outrigger, up to five seats for two men each

Ubot: boat

Equipment No Longer Used:

(Ha)hatoa: fishing kite

Hualing: bow

Lalak: fishing spear

Suup: fish trap

Tok Pisin and Hapororan Kin Terms

Table C.1 • Tok Pisin and Hapororan Kin Terms

Tok Pisin	Genealogical position relative to ego	Hapororan	Genealogical position relative to ego
<u>Bubu</u>	MM, MF, FM, FF, DD, DS, SD, SS	*Tubugi*	MM, MF, FM, FF, MMZ, MMB, MFB, MFZ, FMZ, FMB, FFB, FFZ
		Tubunei	DD, DS, SS, SD; all children in the village two generations below ego
<u>Mama</u>	M; polite address for WM, HM	*Muntsinan*	M
		Kawa	Address for M, MZ, FZ, MB
<u>Papa</u>	F; polite address for WF, HF	*Muntaman*	F
		Titi	Address for F, FB
<u>Auntie</u>	MZ, FZ; loosely: whomever M or F address as susa	*Hatsinan*	MZ, FZ
<u>Uncle</u>	MB, FB; Loosely: whomever M or F address as brata	*Sungut*	MB
		Hasungut	All men of ego's matrilineage in the generation above ego
		Hataman	FB
<u>Susa/Sista</u>	Z; female cousin (usually parallel cousin, but can be used for cross-cousin). Old people: cross-sex sibling/ parallel cousin	*Motohan*	Opposite-sex sibling
		(Ha)Motohan	Opposite-sex parallel cousin

Table C.1 • Tok Pisin and Hapororan Kin Terms *(continued)*

Tok Pisin	Genealogical position relative to ego	Hapororan	Genealogical position relative to ego
Brata	B; male cousin (usually parallel cousin, but can be used for cross-cousin). Old people: same-sex sibling/parallel cousin	*Munasin*	Same-sex sibling
		(Ha)Munasin	Same-sex parallel cousin
Cousin	Cross-cousin, (parallel cousin)	*Hinas*	Cross-cousin
Pikinini	D, S	*Munatun, a pian tson/a pian hihin*	D/S; used by *tsunon* for all members of the *pinaposa* in the generation below ego
Meri/misis bilong mi	My wife	*A hihin tagoan*	My wife
Man bilongmi	My husband	*A tson tagoan*	My husband
Tambu	WM, WF, WZ, WB, HM, HF, HZ, HB	*Suhan*	WM, WF, HM, HF, (WB, WZ, HZ, HB, SW, DH, BW, ZH)
		Halis	ZH, DH
		Ehis	SW; in-married woman in the generation below ego
		Ehan	BW; in-married woman in the same generation as ego
Hap tambu		*Hahagon*	Whomever Z or B call Halis

Stories and Solomon

1. Stories

a) Origin of the Western Islands:

The following story, which describes the origin of all Western Islands, is sometimes told as an alternative to the story of rubbish floating from the Gagan River, which accounts for the emergence of Pororan in particular. I heard slightly different versions of the story on both Pororan and Petats. Another version can be found in the notebooks of Beatrice Blackwood, in the Beatrice Blackwood Collection at the Pitt Rivers Museum, Oxford. Presented below is the version that Kil told me as we travelled along the Buka shoreline by boat:

> A man and two women travelled in a canoe. They travelled along, and the shoreline [of Buka] emerged behind them as they travelled. The man was chewing betel nut. He chewed and threw the skin away into the sea. That's it, every piece of skin turned into an island. You see, this shoreline here is very straight, this is where the man was steering. He kept chewing betel to keep himself awake. He kept throwing skins away, and these islands emerged: Sal and Matsungan, and Petats and Yaming, and then us, Pororan, and Hitou. But there, you see, at Bei, the women took over steering. And they were quarrelling, you know, and so the shoreline was no longer straight. Then over there at Kessa, the man took over steering again, so the coast in Haku and Halia are very straight. That way, they came back, they went around and around and made all of Buka Island.

b) Brutsiangin:

This is the story of the pig, one of the most popular stories on Pororan, as Tsireh told it to me. Gordon Thomas collected another version of this story on Pororan in the 1920s (see Blackwood n.d.). He calls the pig Brutziengi. The story is also told on the Buka west coast and on Nissan Island, although I do not know if the versions are the same. For a similar story from the Massim, see Battaglia 1990: 50–51; and from Tanna, see Bonnemaison 1994: 137–38.

> Brutsiangin is this big pig. Really big, and everyone is afraid of him. They were so afraid, they decided to leave the island. But when they set off, their canoes were too full. Two old women were left behind. They are afraid, too, of the pig. They make a small banana garden for themselves. Their bananas grow and look beautiful. So each of the women marries a banana from the garden. Then, they become pregnant. They use *eitah* [fans made of coconut fronds] to make the babies grow faster. They give birth now, each to a boy. Again, the women fan the boys to make them grow fast. They grow very fast. They are strong now. The women say to each other: 'Let's show them how to use bow and arrow.' The women make many spears and bows and arrows and the boys practice. You see, this mark on the *uotsil* [a kind of tree]? This is where they practiced. Then, when the boys can hit now, the women give them lots of arrows and tell them to go and fight the pig. The boys go now to fight the pig. They stand on a tree and they shout 'Hey, you come now! You come out! Are you afraid of us? Hehe, you are afraid!' That's it, the pig comes out now, and they fight. The older brother shoots first. Then the younger. Then the older again. The pig is dead. The two women are very happy now. They cut the pig. Then they beat the *tui* [slit-gong] to call back the people who left. The others hear the beating of the *tui* now and come back. 'Who has killed the pig?', they ask. The women show them their sons, the sons of the bananas. That's it. All the women now want to marry the two boys who killed the pig. The pig is huge! Have you seen the hole in the ground, up on the cliff [pointing directions]? And the hole on the reef out there [pointing again]? This is where the pig stomped its legs.

2. *Solomon*

Solomon are a genre of songs that were sung competitively by 'bamboo bands' in the area in 2004–05, and that were said to continue a tradition of competitive singing and dancing at feasts in the colonial past. *Solomon* were dreamt by old men at particular locations, and often (but not always) described characteristics of the place. The examples below come from Pororan and Hitou. They draw attention to the importance of the marine environment, of fishing, and of movements and looks.

a) 'Little Mudcrab'

Francis learned this *solomon* when sitting on the beach at his hamlet. Plisoh children used to sing it in 2004–05. It describes the way that mud-crabs stand on their legs and move their arms as if waving out to the sea:

A tsi kuk a tsi kekerek :‖	A little mudcrab:‖
Tsitsing ikotolan :‖	Stands up on the beach :‖
Ngakano utasi :‖	Calls out to the sea :‖
Matoutuno umalei :‖	[Because it] fears the birds :‖

b) *"Tosabau"* [a fish species, caught with lines]

Sung by Hitou women at Telatu Village, Solos language area, to welcome American tourists:

Sun utsineh, tosabau te rumunum ehe.
Eri esua, sua ba ba, eri esua tere tosabau.
Eri esua, sua ba ba, sua ba ba tere tosabau,
Hamok upan ahon, ba tosabau te lu e n'ahon.

Paddle the canoe, *tosabau*, you are around over there.
We paddle, paddle on, we paddle for the *tosabau*.
We paddle, paddle on, paddle on for the *tosabau*,
Throw out now the string, so that the *tosabau* takes the string.

c) 'Kesa' [Shellfish]

Sung by Hitou women at Telatu Village, Solos language area, to welcome American tourists:

Tasi te posanam
Eri esu, su ba ba tsineh.
Tsina nigao, o kesa te pirakan itasi. :‖

The sea is high
We paddle, paddle the canoe.
Good mother, shellfish is plentiful at sea.

d) Lulutsi

Sung by the Lulutsi children:

A Lulutsi esileri :‖	We, the Lulutsi move along :‖
Etsil esileri:‖	We get up and move along :‖
Hobot itarara.	Everyone sees us.

BIBLIOGRAPHY

• • • • • • • • • • • • • •

Akimichi, T. 1995. 'Indigenous Resource Management and Sustainable Development: Case Studies from Papua New Guinea and Indonesia'. *Anthropological Science* 103: 321–27.

Amnesty International. 1993. 'Under the Barrel of a Gun: Bougainville 1991–1993'. ASA index 34/05/93. http://www.amnestyusa.org/countries/papua_new_guinea/document.do?id=C791A586DB4977DA802569A6006041FE. Accessed 10 November, 2005.

Anderson, B. 1991. *Imagined Communities: Reflections on the Origin and Spread of Nationalism*. London: Verso (orig. pub. 1983).

Archer, F. P. 1945–46. Notes on Villages Visited on Buka Patrol, 24 Dec 1945–17 Jan 1946, and census. Patrol Reports, Pacific Manuscript Bureau, Research School of Pacific and Asian Studies. Canberra: Australian National University.

Astuti, R. 1995. *People of the Sea: Identity and Descent among the Vezo of Madagascar*. Cambridge: Cambridge University Press.

Aswani, S. 1999. 'Common Property Models of Sea Tenure: A Case Study from Roviana and Vonavona Lagoons, New Georgia, Solomon Islands'. *Human Ecology* 27: 417–53.

Bamford, S. 2004. 'Conceiving Relatedness: Non-Substantial Relations among the Kamea of Papua New Guinea'. *Journal of the Royal Anthropological Institute* 10: 287–306.

Bamford, S. and J. Leach, eds. 2009. *Kinship and Beyond: The Genealogical Model Reconsidered*. London: Berghahn Books.

Barnes, J. 1962. 'African Models in the New Guinea Highlands'. *Man (N.S.)* 62: 5–9.

Basso. 1996. *Wisdom Sits in Places: Landscape and Language among the Western Apache*. Albuquerque: University of New Mexico Press.

Battaglia, D. 1983. 'Projecting Personhood in Melanesia: The Dialectics of Artefact Symbolism on Sabarl Island'. *Man (N.S.)* 18: 289–304.

———. 1990. *On the Bones of the Serpent: Person, Memory, and Mortality in Sabarl Island Society*. Chicago: University of Chicago Press.

———. 1993. 'At Play in the Fields (and Borders) of the Imaginary: Melanesian Transformations of Forgetting'. *Cultural Anthropology* 8: 430–42.

———. 1999. 'Toward an Ethics of the Open Subject: Writing Culture in Good Conscience'. In *Anthropological Theory Today*, ed. H. L. Moore. Cambridge: Polity Press.

Bell, F.L.S. 1953. 'Land Tenure in Tanga'. *Oceania* 24: 28–57.

Bell, J. A., and H. Geismar, eds. 2009. 'Materializing Oceania'. *The Australian Journal of Anthropology* 20 (special issue): 3–27.

Bender, B., ed. 1993. *Landscape: Politics and Perspectives*. Oxford: Berg.

Blackwood, B. 1935. *Both Sides of Buka Passage*. Oxford: Clarendon.

———. n.d. Petats Field Notebooks. Beatrice Blackwood Collection. Oxford: Pitt Rivers Museum.

Bolton, L. 1999. 'Women, Place and Practice in Vanuatu: A View from Ambae'. *Oceania* 70: 43–55.

———. 2003. *Unfolding the Moon: Enacting Women's Kastom in Vanuatu*. Honolulu: University of Hawai'i Press.

Bonnemaison, J. 1984. 'The Tree and the Canoe: Roots and Mobility in Vanuatu Societies'. *Pacific Viewpoint* 25: 117–51.

———. 1994. *The Tree and the Canoe: History and Ethnogeography of Tanna*. Honolulu: University of Hawai'i Press.

British and Foreign Bible Society. 1934. *U Bulugan u Raeh ter e Jisas Krais te Keleg e nin e Mak. St. Mark's Gospel in Petats*, tentative ed. London: British and Foreign Bible Society.

Carrier, J. G. 1981. 'Ownership of Productive Resources on Ponam Island, Manus Province'. *Journal de la Société des Océanistes* 37: 205–17.

Carrier, J. G. and A. H. Carrier. 1983. 'Profitless Property: Marine Ownership and Access to Marine Resources'. *Ethnology* 22: 133–51.

———. 1985. 'A Manus Centenary: Production, Kinship and Exchange in the Admiralty Islands'. *American Ethnologist* 12: 505–22.

———. 1989. *Wage, Trade and Exchange in Melanesia: A Manus Society in the Modern State*. Berkeley: University of California Press.

Carsten, J. 1997. *The Heat of the Hearth: The Process of Kinship in a Malay Fishing Community*. Oxford: Clarendon.

Carsten, J., ed. 2000. *Cultures of Relatedness: New Approaches to the Study of Kinship*. Cambridge: Cambridge University Press.

Connell, J. 1978. *Taim Bilong Mani: The Evolution of Agriculture in a Solomon Island Society*. Canberra: Australian National University Press.

———. 1997. *Papua New Guinea: The Struggle for Development*. London: Routledge.

Corsín Jimenéz, A. 2003. 'On Space as a Capacity'. *Journal of the Royal Anthropological Institute* 9: 137–59.

Crocombe, R. G., ed. 1971. *Land Tenure in the Pacific*. Melbourne: Oxford University Press.

Crook, T. 2007. *Anthropological Knowledge, Secrecy and Bolivip, Papua New Guinea: Exchanging Skin*. Oxford: Oxford University Press.

Davies, H. L. 2005. 'The Geology of Bougainville'. In *Bougainville Before the Conflict*, ed. A. J. Regan and H. Griffin. Canberra: Pandanus Books.

Dorney, S. 1998. *The Sandline Affair: Politics and Mercenaries and the Bougainville Crisis*. Sydney: ABC Books.

Dove, J., T. Miriung and M. Togolo. 1974. 'Mining Bitterness'. In *Problem of Choice: Land in Papua New Guinea's Future*, ed. P. Sack. Canberra: Australian National University Press.

Epstein, A. L. 1969. *Matupit: Land, Politics and Change among the Tolai of New Britain*. Canberra: Australian National University Press.

Fajans, J. 1997. *They Make Themselves: Work and Play among the Baining of Papua New Guinea*. Chicago: Chicago University Press.

Feil, D. K. 1984. 'Beyond Patriliny in the New Guinea Highlands'. *Man (N.S.)* 19: 50–76.

Feld, S., and K. H. Basso, eds. 1996. *Senses of Place*. Santa Fe: School of American Research Press.

Filer, C. 1990. 'The Bougainville Rebellion, the Mining Industry and the Process of Social Disintegration in Papua New Guinea'. *Canberra Anthropology* 13: 1–39.

———. 1992. 'The Escalation of Disintegration and the Reinvention of Authority'. In *The Bougainville Crisis: 1991 Update*, ed. D. Spriggs. Canberra: Department for Political and Social Change, RSPAS, ANU and Crawford Press.

———. 1997a. 'Compensation, Rent and Power in Papua New Guinea'. In *Compensation for Resource Development in Papua New Guinea*, ed. S. Toft. Canberra: Law Reform Commission of Papua New Guinea and Research School of Pacific and Asia Studies, Australian National University.

Filer, C., ed. 1997b. *The Political Economy of Forest Management in Papua New Guinea*. Port Moresby: National Research Institute and International Institute for Environment and Development.

Filer, C., and N. Sekhran, eds. 1998. *Loggers, Donors and Resource owners*. London: International Institute for Environment and Development.

Foale, S. 2005. 'Sharks, Sea Slugs and Skirmishes: Managing Marine and Agricultural Resources on Small, Overpopulated Islands in Milne Bay, PNG'. Working Papers, Resource Management in Asia Pacific Programme, Research School of Pacific and Asian Studies. Canberra: Australian National University.

Fortes, M. 1950. 'Kinship and Marriage among the Ashanti'. In *African Systems of Kinship and Marriage*, ed. A. R. Radcliffe-Brown and D. Forde. London: Oxford University Press.

———. 1984. Foreword to *The Garia*, ed. P. Lawrence. Melbourne: Melbourne University Press.

Fortune, R. 1963. *Sorcerers of Dobu: The Social Anthropology of the Dobu Islanders of the Western Pacific*. New York: Dutton (orig. pub. 1932).

Foster, R. 1992. 'Commoditization and the Emergence of Kastam as a Cultural Category: a New Ireland Case in Comparative Perspective'. *Oceania* 62: 284–94.

———. 1995. *Social Reproduction and History in Melanesia: Mortuary Ritual, Gift Exchange and Custom in the Tanga Islands*. Cambridge: Cambridge University Press.

Fox, J. J. 1971. 'Sister's Child as Plant: Metaphors in an Idiom of Consanguinity'. In *Rethinking Kinship and Marriage*, ed. R. Needham. London: Tavistock.

Fox, J. J., and C. Sather, eds. 1996. *Origins, Ancestry and Alliance: Explorations in Austronesian Ethnography*. Canberra: Australian National University Press.

Friederici, H. 1910. 'Die Insel Buka'. *Deutsche Kolonialzeitung* 27: 788.

Ghai, Y., and A. J. Regan. 2000. 'Bougainville and the Dialectics of Ethnicity, Autonomy and Separation'. In *Autonomy and Ethnicity: Negotiating Competing Claims in Multi-Ethnic States*, ed. Y. Ghai. Cambridge: Cambridge University Press.

———. 2002. 'Constitutional Accommodation and Conflict Prevention'. In *Accord. Weaving Consensus. The Papua New Guinea—Bougainville Peace Process*, ed. A. Carl and L. Garasu. London: Conciliation Resources.

Gillison, G. 1993. *Between Culture and Fantasy: A New Guinea Highlands Mythology*. Chicago: University of Chicago Press.

Griffin, J. 1973. Bougainville—Em Kantri Bilong Yumi. *New Guinea* 1: 41–50.

———. Bougainville—Occultus Sed Non Ignatus. *New Guinea* 10: 43–50.

———. 1977. Local Government Councils as an Instrument of Political Mobiliza-
tion in Bougainville. In *Local Government Councils in Bougainville*, ed. J. Connell.
Christchurch: University of Canterbury.

Hagai, F. 1966. Explaining Hahalis. *New Guinea* 1: 12–14.

Hahl, A. 1904. 'Reise auf die Salomonsinsel'. *Deutsches Kolonialblatt* 15: 61–64.

Handler, R. 1984. 'On Sociocultural Discontinuity: Nationalism and Cultural Objectification in Quebec'. *Current Anthropology* 25: 55–71.

Hannett, L. 1969a. 'Down the Kieta Way: Independence for Bougainville?' *New
Guinea* 4: 8–14.

———. 1969b. 'Resuming Arawa: Discrimination Against the Whites?' *New Guinea*
4: 72–74.

Hanson, A. 1989. 'The Making of the Maori: Culture Invention and its Logic'. *American Anthropologist* 91: 890–902.

Harding, T. G. 1967. *Voyagers of the Vitiaz Strait: Study of a New Guinea Trade System*. Seattle: University of Washington Press.

Harrison, S. 1990. *Stealing People's Names: History and Politics in a Sepik River Cosmology*. Cambridge: Cambridge University Press.

———. 1993. *The Mask of War: Violence, Ritual, and the Self in Melanesia*. Manchester: Manchester University Press.

Havini, M. 2000. Bougainville: Peoples Integrated Development Peace and Economic Self-reliance. NFIP Forum on Peace and Human Security in the 21st century. Peace Boat M.V. Oliva, Brisbane, Auckland, NZ.

Hayes, G. 1993. '"MIRAB" Processes and Development on Small Pacific Islands: A
Case Study from the Southern Massim, Papua New Guinea'. *Pacific Viewpoint*
34: 153–78.

Hirsch, E., and M. O'Hanlon, eds. 1995. *Anthropology of Landscape: Perspectives on
Place and Space*. Oxford: Oxford University Press.

Hirsch, E., and M. Strathern, eds. 2004. *Transactions and Creations: Property Debates
and the Stimulus of Melanesia*. Oxford: Berghahn.

Hobsbawm, E. J., and O. O. Ranger, eds. 1983. *The Invention of Tradition*. Cambridge:
Cambridge University Press.

Hocart, A. M. 1922. 'The Cult of the Dead in Eddystone of the Solomons'. *Journal of
the Royal Anthropological Institute of Great Britain and Ireland* 52: 71–112.

Hogbin, I., and P. Lawrence, eds. 1967. *Studies in New Guinea Land Tenure*. Sydney:
Sydney University Press.

Hviding, E. 1996. *Guardians of Marovo Lagoon: Practice, Place, and Politics in Mari-
time Melanesia*. Honolulu: University of Hawaii Press.

Hviding, E. and T. P. Bayliss-Smith. 2000. *Islands of Rainforest: Agroforestry, Logging
and Eco-Tourism in Solomon Islands*. Aldershot: Ashgate.

Hyndman, D. 1993. 'Sea Tenure and the Management of Living Marine Resources in
Papua New Guinea'. *Pacific Studies* 16: 99–114.

Ingold, T. 1986. *The Appropriation of Nature: Essays on Human Ecology and Social
Relations*. Manchester: Manchester University Press.

———. 2000. *The Perception of the Environment: Essays on Livelihood, Dwelling and
Skill*. London: Routledge.

Ivens, W. G. 1930. *The Island Builders of the Pacific*. London: Seelsy, Service & Co.
Ltd.

Jessep, O. 1977. 'Land Tenure in a New Ireland Village'. Unpublished Ph.D. dissertation, Australian National University.

Jolly, M., and N. Thomas, eds. 1992. 'The Politics of Tradition in the Pacific'. *Oceania* 62, no. 4 (special issue).

Kalinoe, L., and J. Leach, eds. 2001. *Rationales of Ownership: Ethnographic Studies of Transactions and Claims to Ownership in Contemporary Papua New Guinea*. New Delhi: UBS Publishers' Distributors Ltd.

Kavop, J. 1977. 'Mipela na Kaunsil: A Case Study of the Council Ward System on the West Coast of Buka'. In *Local Government Councils in Bougainville*, ed. J. Connell. Christchurch: University of Canterbury.

Keane, W. 1997. *Signs of Recognition: Powers and Hazards of Representation in an Indonesian society*. Berkeley: University of California Press.

Keesing, R. M. 1975. *Kin Groups and Social Structure*. New York: Harcourt College.

———. 1992. *Custom and Confrontation: The Kwaio Struggle for Cultural Autonomy*. Chicago: University of Chicago Press.

Keesing, R. M., and R. E. Tonkinson, eds. 1982. 'Reinventing Traditional Culture: The Politics of Kastom in Island Melanesia'. *Mankind* 13 (special issue).

Kenneth, R. 2005. 'Land for Agriculture—Silent Women: Men's Voices'. In *Bougainville Before the Conflict*, ed. A. J. Regan and H. Griffin. Canberra: Pandanus Books.

Kinch, J. 2003. Customary Marine Tenure and Rights to Resources in the Milne Bay Province, Papua New Guinea. 2nd Pacific Regional Conference of the International Association for the Study of Common Property Conference, Brisbane.

Konrad, M. 2005. *Nameless Relations: Anonymity, Melanesia, and Reproductive Gift Exchange between British Ova Donors and Recipients*. Oxford: Berghahn.

Küchler, S. 1987. 'Malangan: Art and Memory in Melanesian Society'. *Man (N.S.)* 22: 238–55.

———. 1988. 'Malangan: Objects, Sacrifice, and the Production of Memory'. *American Ethnologist* 14: 626–39.

———. 1993. 'Landscape as Memory: The Mapping of its Process and its Representation in a Melanesian Society'. In *Landscape: Politics and Perspectives*, ed. B. Bender. Oxford: Berg.

———. 2002. *Malanggan: Art, Memory, and Sacrifice*. Oxford: Berg.

Langness, L. L. 1964. 'Some Problems in the Conceptualization of Highlands Social Structures'. *American Anthropologist* 66: 162–82.

Laracy, H. 1976. *Marists and Melanesians: A History of Catholic Missions in the Solomon Islands*. Canberra: Australian National University Press.

Larmour, P., ed. 1991. *Customary Land Tenure: Registration and Decentralisation in Papua New Guinea*. Port Moresby: National Research Institute.

Lawrence, P. 1984. *The Garia: an Ethnography of a Traditional Cosmic System in Papua New Guinea*. Melbourne: Melbourne University Press.

Leach, E. 1961. *Rethinking Anthropology*. London: Robert Cunningham and Sons Ltd.

Leach, J. 2000. 'Situated Connections: Rights and Intellectual Resources in a Rai Coast Society'. *Social Anthropology* 8: 163–79.

———. 2003a. *Creative Land: Place and Procreation on the Rai Coast of Papua New Guinea*. New York: Berghahn Books.

———. 2003b. 'Owning Creativity: Cultural Property and the Efficacy of Kastom on the Rai Coast of PNG'. *Journal of Material Culture* 8: 123–43.

———. 2004. 'Modes of Creativity'. In *Transactions and Creations: Property Debates and the Stimulus of Melanesia*, ed. E. Hirsch and M. Strathern. Oxford: Berghahn Books.

Lederman, R. 1986. *What Gifts Engender: Social Relations and Politics in Mendi, Highland Papua New Guinea*. Cambridge: Cambridge University Press.

Linnekin, J., and L. Poyer, eds. 1990. *Cultural Identity and Ethnicity in the Pacific*. Honolulu: University of Hawai'i Press.

Luana, C. 1969. 'Bek long Bougainville: Gavman i Pulim Mipela Long Wanpela Rot—Tasol.' *New Guinea* 4: 76–80.

Magowan, F. 2001. 'Waves of Knowing: Polymorphism and Co-Substantive Essences in Yolngu Sea Cosmology'. *The Australian Journal of Indigenous Education* 29: 22–35.

Malinowski, B. 1922. *Argonauts of the Western Pacific: An Account of Native Enterprise and Adventure in the Archipelagoes of Melanesian New Guinea*. London: Routledge & Kegan Paul Ltd.

———. 1929. *The Sexual Life of Savages*. New York: Harcourt Brace and World.

Mamak, A., and R. Bedford. 1974. *Bougainvillean Nationalism: Aspects of Unity and Discord*. Christchurch: University of Canterbury.

Mauss, M. 1990. *The Gift*. Oxon: Routledge (orig. pub. 1950).

May, R. 1982. 'Micronationalism in Perspective.' In *Micronationalist Movements in Papua New Guinea*, ed. R. May. Canberra: Australian National University Press.

McKinnon, S. 1991. *From a Shattered Sun: Hierarchy, Gender, and Alliance in the Tanimbar Islands*. Madison: University of Wisconsin Press.

Melk-Koch, M. 2000. 'Die Nördlichen Solomonen'. In *Die Deutsche Südsee 1884–1914: Ein Handbuch*, ed. H. Hiery. Paderborn: Verlag Ferdinand Schöningh.

Merleau-Ponty, M. 1966. *Phänomenologie der Wahrnehmung*. Berlin: de Gruyter & Co. (orig. pub. 1945).

Miller, D. 1987. *Material Culture and Mass Consumption*. Oxford: Basil Blackwell.

Mimica, J. 1988. *Intimations of Infinity: The Mythopoeia of the Iqwaye Counting System and Number*. Oxford: Berg.

Miriori, M. 2002. 'A Bougainville Interim Government (BIG) Perspective on Early Peace Efforts'. In *Accord. Weaving Consensus. The Papua New Guinea—Bougainville Peace Process*, ed. A. Carl and L. Garasu. London: Conciliation Resources.

Mitchell, D. 1982. 'Frozen Assets in Nagovisi'. *Oceania* 53: 56–66.

Mitchell, T. 1988. *Colonising Egypt*. Cambridge: Cambridge University Press.

Momis, J. 1974. 'Taming the Dragon'. In *Problem of Choice: Land in Papua New Guinea's Future*, ed. P. Sack. Canberra: Australian National University Press.

Momis, J., and E. Ogan. 1973. 'A View from Bougainville'. In *Priorities in Melanesian Development*, ed. R. May. Papers delivered at the 6th Waigani Seminar, Canberra, Australian National University.

Mosko, M. 1985. *Quadripartite Structures: Categories, Relations, and Homologies in Bush Mekeo Culture*. Cambridge: Cambridge University Press.

———. 1992. '"Divine Kings" and "Partible Persons" in Melanesia and Polynesia'. *Man (N.S.)* 27: 697–717.

———. 1995. 'Rethinking Trobriand Chieftainship'. *Journal of the Royal Anthropological Institute* 1: 763–85.

Mosko, M., and F. Damon, eds. 2005. *On the Order of Chaos: Social Anthropology and the Science of Chaos*. New York: Berghahn Books.

Munn, N. 1986. *The Fame of Gawa: A Symbolic Study of Value Transformation in a Massim (Papua New Guinea) Society*. Cambridge: Cambridge University Press.

Murdock, G. 1949. *Social Structure*. New York: Macmillan Company.

Narokobi, B. 1983. *The Melanesian Way*. Boroko: Institute of Papua New Guinea Studies.

Nash, J. 1974. *Matriliny and Modernisation: The Nagovisi of South Bougainville*. Canberra: Australian National University.

Nelson, H. 2005. 'Bougainville in World War II'. In *Bougainville Before the Conflict*, ed. A. J. Regan and H. Griffin. Canberra: Pandanus Books.

Nussbaum, M. 1995. 'Objectification'. *Philosophy and Public Affairs* 24: 249–91.

Ogan, E. 1970. 'The Nasioi Vote Again'. *Human Organization* 29: 178–89.

———. 1971. 'Nasioi Land Tenure: An Extended Case Study'. *Oceania* 42: 81–93.

———. 1972. *Business and Cargo: Socio-Economic Change among the Nasioi of Bougainville*. Port Moresby, New Guinea Research Unit, Australian National University.

———. 1996. 'Copra Came before Copper: The Nasioi of Bougainville and Plantation Colonialism, 1902–1964'. *Pacific Studies*, 19, 31–50.

———. 1999. 'The Bougainville Conflict: Perspectives from Nasioi'. Discussion Paper. State, Society and Governance in Melanesia Project. Canberra: Australian National University.

Oliver, D. 1973. *Bougainville: A Personal History*. Melbourne: Melbourne University Press.

Otto, T. 1992. 'The Ways of Kastam: Tradition as Category and Practice in a Manus village'. *Oceania* 62: 264–83.

———. 1998. 'Resource Management in Lavongai and Tigak Islands: Changing Practices, Changing Identities'. In *Pacific Answers to Western Hegemony: Cultural Practices of Identity Construction*, ed. J. Wassmann. Oxford: Berg.

Parkinson, R. 1907. *Dreissig Jahre in der Südsee: Land und Leute, Sitten und Gebräuche im Bismarckarchipel und auf den Deutschen Salomoinseln*. Stuttgart: Strecker & Schroder.

Piot, C. 1999. *Remotely Global: Village Modernity in West Africa*. Chicago: University of Chicago Press.

Pomponio, A. 1990. 'Seagulls Don't Fly into the Bush: Cultural Identity and the Negotiation of Development on Mandok Island, Papua New Guinea'. In *Cultural Identity and Ethnicity in the Pacific*, ed. J. Linnekin and L. Poyer. Honolulu: University of Hawaii Press.

———. 1992. *Seagulls Don't Fly into the Bush: Cultural Identity and Development in Melanesia*. Belmont: Wadsworth.

Powell, H. A., and M. Mosko. 1997. 'Trobriand Chiefs and Fathers'. *Journal of the Royal Anthropological Institute* 3: 154–59.

Premdas, R. 1977. 'Secessionist Politics in Papua New Guinea'. *Pacific Affairs* 50: 64–85.

Reed, A. 2003. *Papua New Guinea's Last Place: Experiences of Constraint in a Postcolonial Prison*. New York: Berghahn Books.

Regan, A. J. 2000. '"Traditional" Leaders and Conflict Resolution in Bougainville: Reforming the Present by Re-Writing the Past?' In *Reflections on Violence in Melanesia*, ed. S. Dinnen and A. Ley. Canberra: Hawkins Press, Asia Pacific Press.

———. 2002. 'Phases of the Negotiation Process'. In *Accord. Weaving Consensus: The Papua New Guinea—Bougainville Peace Process*, ed. A. Carl and L. Garasu. London: Conciliation Resources.

———. 2005. Preface to *Bougainville Before the Conflict*, ed. A. J. Regan and H. Griffin. Canberra: Pandanus Books.

Richards, A. I. 1939. *Land, Labour and Diet in Northern Rhodesia: An Economic Study of the Bemba Tribe*. Oxford: Oxford University Press.

———. 1941. 'A Problem of Anthropological Approach'. *Bantu Studies: A Journal Devoted to the Scientific Study of Bantu, Hottentot and Bushman* 15: 45–52.

———. 1950. 'Some Types of Family Structure among the Central Bantu'. In *African Systems of Kinship and Marriage*, ed. A. R. Radcliffe-Brown and D. Forde. London: Oxford University Press.

———. 1956. *Chisungu: A Girls' Initiation Ceremony Among the Bemba of Northern Rhodesia*. London: Faber & Faber.

Riles, A. 2001. *The Network Inside Out*. Ann Arbour: University of Michigan Press.

———. 2004. 'Property as Legal Knowledge: Means and Ends'. *Journal of the Royal Anthropological Institute* 10: 775–95.

Rimoldi, M. 1971. 'The Hahalis Welfare Society of Buka, New Guinea'. Unpublished PhD dissertation, Australian National University.

Rimoldi, M., and E. Rimoldi. 1992. *Hahalis and the Labour of Love: A Social Movement on Buka Island*. Oxford: Berg.

Rio, K. M. 2007. *The Power of Perspective: Social Ontology and Agency on Ambrym, Vanuatu*. New York: Berghahn Books.

Rodman, M. C. 1985. 'Moving Houses: Residential Mobility and the Mobility of Residences in Longana, Vanuatu'. *American Anthropologist* 87: 56–72.

———. 1987. *Masters of Tradition: Consequences of Customary Land Tenure in Longana, Vanuatu*. Vancouver: University of British Columbia Press.

———. 1992. 'Empowering Place: Multilocality and Multivocality'. *American Anthropologist* 94: 640–56.

Rumsey, A., and J. Weiner, eds. 2001. *Emplaced Myth: Space, Narrative and Knowledge in Aboriginal Australia and Papua New Guinea*. Honolulu: University of Hawaii Press.

———. 2004. *Mining and Indigenous Lifeworlds in Australia and Papua New Guinea*. Wantage: Sean Kingston.

Rutherford, D. 2003. *Raiding the Land of the Foreigners: The Limits of the Nation on an Indonesian Frontier*. Princeton: Princeton University Press.

Sack, P. 1973. *Land Between Two Laws: Early European Land Acquisitions in New Guinea*. Canberra: Australian National University Press.

———. 2005. 'German Colonial Rule in the Northern Solomons'. In *Bougainville Before the Conflict*, ed. A. J. Regan and H. Griffin. Canberra: Pandanus Books.

Sagir, B. 2003. 'The Politics and Transformations of Chieftainship in Haku, Buka Island, Papua New Guinea'. Unpublished PhD dissertation, Australian National University.

———. 2005. 'We Are Born Chiefs: Chiefly Identity and Power in Haku, Buka Island'. In *Bougainville Before the Conflict*, ed. A. J. Reagan and H. Griffin. Canberra: Pandanus Books.

Sahlins, M. 1985. *Islands of History*. Chicago: University of Chicago Press.

Salisbury, R. 1964. 'New Guinea Highland Models and Descent Theory'. *Man (N.S.)* 64: 168–71.

Sarei, A. H. 1974. *Traditional Marriage and the Impact of Christianity on the Solos of Buka Island*. Canberra: New Guinea Research Unit, Australian National University.

Schneider, D. 1961. 'The Distinctive Features of Matrilineal Descent Groups'. Introduction to *Matrilineal kinship*, ed. D. Schneider and K. Gough. Berkeley: University of California Press.

———. 1965. 'Some Muddles in the Models: Or, How the System Really Works'. In *The Relevance of Models for Social Anthropology*, ed. M. Banton. London: Tavistock.

———. 1968. *American Kinship: A Cultural Account*. Englewood Cliffs: Prentice-Hall.
———. 1984. *A Critique of the Study of Kinship*. Ann Arbour: University of Michigan Press.
Scott, J. C. 1998. *Seeing Like a State: How Certain Schemes to Improve the Human Condition Have Failed*. Yale: Yale University Press.
Scott, M. W. 2000. 'Ignorance is Cosmos: Knowledge is Chaos: Articulating a Cosmological Polarity in the Solomon Islands'. *Social Analysis* 44: 56–83.
———. 2007. *The Severed Snake: Matrilineages, Making Place, and a Melanesian Christianity in Southeast Solomon Islands*. Durham: Carolina Academic Press.
Seidel, H. 1911. 'Die Deutsche Salomoinsel Buka'. *Deutsche Kolonialzeitung*, 28: 208–09.
Sharp, N. 2002. *Saltwater People: The Waves of Memory*. Toronto: University of Toronto Press.
Sohia, P. 2002. 'Early Interventions'. In *Accord. Weaving Consensus. The Papua New Guinea—Bougainville Peace Process*, ed. A. Carl and L. Garasu. London: Conciliation Resources.
Spriggs, M. 1997. *The Island Melanesians*. Oxford: Blackwell.
———. 2005. 'Bougainville's Early History: An Archaeological Perspective'. In *Bougainville Before the Conflict*, ed. A. J. Regan and H. Griffin. Canberra: Pandanus Books.
Stafford, C. 2000. *Separation and Reunion in Modern China*. Cambridge: Cambridge University Press.
Strathern, A. J. 1973. 'Kinship, Descent and Locality: Some New Guinea Examples'. In *The Character of Kinship*, ed. J. Goody. Cambridge: Cambridge University Press.
Strathern, M. 1980. 'No Nature, No Culture: The Hagen Case'. In *Nature, Culture and Gender*, ed. C. MacCormack and M. Strathern. Cambridge: Cambridge University Press.
———. 1984. 'Subject or Object? Women and the Circulation of Valuables in Highlands New Guinea'. In *Women and Property—Women as Property*, ed. R. Hirschon. London: Croom Helm.
———. 1988. *The Gender of the Gift: Problems with Women and Problems with Society in Melanesia*. Berkeley: University of California Press.
———. 1991. *Partial Connections*. Savage, MD: Rowland & Middlefields.
———. 1992a. *After Nature: English Kinship in the Late Twentieth Century*. Cambridge: Cambridge University Press.
———. 1992b. *Reproducing the Future: Essays on Anthropology, Kinship and the New Reproductive Technologies*. Manchester: Manchester University Press.
———. 1992c. 'The Decomposition of an Event'. *Cultural Anthropology* 7: 244–54.
———. 1992d. 'Qualified Value: The Perspective of Gift Exchange'. In *Barter, Exchange and Value: An Anthropological Approach*, ed. C. Humphrey and S. Hugh-Jones. Cambridge: Cambridge University Press.
———. 1996. 'Cutting the Network'. *Journal of the Royal Anthropological Institute* 2: 517–35.
———. 1998. 'Divisions of Interest and Languages of Ownership'. In *Property Relations: Renewing the Anthropological Tradition*, ed. C. M. Hann. Cambridge: Cambridge University Press.
———. 1999. *Property, Substance and Effect: Anthropological Essays on Persons and Things*. London: Athlone.
———. 2001. 'The Patent and the Malanggan'. In *Beyond Aesthetics: Art and the Technologies of Enchantment*, ed. C. Pinney and C. Thomas. Oxford: Berg.

————. 2005. *Kinship, Law and the Unexpected: Relatives Are Always a Surprise*. Cambridge: Cambridge University Press.

Strathern, M., ed. 2000. *Audit cultures: Anthropological studies in Accountability, Ethics and the Academy*. London: Routledge.

Summer Institute of Linguistics. 1976. *U Mak, u Jemis na u Hopis u Jon. Mark and the Epistles of James and John. Petats Language*. Kangaroo Ground, Victoria: Wycliffe Bible Translators.

Sykes, K. 2001. 'Paying a School Fee is a Father's Duty: Critical Citizenship in Central New Ireland'. *American Ethnologist* 28: 5–31.

Thomas, G. 1931. 'Customs and Beliefs of the Natives of Buka.' *Oceania* 2: 220–31.

Tryon, D. 2005. The Languages of Bougainville. In *Bougainville Before the Conflict*, ed. A. J. Regan and H. Griffin. Canberra: Pandanus Books.

Tsibim, D. 1967. 'The Bougainville Affair'. *New Guinea* 1: 33–35.

Tsing, A. 1995. *In the Realm of the Diamond Queen: Marginality in an Out-of-the-Way Place*. Princeton: Princeton University Press.

————. 2005. *Friction: An Ethnography of Global Connection*. Princeton: Princeton University Press.

Wagner, R. 1967. *The Curse of Souw: Principles of Daribi Clan Definition and Alliance in New Guinea*. Chicago: Chicago University Press.

————. 1972. *Habu: The Innovation of Meaning in Daribi Religion*. Chicago: Chicago University Press.

————. 1974. 'Are There Social Groups in the New Guinea Highlands?' In *Frontiers of Anthropology*, ed. M. J. Leaf. New York: D. van Nostrand Company.

————. 1977a. 'Analogic Kinship: A Daribi Example'. *American Anthropologist* 4: 623–42.

————. 1977b. 'Scientific and Indigenous Papuan Conceptions of the Innate: A Semiotic Critique of the Ecological Perspective'. In *Subsistence and Survival: Rural Ecology in the Pacific*, ed. T. P. Bayliss-Smith and R. G. Feachem. London: Academic Press.

————. 1981. *The Invention of Culture*. Englewood Cliffs, Prentice-Hall (orig. pub. 1975).

————. 1986a. *Symbols That Stand for Themselves*. Chicago: Chicago University Press.

————. 1986b. *Asiwinarong: Ethos, Image, and Social Power among the Usen Barok of New Ireland*. Princeton: Princeton University Press.

————. 1987. 'Figure-Ground Reversal among the Barok'. In *Assemblage of Spirits: Idea and Image in New Ireland*, ed. L. Lincoln. New York: George Braziller and the Minneapolis Institute of Arts.

————. 2001. *The Anthropology of the Subject: Holographic Worldview in New Guinea and Its Meaning and Significance for the World of Anthropology*. Berkeley: University of California Press.

Wehner, M., and D. Denoon, eds. 2001. *Without a Gun: Australian Experiences Monitoring Peace in Bougainville 1997–2001*. Canberra: Pandanus Books.

Weiner, A. 1976. *Women of Value, Men of Renown: New Perspectives in Trobriand Exchange*. Austin: University of Texas Press.

Weiner, J. 1988. *The Heart of the Pearl Shell: The Mythological Dimension of Foi Sociality*. Berkeley: University of California Press.

————. 1991. *The Empty Place: Poetry, Space, and Being among the Foi of Papua New Guinea*. Bloomington: Indiana University Press.

———. 1998. The Incorporated Ground: The Contemporary Work of Distribution in the Kutubu Oil Project Area, Papua New Guinea. Working Paper No. 17, Resource Management in Asia-Pacific Project, Division of Pacific and Asian History, Research School for Pacific and Asian Studies, Australian National University, Canberra.

———. 2001a. *Tree Leaf Talk: A Heideggerian anthropology*. Oxford: Berg.

———. 2001b. The Foi Incorporated Land Group: Law and Custom in Group Definition and Collective Action in the Kutubu Oil Project Area, PNG. Working Paper 2001/2, State, Society and Governance in Melanesia Project. Research School of Pacific and Asian Studies, Australian National University, Canberra.

Wickler, S., and M. Spriggs. 1988. 'Pleistocene Human Occupation of the Solomon Islands, Melanesia'. *Antiquity* 62: 703–06.

Woodmansee, M., and P. Jaszi. 1994. *The Construction of Authorship: Textual Appropriation in Law and Literature*. Durham: Duke University Press.

Worsley, P. 1968. *The Trumpet Shall Sound: A Study of 'Cargo' Cults in Melanesia*. London: MacGibbon & Kee (orig. pub. 1957).

ancestors, 11, 13, 39, 41, 83–84, 126, 128, 133, 134n3, 175, 179, 185n3, 197–98
  ancestral migration, 11, 112, 114, 122–24
  ancestral settlement of Pororan, 82, 86, 90, 99n3, 109–110
  ancestral spirits, 94, 96, 149
  Christian lifestyle, 3, 162n2
  habits/ways of the ancestors 8, 14, 57, 84
Arawa, 4, 6, 61, 64, 107, 115, 167, 177
Archer, Fred, 3, 22
arm movement, *see* gesture
Arosi, 173–175
Astuti, Rita, 1, 49n6, 171
attraction, 44, 47–48, 75, 120–21, 143, 185, 189. *See also* looks
  and stones, 91, 96–97
  and talk, 175
  and tsunon, 93, 108, 154
  of fish, 35, 37, 41–42, 96–97
Australians (in Bougainville), 3–4, 7, 89, 169
Austronesian ethnographic comparison 79n6, 96, 133–34, 189
Austronesian languages and settlement (of Buka and Bougainville), 2, 23n15
Autonomous Region of Bougainville, 4–7, 178, 185
autonomy, 6–7, 167, 177–78, 182, 184

bait, 34–35, 37, 41, 208
bananas 9, 45, 78, 120, 138–39, 158, 171
  and *pinaposa* (mainland), 124–125, 190
  and gender, 74, 212
  in mainland gardens, 13, 31, 117–118
Barok, 55, 156–57, 161, 193
'baskets' (women captured in warfare), 111–112

Battaglia, Debbora, 16, 78, 137, 145, 148, 150, 152, 212
betel nuts, 10, 31, 55–56, 60–61, 80, 138, 142, 153–54, 202, 211
Bishop Wade, 88
Blackwood, Beatrice, 23n17, 46, 49n1, 49n8, 50nn10–11, 50nn13–14, 79n2, 96, 99n2, 133, 135n11, 200, 211–212
boats
  and boat owners, 8, 10, 12, 15, 92, 203
  and fishing, 27, 38, 42, 208
  and interactions with relatives, 115–117, 119–20, 123, 138–39, 142
  listening to and watching, 18, 25, 116
  Tanimbar stone boats, 96–97
  travel to Town, 54, 62, 72, 80–81, 92, 117, 203–5
body, 69
  after death, 146–150, 152–153, 157, 192
  as object during *sinahan*, 143, 145, 155, 191
body language, 44, 188. *See also* gestures
Bolton, Lissant, 17, 74, 164–65
bonito 37–42, 44, 50n13, 96–97, 104, 207–208
Bonnemaison, Joel, 22n1, 98, 100n12, 113, 187, 197, 212
Bougainville Crisis, 5–7, 13–15, 28, 115–116, 119, 135n6, 166, 169–70, 172–73, 177–78, 181, 190, 205
Bougainville Revolutionary Army (BRA), 5–6, 79n5, 119
Bougainvillean separatism, 5, 172
boundaries
  at sea, 26, 49n4, 195–96
  of *pinaposa*, 107, 110, 112
  on Pororan, 179, 191
  on the mainland, 12–13, 178

Buka history, 2–8
Buka Liberation Front (BLF), 6
bung malot, 146, 153–57, 161–62, 194, 199
burial, 146, 148, 151, 157–58, 199
Burunotoui, 3, 162n2

canoes, 25, 49n1, 201–2, 211–213
    as a means of escaping village life, 29, 48, 65
    in *hahur*, 158, 160, 184, 192
    in Tanna, 197
    use for travel, 8, 204
    use in fishing, 11, 25, 27, 33, 35–36, 208
    movements of, 38–40, 187
    war canoes, 84. *See also mon*
cargo cults, 3
Carteret Islands, 112
cassava, 3, 9, 12, 117–18, 120, 139, 146, 158
centre (and periphery), 95–99, 122, 125
children
    and fishing, 25, 27–29, 33–35, 37, 40, 43
    and fathers, 67–73, 75, 77, 131, 189, 202. *See also* father's child
    and mothers, 52, 55, 57–62, 66, 75, 77, 131, 190. *See also* mothers
    and rank, 126, 128–30, 135n11
    as messengers, 45, 146–47
    in marriage and mortuary rites, 138–40, 149, 151
church, 12, 23, 86–87
    and mortuary rites, 146, 150–52, 162
    and Sundays, 28, 49, 63–64, 66, 148–9, 162n2, 162n4
clamshell (*mamop*), 33–34, 50, 207
coconut
    as locational marker, 26
    and human beings, 46, 139
    oil, 141
    plantations, 10, 12, 30, 83, 134, 139, 200
    use of fronds, 31, 34–35, 212
    use of shells, 34, 122
colonial resettlement, 1, 86–90, 93, 99n5, 114, 132, 180, 189
colonial history, 2–3, 5, 28, 94, 134, 157, 172, 187, 212
community, 8, 151, 157, 176
    community facilities, 6, 119
    community work, 10, 28
Corsín Jiménez, Alberto, 17, 195

Council of Chiefs, 167. *See also* traditional leadership
Crook, Tony, 23, 55, 77, 193
crying (over the body), 146–47, 149, 153

death
    and messengers, 119, 147
    and mortuary rites, 145–53, 162n4, 163n7, 199
    and the Bougainville Crisis, 6, 14
    and tsunon 126–28, 157–59, 163n9, 192, 199
    causes of, 49n7, 96, 202
decomposition, 20, 96, 122, 129, 189
decoration
    'for decoration only', 96–97
    of bodies, 85, 139–41, 143–45, 155, 182, 191
    of *mon*, 50n10, 85, 182
definition and relation, 76–78, 131–132
dolphin, 26, 37, 201
drifting, 11, 65, 82, 85–88, 98, 113, 139, 142, 198
driftwood, 11–12, 15–17, 87–89, 186
dugong, 26, 96–97

eating
    and kin relations, 31, 49n7, 51, 63–64, 68, 141
    and looking and wanting, 42, 44, 47, 160, 187
    and mortuary rites, 146–47, 153–55, 158
    and witnessing, 126–29
    fish, 29, 32–34, 42, 44, 47, 49n7, 51, 121, 187
    on the mainland, 12–13
elections, 7, 92, 182–83, 185
employment, 8–9, 47
Ernst, Max, 163n10

Fajans, Jane, 161–62, 192–93
fathers, father's people 50n14, 51–52, 54, 57, 59, 62–63, 72–73, 79, 89, 91, 124, 131, 133, 188
    and houses, 67–70, 72, 77
    and *tsunon*, 81, 99n1, 112
    father's face, 68, 71–72, 78
    father's child *(pian hatuhan)*, 63, 91, 151, 202
    making grow *(hatuhan)*, 66–72, 74–75, 77–78, 81–82, 144

feasting
  and fishing, 26, 28, 36–37
  and house building, 67, 132
  and marriage, 142
  and mortuary rites, 146, 149, 153–57,
    162, 163n7, 199. *See also bung
    malot*
  and *pinaposa* relations, 28, 32, 26,
    114–118, 120–121, 132
  and reconciliation, 116–18, 120, 132
  and *tsuhan*, 88, 93, 202
  and *tsunon*, 89–91, 107, 109, 111, 123,
    127, 132, 175, 181
finishing/closing relations, 16, 152, 161–
  162, 185
fire sacrifice *(hahats)*, 38, 96–97, 146, 199
firewood, 10, 57, 60–61
firstborn, 58, 126, 128, 139, 199. 200, 202
fish
  eating, *see* eating
  tense moments of handing over, 43–45,
    160, 187
  species caught, 207
fish trap, 35, 208
fishing, 33–41
  and gender, 25, 29–30, 32, 45–47,
    74–75. *See also* gender
  and space and time, 26–30, 32–33,
    38–40, 42
  at night, 25, 27–28, 34, 36–37, 45, 71,
    116, 207
  camps, 8, 27, 82, 84, 109, 113
  hook, 34, 36–38, 41, 42, 44–45, 47,
    50n12, 50n16, 79n7, 187, 207–8
  knowledge, 27, 38, 40–41
  net, 25–26, 35–36, 207–8
  spots, 26, 36, 39, 96, 195
forgetting, 39–41, 99n11, 55, 72, 119,
  137, 145, 150–53
freedom, 28–29, 30, 32, 39, 77, 182, 188,
  196
friends, 33, 48, 62, 89, 134n6, 140, 147,
  151–52, 202

Gagan (village), 1, 12–14, 74, 205
Gagan River, 11–12, 27, 41, 82, 83, 123,
  205, 211
gardening
  and fishing, 1, 28, 30–33, 49–50n9,
    74–75
  and gender, 29, 74–75
  and *tsunon*, 31–32, 81, 93–94, 181

on Pororan, 28–29, 32, 45, 64, 68
  on the mainland, 30–32
gardens
  made by the Pororans, 8–9, 19, 23n12,
    72, 82, 115, 200, 212
  on the mainland, 3, 7, 12–13, 23n14,
    32, 55, 116–118, 120
gender, 16, 20, 23n18, 32–33, 46–48, 97,
  129, 159, 163n9, 164, 186, 198. *See
  also* gardening and gender; fishing
  and gender
Germans (in Buka), 2–3, 28, 86–88,
  100n11, 172
gesture (arm movement, hand movement), 49, 57–59, 66–69, 75, 77,
  79n7, 81, 83, 87–88, 113, 123,
  131–133, 136, 143, 145, 186–88. *See
  also* body language
gogoa, 122, 183, 199
Gogohei (village), 3, 52–53, 55–56, 70,
  74, 77
Griffin, James, 4, 22n8
gum (in mourning), 158–59, 199

Hahalis (village), 62, 109, 128
Hahalis Welfare Society, 4, 22n5, 132, 172
hahini, 11, 58, 60, 63, 65, 67, 77, 79n3,
  81, 90, 107, 109, 113, 121–22,
  126–30, 135n10, 137–38, 140, 157,
  163n9, 165, 180, 190, 199
hahur, 39–40, 146, 157–62, 163n8, 184,
  192, 199, 202
Haku (language area), 6, 12, 23n15,
  54, 64, 115–16, 118, 150–52, 172,
  204–5, 211,
halat, 27, 34, 199
Halia (language area), 23n15, 211
Hanahan (village), 81, 109, 115, 152
hand movement, *see* gesture
Harrison, Simon, 41, 125
hatsunon, *see* tsunon
Havini, Moses, 169
headhunting, 39, 84–85, 87, 123, 185n3,
  187, 189, 201
help and kin relations, 28, 55–58, 60–62,
  66, 77–78, 107, 112, 115, 118, 131–
  32, 171, 188, 191
hiningal, 27, 33, 34, 36, 200
hitaku, 84, 87, 90–91, 93, 95, 11, 200
hitots, 37, 47, 80
Hitou (island); 8, 23n15, 40, 64, 66, 137–
  40, 142, 205, 211, 213

Hviding, Edvard, 1–2, 17, 22n1, 24n20, 26, 114, 195–96

image, 55, 72–73, 145, 156–57, 159, 161–62, 171, 183–84, 192–93
indeterminacy, *see* movements, indeterminacy of
indirect rule, 2, 86
Ingold, Tim, 24n19, 195
in-law, 22, 31–32, 44, 51–57, 61–65, 69–71, 75, 80, 101, 116–18, 120, 137–40,142–45, 147, 149, 157, 191

Japanese, 3, 22n3, 23n14, 50n16, 89

kal atoh, 88, 91, 200. *See also tsuhan*
Karoola (village), 23n12, 28, 80–81, 107, 115, 204–5
Kastom 7–8, 19–20, 132, 164–69, 173, 176, 178, 181–85, 190–91, 195
Keketin (ancestral place), 19, 90, 180
Kenneth, Roselyn, 12, 14, 16, 25, 73, 119
Kessa (market site), 12, 28, 31, 115, 139, 204–5, 211
kin terms, 54–56, 79n1, 151, 209–10
kite fishing, 35, 44, 208
Kohiso (village), 28, 205
Küchler, Susanne, 1, 16, 114, 145, 152, 171
kukubei, 27, 47, 49n5,
Kuri Village Resort, 91–93, 96–97, 105, 182–83

land tenure, 17, 168, 177–79, 196. *See also* boundaries; straightening the ground
Leach, James, 17, 23n18, 24nn19–20, 46, 50n9, 74, 76, 78, 164–65, 189, 193
Leitana, 12, 93, 189
lies/lying, 10, 55–56, 122, 194
Local Government Councils, 4, 172
Lontis (village), 12–15, 74, 125, 150–52, 163, 205
look, *see ngot*

magic
    fishing magic, 35–37, 50nn13–14
    magic working on people, 44, 47, 66, 71, 73, 85, 120, 144, 154, 201
    not needed on Pororan, 66, 120

Magowan, Fiona, 197, 198n1
mainland women married on Pororan, 32, 52–55, 61–63, 69–71, 77
mak
    of a *tsuhan*, 91
    of being human, 157, 159–60
Malasang (village), 3, 49n2, 115–16, 118, 121–24
Malinowski, Bronislaw, 69, 75, 78
Manuan (island), 27, 179
marine tenure 17, 134, 195–96, 198. *See also* boundaries
markers (locational), 26, 195–196
market (in Buka), 9–10, 28, 31, 33, 36–37, 48, 60, 65, 92, 99n2, 107, 114–15, 152, 204–5
marriage, 19, 31, 66, 71–73, 75–76, 79n2, 89, 108, 114, 120, 128, 136–39, 141, 144, 165, 175, 180, 187, 191, 200. *See also sinahan*
masalai, *see* spirits
matrilineal group, 8–9, 63, 73, 77, 133, 138, 141, 171, 176, 189, 199, 201. *See also ngorer; pinaposa*
matrilineal kinship, 7, 55, 57, 68, 73, 75, 78, 79n8, 108, 111, 114, 131,-32, 134, 159–160, 169, 171, 177–78, 181, 189–91
matrilineal relatives, 14–15, 19, 126–130, 132, 146–47, 151–53, 158, 170, 188
matrilineal spirits, 162n4. *See also* ancestral spirits
mausman, 56, 83, 201
McKinnon, Susan, 23n18, 96–98, 122, 171, 187, 189
migration (ancestral), 11, 19, 95, 112, 114, 117, 121–22, 125, 130, 132–33, 134n5, 165–66, 173-5, 186,
Milne Bay, 11, 49n4
mission (Marist), 3, 86, 99n2, 99n4, 146, 155, 162n2
mon, 37, 50n10, 84–85, 92, 106, 182–85, 201, 208
mortuary rites, 19, 137, 145–46, 153, 156, 165, 187, 191
Mosko, Mark, 20, 23n18, 69, 99n1, 129, 189,
mother
    all the mothers, i.e. senior women, 92, 100n13, 184
    and child, *see* children

and daughter-in-law, 31, 67, 70–71. *See also* in-law
and rank, 126, 133
following/returning to one's mother, 11, 51–54, 57–63, 66, 73, 77, 120, 124, 171 190
'one mother', 107–10, 171. *See also* *pinaposa*
movements
  and relations, 52, 58–59, 64, 73, 75–78, 88, 111–13, 131–33, 151–52, 157, 182. *See also* objectification
  at sea, 25, 38–41, 46, 158–61, 187–88, 196, 198
  attracting fish, 35–37, 44
  controlling/directing, 29–30, 77, 83, 89, 99n1, 137, 142, 153
  defining and relating, *see* definition and relation
  giving shape to, 69, 77, 82, 133–34, 144
  indeterminacy/open-endedness of, 15–16, 21, 44, 49, 65, 88, 125, 142, 145, 184–85, 189, 198. *See also* *roror*
  methods for studying, 17–19
  transformation of, 46–47, 87, 113, 136–37, 142, 159–61, 187–88, 192, 197–98
  verbal rendering of, 54, 66, 187–88
  watching, 10, 15–18, 21, 25, 40, 52–55, 126, 130, 168–70, 175, 185–89
Munn, Nancy, 16, 73, 78, 145, 149, 150, 198

New Ireland, 55, 65, 95, 101, 152, 171, 192
ngorer, 14, 30–31, 36, 107–9, 112–13, 116, 121, 123, 129, 135n9, 161, 168, 201–2
ngot (look, see), 44, 52, 126, 128, 154–55, 188, 201
nitsunon 93, 129–30, 132–33, 175. *See also* *tsunon*
Nova (village), 51, 52, 62, 111
Nova II (hamlet), 116

object (material), 78
objectification, 20–21, 80, 126, 136, 144–50, 159, 164, 168, 172, 175, 189, 194

octopus, 46, 65–66, 94–95, 115–16, 119, 207
origin
  of Buka people, 11, 112–13, 123
  of human beings, 46–47, 184, 188. *See also* Sia and Hulu
  of Pororan Island, 11, 82, 211

pacification, 2, 9, 114
Panguna copper mine, 4–5, 7
passage (in the reef), 25–27, 29, 36, 41, 49n5, 95, 110, 134n4, 195–96, 201, 207
paternal relatives, 52–53, 59, 62, 72, 76, 126–27, 146–53, 158, 183. *See also* father's people
peace process, 6, 15, 91, 134n6, 167, 172, 177, 183–4, 190
personification, 146–50
Petats (island), 22n3, 23n17, 27, 33, 35, 39, 49n1, 49n5, 84, 96–97, 110, 115–16, 134nn3–4, 203, 211
Philippines, 11, 65, 139, 142
pian hatuhan, *see* fathers
pig, 46, 50n10, 86, 93, 99n9, 109, 126–30, 146, 149, 163n7, 194, 211–12
pinaposa
  and <u>masalai</u>, 94–95, 127
  and rank, 132–34
  and *tsunon*'s talk, 108–12
  by the hair, 107
  locations of, 83, 90, 93, 179–82
  names of, 63, 88
  relations across Buka, 112–25, 132, 165
  'their children are stuck together', 57, 63, 108
  writing down, 170–171
pinaposa meetings, 63–65, 78, 87, 90, 107
place, places
  and kinship, 51–52, 57, 61–62, 69–70, 74–78, 189–90, 193
  on Pororan, 80–94, 100n11, 107, 111–13, 130, 134, 179–80, 189
  on the mainland and of relevance to the Pororans, 115, 121–126, 130
  on the mainland *versus* on Pororan, 12–14, 25, 29, 31–32, 61, 93–95, 121–126, 130, 132, 134, 169, 178, 189–90
post-Crisis, 7, 79n5, 173

pre-colonial history (Buka), 1–2, 9, 19, 39, 49n5, 81, 86, 90
processual analysis, 17, 171
pulling
  and stones, 96–97
  a wife (fathers), 67–70, 77, 133, 188–89
  followers (*tsunon*), 82, 85, 88–89, 92, 93, 107–11, 133, 160, 175, 188–89
  in a fishing line, 39–40
Punein, mountain of, 11, 112, 121–23, 130

Rabaul, 11, 65, 69, 101
radio, 7, 10, 167
rank, 23n13, 40, 56, 60, 66, 83–84, 90, 92–93, 109–12, 116, 121, 126–34, 135n8, 142, 146, 149, 153, 158–61, 168, 173–76, 180, 182, 186, 188, 190–94, 199, 201
reconciliation, 7, 116–120, 132, 134n6, 183
Reed, Adam, 48
reef, 11, 16, 19, 25–27, 33–41, 46, 50n15, 53, 58, 60, 77, 81–82, 85, 95–98, 113, 123, 138, 158, 160, 183–84, 188–89, 195–98, 201, 207–8, 212
Regan, Anthony, 4, 6, 22n6, 22n8, 172
relation *see* definition and relation
respect, 15, 44–45, 57, 60, 65, 85, 89, 94, 115, 126, 149, 169, 188, 190, 200
  and fathers, 52, 67–68, 73, 120
  and mothers, 57, 60
  and *tsunon*, 60, 81, 94, 110–11, 149, 175
rest, 26, 28–30, 32, 42–43, 121, 187, 200
return, 19, 21, 54, 57, 65, 187, 191
  from the sea, 42–48, 120, 128, 144, 155, 157, 187–88
  of help, 116, 120–21, 132, 136, 155
  of power, 129–30
  to one's mother, *see* mother, following/returning to
  to the mainland, 82–83, 113, 120–21, 123–24, 129–30, 132, 136, 190
Richards, Audrey, 75–76, 79n8
Rimoldi, Max and Eleanor, 3–4, 16, 22n5, 89, 93–95, 99n10, 128, 132–33, 172
Rio, K, 162n1
road
  and *roror*/indeterminate movements, 16–17, 21, 52, 54, 86–89, 120, 130–32, 186–190, 196–98

ancestral roads, 112–14, 117, 121–26, 130–32
Buka main road/east coast road, 12, 80–81, 123, 152, 182–84
'*kura maror*' (following roads) on the mainland, 14–16, 54, 169, 178, 186, 189
roror (going around), 9, 32–33, 38, 42, 44, 46–48, 50n18, 52, 54, 71, 75, 120–21, 126, 132, 152, 160, 184–189, 196–98, 202. *See also* movements, indeterminacy of
Rutherford, Danilyn, 16, 49n6, 89, 171

Sabarl (island), 148, 150, 153
Sagir, Bill, 3, 16, 128, 133, 172
saltwater, saltwater people, 1, 12, 16, 17, 21, 29–32, 47–48, 65, 71, 74, 77, 125, 133–134, 137, 145, 164, 176–77, 181–82, 189–91, 194–97
Sarei, Alexis, 16, 79n2
school, 28, 33, 37, 63, 72, 77, 162n2, 166, 207
school fees, 68, 70, 79n4
Scott, Michael, 173–75, 194
sea cucumber, 9, 49n5
shark, 36, 42, 50n17, 94–95, 110, 134n4, 207
Sharp, Nonie, 22n1, 26, 195–96
shellfish, 9, 19, 25, 27–28, 33–34, 39–40, 46, 60, 117, 119, 207, 213
shell money (*beroan*), 67, 138, 141, 148, 199
ship, 2–3, 87–88, 99n7, 139
Sia and Hulu, 46–48, 123, 159–60, 184, 188
siblings, 43, 46, 54, 116, 128, 151, 188
slit-gong, 88, 91, 158, 183, 199, 202, 212
solomon, 211–13
Solomon Islands, 1, 22n1, 174
Solos (language area), 12–13, 15, 23n15, 84, 99n4, 112, 121, 205, 213
space
  and cutting up the island, 180–82
  and paper, 170
  and place (in anthropology), 16–17, 195–197
  and *roror*, 187
  in fishing *see* fishing, and space and time
  in fishing and *hahur*, 42, 160

spear-fishing, 25, 38, 34, 36–37, 116, 207–8
spirits,
    ancestral spirits and spirits of the dead,
        90, 97, 100n11, 126–28, 146–49,
        154–59, 162, 162n4, 163n6, 185,
        187, 200, 201, 204
    at sea, 41, 50n15
    eating with the *tsunon*, 126–28, 153
    <u>masalai</u>, 94, 99n11, 127, 134n4, 200, 201
    in the bush, 81
    throwing out/sending off spirits, 137,
        150–56
Stone, 96–99
    ancestral stones, 134n3
    around which the island grew, 82–83
    fishing spots, 26, 36
    for attracting bonito, 37
    old men, 83
    on Tanna, 100nn12–13, 197–98
stories
    of fishing, 26, 37, 66
    of headhunting, *see* headhunting
    of island settlement, 11, 18, 82–89,
        110–11, 173, 175, 179–80
    of migration, 19, 141–171, 121–126,
        133, 165–66, 190
    origin stories, *see* origin; Sia and Hulu
St. Paul, 88, 91
straightening relations, 13, 56, 151, 176,
    191
straightening the ground, 168, 177–182,
    191. *See also* land tenure
Strathern, Marilyn, 16, 20–21, 23n18, 47,
    73, 76, 98, 129
surprise
    and fishing, 16, 27, 38, 42, 49n6
    encounters, 64, 119, 130, 171
sweet potatoes, 3, 8–12, 23n14, 29, 31,
    38, 55, 57–61, 65, 68, 74, 77, 113–
    120, 131, 138–39, 153, 186

tadak, 95, 192–93
talk
    elicitory, 55–56, 112, 166, 194
    of the tsunon, 56, 85, 94, 108–112,
        122, 166, 175, 191
    limitations of, 193–95
Tanimbar, 96–98, 171
Tanna, 98, 100n12, 197, 212
taro, 3, 12, 23n14, 31, 76, 116–18, 139,
    141, 152, 162n5

Thomas, Gordon, 23n17, 46, 50n11,
    50n14, 88, 211
throwing away/down, 18, 44, 92, 112,
    130, 144, 175, 188, 200, 211
Tikana, 171
time, *see* fishing, and space and time
Torres Strait, 1, 22n1
Town (Buka Town), 1, 8–10, 12, 27,
    20–31, 38, 42, 50n18, 51, 54–55,
    59–62, 69–72, 77, 80, 91–92, 101,
    104, 115–19, 123, 134n6, 147,
    152, 165–69, 177–78, 183–85, 189,
    202–5
tracing/following the footsteps
    of the ancestors, 15, 83, 113–14
    of the deceased, 146, 151–53, 157
traditional leadership/leaders, 6–7, 19,
    134, 165–69, 172–78, 181, 190–91,
    202. *See also tsunon; hahini*
transformation, *see* movements, transfor-
    mation of
Trobriand fathers, 69, 99n1
trolling, 27, 37–39, 41–45, 104, 208
truck, 12, 18, 22n10, 54, 80–81, 115, 141,
    152, 204–5
tsuhan, 87–95, 99n5, 99nn9–10, 109–10,
    116, 122–23, 134n2, 135n9, 146,
    157–61, 165, 180–81, 184, 199–200,
    202
tsunon
    power of (*nitsunon*), 78, 81–95, 99n1,
        107, 128–31, 166, 174–76, 181–
        82, 189, 191
    head/hair of, 107, 127, 157, 183, 199
    hatsunon, 126–131
    tasks of, 56, 80–81, 84, 93, 189
turtle, 26, 36–37, 93, 207–8

Vanuatu, 1, 22n1, 74, 98, 162n1, 164–65
village court, 28–29, 48, 56
village meeting, 28

Wagner, Roy, 16, 23n18, 42, 48, 55, 76,
    95, 136, 145, 148, 156–57, 160–61,
    188, 192–93
Weiner, James, 17, 23n18, 24nn19–20, 48,
    187, 194
will (of a person in fishing), 41
wind, 9, 27, 41, 184, 187, 198, 203
witnessing, 92, 126–130, 133–34, 135n11,
    153, 175

World War II, 3–4, 23n14, 50n16, 88–89, 94

writing down (*pinaposa*, traditional leadership and land ownership), 166–70, 176, 191

Yaming (island), 22n3, 27, 96–97, 110, 134n3, 211

Yaparu (village), 8, 64, 71–73, 101, 117–18, 205

Yolngu, 197